D1291896

THE PRESS IN INDIA

THE PRESS IN INDIA

R. C. S. SARKAR,

Formerly Law Secretary, Government of India
and
Chairman, Union Public Service Commission

1984

S. CHAND & COMPANY LTD
RAM NAGAR, NEW DELHI-110055

S. CHAND & COMPANY LTD

Head Office : RAM NAGAR , NEW DELHI-110055

Show Room : 4/16-B, Asaf Ali Road, New Delhi-110002

Branches :

Mai Hiran Gate, Jalandhar-144008	285/J, Bipin Behari Ganguly Street,
Aminabad Park, Lucknow-226001	Calcutta-700012
Blackie House,	Sultan Bazar, Hyderabad-500001
103/5, Walchand Hirachand Marg,	3, Gandhi Sagar East,
Opp. G.P.O., Bombay-400001	Nagpur-440002
Khazanchi Road, Patna-800004	KPCC Building,
613-7, M.G. Road,	Race Course Road, Bangalore-560009
Ernakulam, Cochin-682035	152, Anna Salai, Madras-600002

First Published 1984

Published by S. Chand & Company Ltd., Ram Nagar, Nuw Delhi-110055
and printed at Rajendra Ravindra Printers (Pvt) Ltd.
Ram Nagar, New Delhe-110055

Preface

This book presents a comprehensive and critical study of the working of the Press in India. It deals with the existing state of the Press, its growth and development, the constitutional and legal framework within which it functions as well as important issues facing the Press. New issues have come to the fore replacing the old and the role of the Press in free India has become the subject of keen debate. After a detailed study of the subject, the Second Press Commission has made as many as two hundred and seventy eight recommendations covering different aspects of the working of the Press. A critical examination has been made of the recommendations of the Commission taking into account the views of its dissenting members and the author has also expressed his personal opinion on them.

In a modern society, freedom of the Press cannot be absolute or unfettered. It is subject to restraints under the Constitution and laws of the country. Government may also exercise executive control over the Press. Press freedom is also subject to contempt of court and privileges of Parliament. This book deals with those topics in a thorough and objective manner and tries to evaluate whether within the restraints, numerous as they are, the Press in India is free and independent and whether it is playing its expected role.

The Press is not only a medium of expression but it is also an industry and a business with profit motive. This book deals with monopolistic combines, de-linking and diffusion of ownership, price-page schedule, news-to-advertisement ratio and other matters of topical interest.

The method of treatment adopted in this work is an integrated discussion of each topic in the form of a complete nar-

(*vi*)

rative. It would help the general readers, Indians or foreigners, to understand better the working of the Press in the complex background of Indian society. Journalism has been prescribed as a post-graduate course of study in various Universities. This book provides useful information which would be of great help not only to the students of Journalism but also to students of Law and Political Science.

I take this opportunity of acknowledging the help I received from Shri J. K. Bhattacharya, I.A.S., Joint Secretary, Ministry of Information and Broadcasting for his valuable suggestions in the preparation of this book.

A-14 Chittaranjan Park
NEW DELHI-110 019.

R. C. S. SARKAR

Contents

(*vii*)

Table of Cases

A

V

W

CHAPTER I

Role of the Press

The Press is a responsible part of a democratic society and its role in India after Independence has become the subject of keen debate. Two Press Commissions were appointed to inquire into the problems, growth and status of the Press. Conferences and seminars have been held to discuss the ailments of the Press and their remedies. New issues have come to the fore in place of the old and there is wide divergence of opinion on many issues. But there is unanimous agreement that a free and healthy Press is indispensable to the functioning of a true democracy. In a democracy, whatever may be its form, there should be active participation of the people in all spheres of activity, local or national. They have to exercise their franchise and elect their representatives and even when the government is formed, they must be eternally vigilant to keep the abuses of the government in check. To enable the people to exercise their necessary functions, they have to be kept informed about current affairs and broad issues, political, social and economic. Free exchanges of ideas and free debate are an essential part of the government of a free country.

Role of the Press

The role of the Press is to keep the people well-informed. Its functions are to inform, educate and entertain the public. While the primary function of the Press is to provide comprehensive and objective information on all aspects of the country's social, economic, political and cultural life, it has also an educative and mobilising role. It plays an important role in moulding public opinion and can be an instrument of social change. Mahatma Gandhi in his *Autobiography* defined the duties of a newspaper thus : "One of the objects of a newspaper is to understand the popular feeling and give expression to it; another is to arouse among the people certain desirable sentiments; and the third is fearlessly to express popular defects."

Outlining the duties of journalists, the All India Newspaper Editors' Conference in their memorandum to the First Press Commission have said that "Journalism should strive to inform the people of current events and trends of opinion, to create and sustain an ever widening range of interest, and to encourage discussion of current problems with due regard to all points of view, all of which involve accurate and impartial presentation of news and views and dispassionate evaluation of conflicting ideals."[1] The presentation of news should be truthful, objective and comprehensive without any suppression or distortion and without vulgar sensationalism in presentation. The journalists have an undoubted right to make comments on news but such comments should be based on the firm foundation of verified facts and should be fair and constructive. People want facts and a distinction has to be made between facts presented and comments made. The Press should not only be free but also healthy.

Similar views were expressed also by the first Royal Commission on Press in England. Dealing with the role of the Press in a democracy, it observed : "The democratic form of society demands of its members active and intelligent participation in the affairs of their community. It assumes that they are sufficiently well informed about the issues of the day to be able to form the broad judgment required on an election, and to maintain between the elections the vigilance necessary in those whose governors are their

---

1. *The First Press Commission Report*, Vol. I, p. 339.

servants and not their masters. More and more it demands also an alert and informed participation not only in purely political processes but also in the efforts of the community to adjust its social and economic life to increasingly complex circumstances. Democratic society, therefore, needs a clear and truthful account of events, of their background and their causes; a forum for discussion and informed criticism; and a means whereby individuals and groups can express a point of view or advocate a cause."[2]

A democratic society lives and grows by free and open public discussion. In order to enable the people to form their judgment on various issues, they must have access to all shades of opinion. There can be no single voice of the Press in a free society. It is, therefore, essential that there should be variety of ownership and opinion and different newspapers and magazines should put before the public the varied and different points of view held by different political parties or groups. It should be left to the people to choose their course of action. A free market place of ideas is the best sifting ground between right and wrong.

Journalism, to be meaningful, should have a clear objective. In dealing with the role of the Press, sufficient stress is generally laid on the need for maintenance of professional standards with regard to accuracy, comprehensiveness and objectivity, but there has not been quite enough emphasis on the objective towards which journalism should strive. In this context, the first Press Commission observed : "In our view, it is only a clear perception of the objective which can give a meaning and significance to the vocation of journalism."[3] The Press in India has, however, a clear objective as outlined in the Constitution. The ultimate goal of Indian society has been very clearly defined in the Directive Principles. This is to secure and protect a social order in which justice, social, economic and political shall inform all the institutions of national life. This goal was more explicitly

2. *Report of the First Royal Commission on Press*, pp. 100–1.
3. *The First Press Commission Report*, Pt I, Chapter XIX, p. 339.

defined later by the 42nd Amendment to the Constitution by which the Preamble was amended to describe the Indian State as a "Sovereign Socialist Secular Democratic Republic" in place of "Sovereign Democratic Republic." The Preamble and the Directive Principles set out the kind of society which the country is seeking to achieve. Without the background of such social philosophy, it would not be possible for a journalist to correlate and interpret the multitudinous variety of events that take place every hour.

The Press in India has also a special responsibility. We have a parliamentary system where there is the dominance of the party in power and the opposition is weak and fragmented, incapable of offering any national alternative or keeping the abuses of the government in check. This has raised certain doubts and misgivings about the suitability of parliamentary system itself and a heavy responsibility has devolved on the Press. It has to function as an extra-parliamentary opposition to strengthen the roots of democracy and democratic institutions and to keep the government in check. It has to guard against the erosion of democratic values and create a vocal public opinion for realising the goal of social and economic justice.

Freedom of the Press

To enable the Press to keep the people informed and to provide a forum for public discussion and informed criticism, the Press must be free and independent. These two attributes are inseparable and both are equally important. A free Press must also be an independent Press.

A free Press is the very basis of democracy. But there had been persistent opposition to freedom of the Press and to all democratic movements from the governments all over the world and repressive measures were undertaken to suppress them. Freedom of the Press, as it is today, is the result of a few centuries of hard-won fight in the name of the people. In England, with the emergence of newspapers in the 17th century, opposition against the absolute and unfettered powers of the monarchy gained momentum but the government tried to suppress the Press in various ways through licensing, censorship and prohibitions. In spite of repressive measures, the agitation continued and intellectuals like Milton and Mill lent their support to the cause of a free Press. Milton wrote in his *Areopagitica* that free men must have the "liberty to know, to utter, and to argue freely according to conscience." Suppression of opinion was abhorrent to Mill and he said : "the peculiar evil of silencing the expression of opinion is that it is robbing the human race, posterity as well as the existing generation : those who dissent from the opinion, still more than those who hold it. If the opinion is right, they are deprived of the opportunity of exchanging error for truth : if wrong, they lose... the clearer perception and livelier impression of the truth, produced by its collision with error." The government had to yield to the pressure of public opinion and all controls over the Press were gradually removed. By the middle of the 19th century, freedom of the Press was fairly established in England and the Press came to be known as the Fourth Estate. In U.S.A. also, the Press had to struggle hard for its freedom till it was recognised as a fundamental right by the first amendment to its Constitution which says :

"Congress shall make no law....abridging the freedom ....of the Press".

The struggle for freedom of the Press in India also was long and arduous.[4] Ever since the publication of the first newspaper, *Bengal Gazette* or *Calcutta General Advertiser* in 1780, repressive measures were undertaken by the government to stifle the Press. With the emergence of the nationalist Press which took up the cause of the freedom movement and welfare of the people, a new dimension was added to Indian journalism. The nationalist Press was severely persecuted and suffered great hardship but it had its reward when freedom of speech and expression was guaranteed as a fundamental right in article 19 of our Constitution. The history of the struggle

4. For details see : *The First Press Commission Report*, Part II ; Mudholkar J, *Press Law* (Tagore Law Lectures) Chapter 2 ; and Chapter 2 of the book.

for freedom of the Press is so closely related to the history of the growth of democracy that a free Press is regarded as an institutional limb of modern democracy.

A free Press with its undoubted powers and resources to champion the cause of the weak and oppressed and to point out the shortcomings of the government of the day has been described as the sentinel on the *qui vive*. Exposure of a grave scandal like that of Watergate may even lead to the fall of a government. The Press may also do incalculable harm to the country by abusing its powers. People are generally prone to believe the printed word even when it is not honest. It is this gullibility of most people which gives a tremendous power to the Press and quite often a power for mischief by undermining the character and reputation of the people. Notwithstanding the dangers inherent in a free Press when it abuses its powers or exposes the weaknesses or corruption in the government, its importance has been emphasised by heads of government who cherish democratic values. Thomas Jefferson once said : "If it is left to me to decide whether we should have a government without newspapers or newspapers without a government, I would not hesitate to prefer the latter." Pandit Nehru reiterated the same idea when he said : "I would rather have a completely free Press with all the dangers in the wrongful use of that freedom than a suppressed or regulated Press."

Judicial decisions also both in U.S.A. and India have recognised the importance of a free Press in a free society. The U.S. Supreme Court observed that the right to free speech "is absolutely indispensable for the preservation of a free society in which the government is based upon the consent of an informed citizenry and is dedicated to the protection of all, even the most despised minorities."[5] The same view was taken by Patanjali Sastri, J., when he said : "Freedom of speech and of the Press lay at the foundation of all democratic organisations, for without free political discussions, no

5. *Speiser* v. *Randall*, 357 U.S. 513.

public education, so essential for the proper functioning of the processes of popular government, is possible."[6]

While the need of a free Press in a free society is recognised by the lessons of history, by intellectuals and statesmen as also by judicial decisions, a question arises what does freedom of the Press mean. It is an expression which is both elastic and ambiguous. The term "Press" is used in different senses in different contexts. It may mean an establishment where printing is done. In that sense, it means all plants, machinery, implements and other materials by means of which printing is done. It has been understood in that sense in the Press and Registration of Books Act, 1867.[7] It may also mean a medium of publication, namely, any printed periodical work containing public news or comments on public news. In this sense, it covers newspapers, magazines, news services, etc. in general, or the persons who write them; journalism or journalists. It is understood in this sense when we talk of freedom of the Press.

The content of the expression 'freedom of the Press' is also differently understood by different persons. Some have understood it to mean freedom to publish any matter by printed word without any legal restraint or prohibition. Others have understood it to mean freedom from prejudices and preconceived notions; freedom from executive control of government; freedom from influence of advertisers and pressure groups and freedom from dependence on others for financial assistance. To equate freedom of the Press with freedom from influence of proprietors, advertisers or pressure groups is to confuse the legal concept of freedom of the Press with the idea of independence of the Press. Neither the first Royal Commission on the Press in England nor the Second Press Commission in India headed by Justice Mathew chose to discuss the meaning and significance of this concept. The first Press Commission in India has, however, expressed the view that this expression means "freedom to hold opinions, to receive

6. *Romesh Thappar* v. *State of Madras*, 1950 S. C. R. 594.
7. See. sec. 4 of the Press and Registration of Books Act, 1867.

and to impart information through the printed word without any interference from any public authority."[8] In other words, it is the right of the citizen to publish what he chooses without any prior permission from the government or any other public authority, subject only to the legal liability for what he has chosen to publish.

Freedom of the Press has three essential elements : (i) freedom of access to all sources of information; (ii) freedom of publication; and (iii) freedom of circulation. It is the function of the Press to disseminate correct news and spread the truth. To enable it to do so, the Press should have access to all sources of information. Free flow of information is essential to a democratic society. Freedom to have access to public records is an important aspect of freedom of the Press. In a modern welfare state, the government regulates the social and economic life of the citizens in diverse ways. There is an inherent danger that the vast powers of the executive may not always be used for public welfare but used for private gain or with corrupt motives. If the Press has to rely on what the government chooses to supply to it, the picture may be one-sided and distorted and may not represent the truth. It is necessary, therefore, that the Press should have access to public records. But the government is generally reluctant to allow the Press to have access to public records under the Official Secrets Act, 1923 and various other rules and orders. While openness is essential to the functioning of a democratic society, secrecy is also necessary to protect certain vital interests such as defence, national security, foreign relations, criminal law, personal privacy and trade secrets. It is necessary, therefore, that a proper balance should be drawn between the needs of openness and requirements of secrecy, though this balance may perhaps be tilted a little more in favour of openness than it has been hitherto.

While freedom of thought is a personal freedom, freedom of expression and publication, which the Press enjoys, is a collective freedom. It includes not only the right to pro-

8.　*The First Press Commission Report*, Part I, p. 358.

pagate one's views but also the views of others. It follows that contributors to newspapers and journalists enjoy the same rights and privileges as the Press. If a person has the right to express his views, so have others. It follows as a necessary corollary that this right imposes a duty to tolerate the views of others, even opposed to one's own. Democratic experience has shown that spread of information from different and even conflicting sources in the widest possible manner is important for the welfare of the people. It is also well recognised that freedom of publication is secured by freedom of circulation. Our Supreme Court held as early as 1950 that "liberty of circulation is as essential to the freedom (of expression) as the liberty of publication. Indeed, without circulation, the publication would be of little value."[9] Freedom of expression covers both content and circulation, if any law unreasonably curtails, directly or indirectly, the right of circulation, it would be void.[10]

Freedom of the Press does not mean that the Press enjoys any special rights or privileges other than those to which a citizen is entitled. This is the position in England and U.S.A. as also in India. As Dicey remarked :

"The law of England does not recognise in general any special privileges on behalf of the Press. The law of the Press as it exists in England is merely part of the law of libel and the so-called liberty of the Press is a mere application of the general principle that no man is punishable except for a distinct breach of law."[11] In India also, the Privy Council held that "the freedom of the journalist is an ordinary part of the freedom of the subject, and.... his privilege is no other and no higher."[12] Under our Constitution also, freedom of the Press being included in the freedom of expression guaranteed to citizens, the Press does not enjoy any special rights or privileges which cannot be exercised or claimed by an ordi-

9. *Romesh Thappar* v. *State of Madras*, 1950 S. C. R. 594.
10. *Express Newspapers* v. *Union of India*, A. I. R. 1958 S. C. 578.
11. *Law of the Constitution*, A. V. Dicey, 9th Edn., p. 240.
12. *Arnold* v. *King Emperor*, (1914) 18 C. W. N. 785 (P.C.).

nary citizen. Though the Constitution of U.S.A. is different
from ours, the law of that country does not confer any privileges on the Press nor does it exempt the Press from any laws.

The Press should have the right to print anything which
it thinks fit for publication. But this freedom is not absolute
or unfettered. In an organised society, the rights of the Press
have to be harmonised with its duties and responsibilities
towards the society. It must be realised that there are certain
limitations on what newspapers can safely publish. Public
order, decency, morality, friendly relations with foreign States
and such other things must be safeguarded. The protective
cloak of Press freedom must not be thrown over its wrong
doings. If a newspaper publishes what is improper, mischievous or illegal and abuses its liberty, it must be punished according to law. The doctrine of absolute freedom of the Press
has its dangers. There is hardly any dispute that certain restrictions are essential for the preservation of freedom of the
Press and such restrictions may be placed by the Constitution
or laws of the country. What is objectionable is not restrictions as such but the imposition of arbitrary and excessive
restrictions which would make the freedom a mockery. To quote
from the report of Mons Lopez to the Economic and Social
Council of the United Nations : "If it is true that human
progress is impossible without freedom, then it is no less true
that ordinary human progress is impossible without a measure
of regulation and discipline. Indeed one might say that restrictions are essential to the preservation of freedom itself
and that what makes freedom usable as a factor of progress
is the existence of essential compensatory limitations."[13]

There is a fundamental difference between prior restraint and subsequent punishment. Any form of prior restraint is a fetter on the free will of the people and an attempt
to control liberty of expression by administrative authorities.
When there is no prior restraint "anything is lawful which
is not unlawful,"[14] as Ivor Jennings put it. A subsequent

13. *Report of Mons Lopez to the Economic and Social Council of the
     U.N.* quoted by *The First Press Commission Report*, Part I, p. 358.
14. Sir Ivor Jennings, *The Law and the Constitution*, 4th Edn., p. 247.

punishment does not put any restraint on freedom of expression; it only takes account of the abuse of freedom by punishing anybody who publishes what is unlawful. In the case of an unjust attack on an individual, the person defamed may sue for damages or file a complaint in a criminal court. In more serious offences like sedition, incitement to criminal offences etc., the State may launch prosecution against the persons concerned and they will be liable to be tried in a criminal court. A subsequent punishment upholds the law and liberty of the Press.

Independence of the Press

A Press to be free must also be independent. Even when a newspaper is free to express its opinion without any restraint from the government, it cannot exercise its freedom unless it keeps itself genuinely independent. Threats to independence of the Press can be both internal and external. The Mathew Commission in Chapter V of its Report has referred to certain external threats. Mr. D. R. Mankekar in an article "Free, Not Independent"[15] has referred to certain internal threats also. We shall briefly examine them.

A Press to be independent must be economically viable. A newspaper struggling for existence and depending upon outside agencies to dole out funds cannot afford the luxury of freedom. Thanks to the technological revolution, equipment for the Press has become very expensive and a poor newspaper is unable to afford it. It cannot also afford to engage trained journalists and the quality of the paper also becomes poor. Such a paper becomes subject to internal and external pressures which it cannot resist. Sound business management and quality of the staff are the necessary ingredients which contribute to the viability of the Press.

Another factor which poses internal threat to independence of the Press is the lack of character. This applies as much to our political life and business as it does to the Press. Journalists are under constant pressure from political par-

15. *"Free, Not Independent"* an article by Mr. D.R. Mankekar in "What ails the Indian Press."

ties, industrialists and other pressure groups. They have also to be on guard against the temptation to enjoy favours, whether from government authorities, employers, advertisers or others. Sometimes they are given government accommodation on concessional terms and the government does not bother even to collect the concessional rent. If the journalists do not have the necessary strength of character to resist the pressures or allurements offered to them, the Press ceases to be free. Lack of character, the enemy within, strikes at the root of the independence of the Press.

Another very important factor which seeks to undermine independence and efficiency of the Press is the editor's loss of autonomy in his own set-up. A newspaper is a private enterprise operating for private profit combined with the right of the journalist to express his views freely. Some of the largely circulated newspapers are owned by commercial houses or industrialists who run the newspapers as a subsidiary to their business interests or for exerting political pressure. The proprietors naturally do not want anything to be published which is against their business interests or the interests of their fellow businessmen. Moreover, as there is pervasive governmental regulation of industry and business in a planned economy, they cannot afford to take the risk of offending the government or other authorities. In such cases, the proprietor leaves the control of the newspaper to an executive or a manager who hardly knows the contours of freedom of the Press. The manager dictates to the editor what to say and what not to say and the editor becomes no more than a mere scribe of the proprietor. In the process, the newspaper loses its freedom and independence. Speaking on the conditions in which the Press in the United States operates, Carl E. Lindstrom, a former editor of Hartford *Courier-Times* remarked : ''We have a reasonably free Press in this country, but there are far too many captive editors who cannot even be heard rattling their chains.'' This is perhaps true in our country also.

The question of editorial autonomy is a controversial topic and has been the subject of debate all over the world. The proprietor of a newspaper has certainly the right to lay down the policy of the paper. He who pays the piper has also the right to order the tune. When an editor accepts his appointment in a newspaper, he accepts also the broad principles of the policy of the paper. He is expected to operate within the four corners of that policy but there should not be any interference in his day-to-day work. Independence of the editor is vital to freedom of the Press. If the editor has to play the second fiddle to the general manager, the paper is bound to be unenterprising and dull. The status and prestige of the editor should be enhanced commensurate with his pivotal role in a newspaper. Various attempts have been made in other countries to define the editor-management relationship and safeguard the autonomy of the editor. In our country also, the editor's sphere of autonomy should be clearly defined, and encroachment on it resisted.

The ownership pattern is another danger which can imperil independence and freedom of the Press. A newspaper owner should have the right to use his paper as on organ of propaganda on his own account or on behalf of the political party he supports. To deny him that right would be to deny the right of freedom of expression. But there is danger if there is monopoly of newspapers in a particular country. Government may then step in and legislation to prevent monopoly may be justified. But what is monopoly ? A monopoly is the enjoyment of some form of exclusive control over the production and sale of some commodity or service as opposed to a system of free competition. Applying this test, there is no democratic country where monopoly of newspapers exists. In every country, there is a number of dailies and periodicals and the reader is free to choose any of them. In India, there are about 1,264 daily newspapers and there are about 17,782 periodical publications. In Delhi alone, there are 6 or 7 dailies and the reader has a wide range of choice and there is a fierce competition among the newspapers. There is no monopoly in India. If there is no monopoly, some complain that there is an oligopoly which means a group of papers or owners joining together to control the news media to the exclusion of other papers. Whether there is any monopoly or oligopoly in the newspaper industry and whether such monopoly or oligopoly would affect freedom of the Press would be an interesting study and we shall discuss it fully later in Chapter 9.

There is yet another internal threat to independence of the Press and that is from the vested interests of trade unions of working journalists. The Mathew Commission in its report has referred to certain cases where the working journalists have hindered the production, publication or distribution of newspapers.[16] In 1975, the employees of an English daily of Delhi began to withhold editorial matter which was not to their liking from being sent to the composing room and the editor felt helpless. In 1979, the workers of *Jugantar* of Calcutta belonging to a trade union sympathetic to the ruling left front prevented the paper from coming out as it contained an article critical of the State Government. More recently in 1981, the trade unions of employees of *Arya Varta* and *Indian Nation* in Patna and of the *Indian Express* and allied publications in Bombay obstructed the printing and distribution of the newspapers, allegedly under incitement of politicians in power. These are unhealthy trends which political parties and trade union leaders are following. Associations of Working Journalists have been captured by anti-democratic elements, and until those are eliminated, it would be difficult to deal with this particular threat to freedom of the Press.

It has been alleged not only in India but in many countries where private enterprise in industry and commerce is allowed that commercial advertisers influence both the news and views columns of newspapers. But the evidence on the subject is so scanty that it is difficult to hold how far this allegation is correct. Government also which is a major advertiser has been subjected to criticism that it exerts pressure through its discriminatory advertisement policy and also through its schemes of distribution of newsprint quotas. The Mathew Commission has received some complaints that the government discriminates in the selection of newspapers for advertisements and also in the rates fixed for such advertisements. It is necessary to investi-

16. *The Second Press Commission Report*, Vol. I, p. 64.

gate these allegations further before any firm conclusion can be drawn.

There is yet another external threat to freedom of expression which is of recent origin and that is from mob pressure. There has been a tendency on the part of some sections of the public, especially students, to take law into their own hands and administer threats to, or engage in violent physical attacks on, the staff or property of a newspaper, apparently feeling aggrieved by a report or comment appearing in its columns. The Mathew Commission refers to some instances of this[17] nature from different parts of India which include : abusive letters and threats addressed to the editor of the *Indian Express*, Delhi in March 1979, for publishing reports which exposed large-scale copying in the examinations conducted by Meerut University; mob attack on the news editor and staff of the *Times of India* in Bombay on 8th September, 1979 in protest against a report on the arrest of a city priest for smuggling; the attack on three newspaper offices in Cuttack, in March 1981, by a group of young men for publishing a report about the alleged molestation of a woman student of the Medical College; the *gherao* of four newspaper offices in Bangalore in September 1980, in protest against the alleged misreporting of an incident involving the Karnataka Chief Minister; the *gherao* of the offices of *Hind Samachar* during July, 1981 and the burning of the effigy of the Chief Editor, Lala Jagat Narain who was subsequently murdered on 9th September, 1981. These misguided elements among the public seek to exercise their disagreement with newspaper reports through physical violence against the premises or property of the newspaper or its editor or employees rather than availing of a remedy provided under the law of the land. This is essentially a law and order problem and unless urgent and effective steps are taken to control it, newspapers will naturally be reluctant to express their opinion freely.

We have already discussed the role of the Press and the need for its freedom. We have seen that freedom of the Press

17. *The Second Press Commission Report*, Vol. I, p. 64.

cannot be absolute or unfettered but must be subject to certain restrictions. We have further discussed possible threats to independence of the Press, internal and external. Freedom of the Press has been guaranteed as a fundamental right under our Constitution but certain restrictions have been imposed on this freedom by the Constitution itself. Statutory curbs have also been placed on Press freedom under various laws such as the Official Secrets Act, 1923, Law of Defamation, the Press and Registration of Books Act, 1867, the Post and Telegraph Acts, Industries (Development and Regulation) Act, 1951 and other laws. Government may also exercise executive control over the Press through its advertisement policy and the scheme of distribution of newsprint quotas. It may also put pressure on the Press by extra-legal action under the vast powers it possesses. Contempt of court and privileges of Parliament put further restrictions on the Press. We propose to examine in subsequent chapters the nature of these restrictions and whether they are within permissible limits so as not to make the constitutional guarantee of freedom of the Press a mockery. It will be interesting to examine whether the Press in India is free and independent and whether it is playing its expected role or what ails the Press.

CHAPTER II

History of the Press in India

The history of the Press in India is the history of its struggle for freedom. It is a story of how repressive measures were undertaken to control the Press and how they were tightened or relaxed to meet newer exigencies and political vicissitudes through which the country passed over two centuries.

The first newspaper in India, the *Bengal Gazette* or *Calcutta General Advertiser,* was published in 1780 at Serampore by one James Augustus Hicky. It was a two-sheet newspaper mainly devoted to scurrilous attacks on the private lives of the servants of the East India Company, including the Governor-General Warren Hastings and his wife and the Chief Justice. His attacks against the highest in the Company soon landed him in trouble. He was involved is a number of libel cases and sentenced to imprisonment and fine. He was also subjected to oppression by the East India Company which left him in utter penury.

The next few years saw a few other newspapers coming up. They were benefited by Hicky's bitter experience and trod warily the trail which Hicky had blazed for them. 1780 saw the publication of *India Gazette,* which was followed by *Calcutta Gazette, Bengal Journal, Oriental Magazine of Calcutta Amusement* and *Calcutta Chronicle.* There were four weekly newspapers and one monthly magazine published from Calcutta within six years of Hicky's maiden effort. In Madras, the first newspaper was *Madras Courier* followed by *Harkaru,*

17

Madras Gazette and *India Herald.* Censorship was first introduced in Madras in 1795 when the *Madras Gazette* was required to submit all general orders of the Government for scrutiny by the Military Secretary before publication. Bombay's
first newspaper was *Bombay Herald* followed by the *Courier*
and *Bombay Gazette.* By and large, the newspapers kept themselves on the right side of the government, the rare recalci-
trants being summarily dealt with on charges of gross libel.
In Calcutta, however, one William Duane who acquired the
Bengal Journal, was persecuted, his house broken into and
searched and he was ultimately sent back to England without
being given any compensation for the property left behind
by him.

In more than one sense, the turn of the eighteenth century marks the end of a phase in journalism. The newspapers
were started by ex-servants of the Company and contained
materials exclusively of interest to, and relating to, the activities of the European population in India. The most significant aspect of this period was that there were no Press laws
as such but Government took summary action against offending newspapers. The pattern of governmental action was to
deport incorrigible editors, deny postal facilities to the unre-
pentant and to require those who persisted in causing dis-
pleasure to the Government to submit either a part or the
whole newspaper for censorship.

Regulations of 1799

Every newspaper is required today to print the names of
the printer, publisher and the editor. The origin of this
requirement may be traced to the Regulations made by the
Governor-General in 1799 requiring the newspapers under
pain of penalty, to print the names of printer, publisher and
the editor and to submit all material published in the paper
for pre-censorship by the Secretary to the Government of
India. Any breach of the regulations was punishable with
deportation from India. But, in fact, the newspapers did not
submit to the requirement of pre-censorship with regularity
and there were other difficulties in enforcing the Regulation.

This Regulation was, therefore, repealed during the time of Warren Hastings.

Pre-censorship having been abolished, James Silk Buckingham and Raja Ram Mohun Roy played an important part in establishing freedom of the Press in this country. Buckingham was an indefatigable fighter for the freedom of the Press and was on several occasions threatened to be deported but was saved by Lord Hastings who advocated a benevolent atti·tude towards the Press because he believed that free discussion by the Press about the activities of the government would serve to strengthen the hands of the administration. Raja Ram Mohun Roy's three papers strongly advocated religious and social reforms which were viewed with apprehension in official circles. The tireless campaign of Buckingham and Ram Mohun Roy convinced many eminent minds both in this country and in England of the useful role a free Press could play by its exposure of lapses in administration and its criticism of government's policies.

Ordinance of 1823

After the departure of Lord Hastings, the new Governor-General John Adam had no faith in a free Press. He did not like the idea that newspapers should sit in judgment on the acts of government or that they should bring public measures and the conduct of public men as well as the conduct of private individuals before what is called "public opinion." He, therefore, issued an Ordinance in 1823 introducing "licensing" of the Press, under which all matters printed in the Press, except commercial matters, required a previous licence from the Governor-General. Such licence could be granted on the submission of an application stating the names and other particulars of the Press, such as the location of the Press, title of the newspaper and the names of the printer, publisher etc. Certain penalties were imposed in cases where the printing or publishing was done without the requisite licence and the Governor-General had the power to revoke the licence. Regulations made under the Ordinance empowered magistrates to dispose of both unlicensed printing presses and presses which continued to function after the notice of re-call. Similar regulations were made in Bombay in 1825 and 1827. It was apparent that these regulations were aimed at the Indian language Press of those days and may be said to be forerunners of the Vernacular Press Act of 1878.

Metcalf's Act of 1835

In the period that followed, both Lord Bentinck and Sir Charles Metcalf adopted a more liberal attitude towards the Press. A new Act was passed in 1835, known as the Metcalf's Act. It repealed the Bengal Regulations of 1823 and the Bombay Regulations of 1825 and 1827. The Act was made applicable to all the territories of the East India Company and required the printer and publisher of every newspaper to give a declaration about the precise location of the premises of its publication. It is said that in India Metcalf liberated the Press and the native Press developed rapidly in the three provinces of Bengal, Bombay and Madras as also in the North-West Provinces (now known as Uttar Pradesh). But the language newspapers devoted themselves generally to questions like the *sati*, caste, widow re-marriage, polygamy, the atrocities of indigo planters and the blunders of young magistrates.

Act of 1857

The revolt of 1857 aroused grave apprehensions in the mind of the Government and it felt that sedition had been poured to an audacious extent into the hearts of the people of India. Lord Canning, therefore, enacted the Act of 1857. The Act reintroduced the main features of the Adam Licensing Regulations of 1825. Under the Act, keeping or using of printing presses without a licence was prohibited and the Government assumed discretionary powers to grant licences and to revoke them at any time. The Act was made applicable to the whole of India and it was applied to all kinds of publication, including books or other printed papers, in any language, English or Indian. An important feature of the law was that it did not draw a line of demarcation between European and Indian publications. It imposed a prohibition that "no newspaper shall contain any observations or statements impunging the motives or designs of the British Government either in England or in India or in any way tending to bring the said Government into hatred or contempt, to excite dissatisfaction or unlawful resistance to its orders or to weaken its lawful authority or the authority of its civil and military servants, or observations or statements having a tendency to create alarm or suspicion among the native population of any intended interference by the Government with their religious opinions and observances or having a tendency to weaken the friendship towards the British Government of native princes . . . . .".

Indian Penal Code, 1860

The Indian Penal Code was passed in 1860. Though the Act was not directed specifically against the Press, it laid down offences which any writer, editor or publisher must avoid, e.g., the offences of defamation and obscenity. Later amendments introduced the offences of sedition (Section 124A); promoting enmity between classes (Section 153A); imputations or assertions prejudicial to national integration (Section 153B); and outraging religious feelings (Section 295A).

The Press and Registration of Books Act, 1867

The earliest surviving enactment specifically directed against the Press was passed in 1867, the Press and Registration of Books Act. The object of the Act was not to establish governmental control over the freedom of the Press. It was a regulatory measure which enabled the government to regulate printing presses and newspapers by a system of registration and to preserve copies of books and other matter printed in India.

Vernacular Press Act, 1878

The rapid growth of the Indian language Press made the Government rather uneasy. The official opinion had hardened towards the language Press and the diehards among them stressed the need for a more effective law than the existing Act of

1857 and Section 124A of the Indian Penal Code. Lord Lytton, therefore, passed the Vernacular Press Act in 1878. The salient provisions of this enactment were to place newspapers published in the languages of India under "better control" and to furnish the Government with more effective means than the existing law provided for punishing and suppressing seditious writing calculated to produce disaffection towards Government in the minds of ignorant population. It empowered the Government, for the first time, to issue search warrants and to enter the premises of any Press, even without orders from any court. While Lord Canning refused to discriminate between "the disloyal native" and the "loyal British" in the Press Act of 1857, Lord Lytton enacted a law which was palpably discriminatory to control the vernacular Press. It is said that the blow was aimed mainly at the *Amrita Bazar Patrika* which by its forceful writing on political matters incurred the wrath of Sir Ashley Eden, the then Lt. Governor of Bengal. He asked Babu Shishir Kumar Ghosh to conduct the paper according to the directions of the government and in return made a tempting offer to him. Shishir Babu, however, refused the generous offer and the Lt. Governor wanted to teach him a bitter lesson by applying the Vernacular Press Act to the *Patrika*, which was then an Anglo-Vernacular paper and fell within the scope of the Act. But Shishir Babu was too clever for Sir Ashley. Before the Act was put into force, Shishir Babu brought out his paper wholly in English and thus circumvented the Act, for a journal conducted in the English language was beyond the jurisdiction of the Vernacular Press Act. There was bitter opposition to the Act both in India and in Britain. Instead of cowing down the language Press, the Act produced exactly the opposite effect. The general tone of the newspapers was one of opposition to Government and Government measures. This hostile attitude continued till, at the instance of Gladstone, the Gagging Act was repealed in 1881.

Criminal Procedure Code, 1898

Though the Criminal Procedure Code, 1898 was a general

law laying down the procedure in criminal matters, it came
to include matters of interest to the Press, e.g., Section 108
particularly after the insertion of Secs. 99A-99G in 1922,
which conferred certain procedural powers upon the Government to search for and forfeit publications which offended
against the provisions of Sections 124A, 153A or 295A of the
Indian Penal Code.

In the eighteenth century, newspapers were started by
ex-servants of the East India Company and contained materials mainly relating to the European population in India.
19th century saw the rapid growth of the Indian Press. There
was a movement for religious and social reforms and there
was a growing political consciousness among the people. In
the latter part of the 19th century, Indian National Congress
came into being and there was political agitation. Indian Press
voiced the demands of the people not only in religious and
social matters but also in political matters. The influence of
the Indian Press on the minds of the people, particularly the
intelligentsia, was considerable. Writing about the Press in the
19th century, Dr. Pattabhi Sitaramayya points out that
"popular agitation gives birth to repression on the ground
that, unless the people are thoroughly beaten, no concession
should be made to popular demands. Lord Lytton's Press Act
of 1878 which was, however, quickly withdrawn, was the real
forerunner of this policy. The Arms Act was another reply
to the growing self-consciousness of the nation and continued
a festering sore."

Acts of 1908 and 1910

With the emergence of the nationalist Press which took
up the cause of the freedom movement, a new dimension was
added to Indian journalism. The nationalist Press and the
Anglo-Indian Press had different, almost conflicting, objectives. Mr. S. Natarajan describes the early part of the 20th
century as an "amazingly hysterical period which the Press
in India passed through." The Anglo-Indian Press was one
with the Government in its policies and it went all out to
belittle the extremist as well as the moderate schools. Naturally,

therefore, the Government did not find any danger in the Anglo-Indian Press. Even if it criticised government policies on certain occasions, they were explained away as "occasional lapses from good taste and right feeling." The nationalist Press, on the other hand, was a bitter critic of the government and lent its support to the freedom movement and was trying to rouse political consciousness among the people and the Government took repressive measures against nationalist Press on the slightest pretext.

A wave of revolutionary movement was passing through the country, particularly in Bengal and with the Government notification in July, 1905 announcing the partition of Bengal, the stage was set for widespread trouble. As open criticism of the government was no longer possible, the movement went underground and terrorist activities increased and the young men took to the cult of the bomb. Tilak who was inspiring the people in the cause of freedom movement through his papers *Kesari* and *Mahratta* was prosecuted and sentenced for sedition twice, once in 1897 and again in 1908. Prominent among the editors prosecuted in Bengal were Aurobindo Ghose of the *Bande Mataram,* Brahmo Bandhab Upadhyaya, editor of *Sandhya* and Bhupendra Nath Dutt, the editor of *Jugantar.* Lajpat Rai and Ajit Singh had already been deported in 1907 and Bengal contributed as many as nine who were singled out for this distinction.

The Government of India was haunted by the spectre of sedition and it enacted laws to control public meetings (1907) followed by the Newspapers (Incitement to Offences) Act, 1908. This Act empowered a Magistrate to seize a Press on being satisfied that a newspaper had printed matters containing any incitement to murder or to any other act of violence or to an offence under the Explosive Substances Act. Proceeding under this Act did not save any person from being prosecuted under any other law and if the Magistrate makes his order of the seizure of the Press absolute, the local government could annul the declaration by the printer or publisher and prohibit any further declaration in respect of the newspaper or any newspaper which was in substance the same as the prohibited newspaper. The effect of this draconian law was that several newspapers, which expressed sympathy with terrorist activities, ceased publication. Any hope that the hardships inflicted by the 1908 Act were temporary was shattered when it was followed by a more comprehensive enactment, the Indian Press Act, 1910.

The Indian Press Act was directed against offences involving violence as well as sedition. It required security deposit by every person keeping a printing press and provided for forfeiture of such deposit in all cases where the matter contained in the newspaper incited violence or sedition. The provisions of forfeiture were attracted when the matter contained in the newspaper had a tendency, directly or indirectly, whether by inference, suggestion, allusion, metaphor, implication or otherwise, to incite to murder or to any offence under the Explosive Substances Act, 1908 or to any act of violence or to seduce any officer from his allegiance or his duty, to put any person in fear or cause annoyance to him, to encourage or incite any person to interfere with the administration of the law or with the maintenance of law and order and so on. When the security deposit was forfeited, a person making a fresh declaration was required to deposit a higher amount than the first and on the third occasion, if an offence was alleged, the security deposited, the printing press used for printing the newspaper and all copies of such newspaper were forfeited.

Enlightened public opinion was very much against the harsh provisions of the Press Act from the very beginning. To demand security deposit from the keeper of every printing press, irrespective of the purpose for which the Press is used, put an unnecessary financial burden on well-intentioned printers and publishers and in cases of small concerns, the burden proved too heavy for printers and they became bankrupt. The Act had become a festering sore affecting the Indian Press. After the bomb attack on Lord Hardinge in 1912 from which he narrowly escaped, the provisions of the Act were being indiscriminately misused.

Criminal Law Amendment Act, 1913 and the Defence of India Regulations, 1914

The rigours of the Act of 1910 were further enhanced by the Criminal Law Amendment Act, 1913 and by the Defence of India Regulations which were promulgated on the outbreak of the First World War in 1914. They were used to stifle criticism and silence agitation. Lord Chelmsford used the Press Act with severity and too often. A notorious instance of the misuse of the Act was the case of Mohamed Ali.[1] A pamphlet published by him under the title of "Come over to Macedonia and help us" was forfeited without the notification stating the grounds for the Government's opinion which was a requirement under the Act. The Calcutta High Court took the view that the pamphlet was not seditious and the Chief Justice Sir Lawrence Jenkins observed that that it would be the duty of the Court to hold, but for Section 22, that there had been no legal forfeiture. He analysed the provisions of the Act and said that they were far too harsh for the publisher of a newspaper and that "much that is regarded as standard literature might undoubtedly be caught". Again, in the case of *New India* edited by Mrs. Besant, the Madras High Court remarked : "Section 3(1) imposes a serious disability on persons desiring to keep printing presses." A deputation of the Press Association headed by Mr. Horniman waited upon Lord Chelmsford on 5th March, 1917 to impress upon him the harsh nature of the law. Lord Chelmsford remained unimpressed and said : "The function of a judge is not to say what the law ought to be, but what it is. Executive action is and must always be based upon information, experience and considerations of policy which find no place in the courts of law. Sir Lawrence Jenkins was not entirely consistent with himself. And I cannot but think that if he had any knowledge of the statistics I have given you, he would have hesitated before describing the keeping of printing presses and the publication of newspapers as an extremely hazardous undertaking."

---

1. In re : Mohamed Ali, A.I.R. 1914 (Cal) 242 (S.B.).

Powers vested in the government were being misused all over India. Mrs. Besant was prohibited from entering into the Bombay Presidency by Lord Willingdon under the Defence of India Act. In Bengal, the number of young men interned ran up to nearly three thousand. The amount collected by the Government by way of securities and forfeitures, most of them by executive orders, the number of presses closed and the publications proscribed would clearly show under what trying conditions the Press functioned and to what extent it was crippled. The numerous protests proved to be of no avail. Immediately on the heels of these repressive measures came the Rowlatt Act. The agitation which followed took a new turn. Proscribed literature was being read publicly and distributed openly and people were courting arrest. There was insistent demand that the repressive laws should be repealed.

When the situation was going out of control, a Press Laws Committee was appointed under the Chairmanship of Sir Tej Bahadur Sapru in 1921 to review the working of the Acts of 1908 and 1910. The Sapru Committee felt that the two Acts had done little to check the evils they were meant to restrain, namely, the promotion of revolutionary conspiracies through the Press and recommended repeal of the two Acts and suggested that the purposes of these Acts would be served by ordinary law and by incorporating the provisions of the Act of 1910 as to seizure and confiscation of seditious publications in the Press and Registration of Books Act, the Sea Customs Act and the Post Office Act by suitable amendments. Accordingly, the Acts of 1908 and 1910 were repealed by the Press Law Repeal and Amendment Act, 1922.

Official Secrets Act, 1923

The next important law on the subject is the Official Secrets Act, 1923. It is a general Act but has an important impact on the Press. It is aimed at maintaining the security of the State against leakage of secret information, sabotage and the like. It is an existing Act still in force and we shall discuss this Act in detail in Chapter 4.

The Gandhian Era and the Indian Press (Emergency Powers) Act, 1931

Gandhiji's advent into politics in 1920 was not a mere event; it was a phenomenon. Drawing essentially from his experiences in South Africa, Gandhiji combined Aurobindo's faith in passive resistance, Tilak's faith in masses and Gokhale's belief that the possibilities of understanding knew no limit. His faith in the masses remained unshaken throughout, and their faith in him was equally deep and abiding. He launched his first non-cooperation movement in 1920 which roused political consciousness among the masses. Though Gandhiji dominated the political scene, there were other leaders also exerting considerable influence who differed from Gandhiji in their approach to national problems. In the twenties, newspapers played an important role by propagating the views of different schools of thought and by moulding public opinion.

In Bengal, the *Amrita Bazar Patrika* gradually worked its way up to the position of the leading paper in the province. It clashed with the *Bengalee* of Surendranath Banerjea. Among Bengali papers, the *Ananda Bazar Patrika* was started in 1922 which had the distinction of having had over a long period the largest circulation of any individual newspaper in the country. There were other papers, the *Nayak, Nabasakti* and the *Basumati*. In 1923, C. R. Das's *Forward* appeared to propagate the Council-entry programme of the Swaraj Party which swept all before it. On the other hand, Shyam Sundar Chakravarty, a staunch follower of Gandhiji started the *Servant* which continued to propagate the cause of Gandhian no-changers. In Bihar also, there were many papers and the publication of the *Searchlight* founded by Sachchidananda Sinha marked the beginning of national as opposed to secterian journalism in the Province. The *Leader* in Allahabad was a moderate paper. In Bombay, there were three Anglo-Indian papers, the *Times of India,* the *Bombay Gazette* and the *Advocate of India.* The Congress felt the need for a paper of its own in Madras and by common consent and its own inclinations, the *Hindu* was permitted to function as a progressive nationalist paper without coming under the direct influence of any party. There was a large number of newspapers all over India to represent different shades of opinion and they performed a useful function by providing a free market of ideas.

After the repeal of the Acts of 1908 and 1910 in 1922, there were no repressive Press laws and newspapers flourished. But the launching of the Civil Disobedience Movement by Gandhiji in 1931 prompted the government to promulgate an Ordinance to "control the Press" which was later enacted as the Indian Press (Emergency Powers) Act, 1931. Originally a temporary Act, it was made permanent in 1935. This Act imposed on the Press an obligation to furnish security at the call of the Executive. The Act (as amended by the Criminal Law Amendment, Act, 1932) empowered a Provincial Government to direct a printing press to deposit a security which was liable to be forfeited, if the printing press published any matter by which any of the mischievous acts enumerated in Section 4 were furthered, e.g., inciting or encouraging the commission of any offence of murder or of any cognizable offence involving violence; expressing, directly or indirectly, approval or admiration of any such offence; bringing the government into hatred or contempt or inciting disaffection towards the government; inciting feelings of hatred and enmity between different classes of subjects; and inciting a public servant to resign or neglect his duty. The government was empowered to forfeit the security or where no security had been deposited, to declare the press to be forfeited. On the second occasion, the security to be deposited by the press could be up to ten thousand rupees. Power was also conferred on the postal and customs authorities to seize articles in the course of transmission, if they were suspected to contain matter of the nature described above. This was a comprehensive and harsh measure.

While the Draft Constitution was under consideration in the Constituent Assembly, the Government appointed a Press Laws Enquiry Committee to "review the Press Laws of India with a view to examine if they are in accordance with the fundamental rights formulated by the Constituent Assembly of India''. This Committee recommended, *inter alia*, the repeal of the Press (Emergency Powers) Act, 1931 and the incorporation of some of its provisions in the general statutes laying down the law of crimes. The Act of 1931 was accordingly repealed and replaced by the Press (Objectionable Matter) Act, 1951.

Post-Independence Period

At present there is no repressive Central law directed against the Press. The Press (Objectionable Matter) Act, 1951 was enacted to provide against the printing and publication of incitement to crime and other objectionable matter. The expression 'objectionable matter' was defined in the Act. The Act provided for demand for security from the keeper of the Press as also from newspapers and newssheets in certain cases. There was also provision for forfeiture of such security. But such demand for security and its forfeiture could be made only after a judicial inquiry by a Sessions Judge; and the person against whom a complaint had been made could demand the matter to be determined with the aid of a jury and had also a right of appeal from the order of the Sessions Judge to the High Court. The Act was a temporary one and was allowed to lapse in February, 1956 and it was also formally repealed by a subsequent Repealing Act of 1957. During the Emergency of 1975, the Prevention of Publication of Objectionable Matter Act, 1976 was passed but it was repealed in 1977 by enacting the Prevention of Publication of Objectionable Matter (Repeal) Act, 1977.

Though there is no specific Press law to control the Press, freedom of the Press is not absolute or unfettered. Restrictions may be imposed on the Press under clauses (2) and (6) of article 19 and also during the Emergency. We shall discuss the nature and scope of these restrictions in Chapter 3. There are various laws which have an impact on the Press; there is also executive control. We shall discuss this matter in Chapter 4. The Press is also subject to various other restrictions, such as contempt of court and contempt of legislatures. We shall discuss them in subsequent chapters.

In 1956, the Newspaper (Price and Page) Act was enacted which was declared void by the Supreme Court in 1962 as being violative of article 19(1)(a). We shall discuss the matter fully in Chapter 9 while dealing with price-page schedule.

From the foregoing brief survey of the history of the Press in India, we have seen that the Indian Press, both English as well as vernacular, had played a leading part in the affairs of the country for over a century. We have seen the trials and tribulations through which the Press had to pass under the British rulers. We have also seen how arbitrary the government action had been towards the newspapers. In particular, the Vernacular Press Act of 1878 which was nicknamed as the Gagging Act and the Indian Press Act of 1910 were notorious and sent many a journalist and publisher to jail or turned them bankrupt. But the journalists of those days had a mission and indomitable courage and because of the sacrifices of those great men of the past, we are enjoying freedom of the Press to an extent which very few democratic countries have.

CHAPTER III

Freedom of the Press Under the Constitution

Guarantee of freedom of expression

The Constitution of India was adopted, enacted and given to themselves by the people of India with a view to constituting India into a sovereign, democratic republic. In our democratic society, pride of place has been given to freedom of speech and expression which is the mother of all liberties. One of the main objectives of the Constitution, as envisaged in the Preamble, is to secure liberty of thought and expression to all the citizens. In order to give effect to this objective, "freedom of speech and expression" has been guaranteed as a fundamental right under article 19(1)(a) available to all citizens, subject only to the restrictions which may be imposed by the State under clause (2) of that article. The relevant portion of article 19 reads as follows :

"19(1) All citizens shall have the right—(a) to freedom of speech and expression;

(2) Nothing in subclause (a) of clause (1) shall affect the operation of any existing law, or prevent the State from making any law, in so far as such law imposes reasonable restrictions on the exercise of the right conferred by the said sub-clause in the interests of sovereignty and integrity of India, the security of the State, friendly relations with foreign States, public order, decency or morality, or in relation to contempt of court, defamation or incitement to an offence."

No separate provision for freedom of the Press

There is no separate provision in our Constitution guaranteeing freedom of the Press as in countries like U.S.A. The first Amendment to the U.S. Constitution says : "Congress shall make no law....abridging the freedom of the speech or.... of the Press". The Constitution makers had before them the experience of the first and fourteenth amendments of the U.S. Constitution as also the judgments of American Supreme Court thereon and they deliberately did not incorporate the language of the First Amendment. Freedom of expression is a term of much wider import and includes all possible forms of expressing thoughts, feelings and convictions. Such expression may be made by writing, printing, picture or by any other manner, and includes expression through the Press. There were demands from many quarters that freedom of the Press should be separately mentioned but these demands were rejected. Dr. Ambedkar stressed that freedom of expression includes freedom of the Press. He said that the Press has no special rights which are not to be given to, or which are not to be exercised by, the citizen in his individual capacity.[1] The Supreme Court has also held in a number of cases that there was no need to mention freedom of the Press separately, because it is already included in the guarantee of freedom of expression.[2] In spite of the clear verdict of the Supreme Court on this question, demands persist that freedom of the Press should be separately mentioned. But it would not be desirable to put freedom of the Press on a higher footing than freedom of expression enjoyed by a citizen in his individual capacity. Mathew Commission also examined this question and came to the conclusion that no useful purpose will be served by inserting a separate provision in the Constitution on freedom of the Press as that concept is already embodied in article 19(1)(a) and by inserting

---

1. See *Constituent Assembly Debates*, Vol. VII, p. 780 (2.12.48).
2. See *Express Newspapers* v. *Union of India* (1959) S.C.R. 12, *Bennet Coleman* v. *Union of India* A.I.R. 1973 S.C. 106.

such a provision, no particular benefit can be conferred on a non-citizen like a company.[3]

As there is no separate guarantee of freedom of the Press in India, certain consequences flow. Since freedom of the Press is derived from article 19(1)(a) which is guaranteed to all citizens, the Press stands on no higher footing than any other citizen and cannot claim any privileges as such as distinct from those of any other citizen. Conversely, the Press cannot be subjected to any special restrictions which could not be imposed on private citizens. Secondly, since the guarantee under article (19)(a) is confined to citizens, a non-citizen running a newspaper is not entitled to the benefit of the liberty of the Press. We shall discuss this aspect of the question more fully later.

Constitutional remedies to enforce freedom of the Press

Since freedom of the Press is a fundamental right guaranteed under article 19(1)(a), it is available to citizens and against State action only. If freedom of the Press is interfered with by a private citizen, there is no constitutional remedy against such interference, though the Press may have a remedy under ordinary law of the land. But if a person is aggrieved by an infringement of this right by any law or by an executive order of the government, he may apply for relief to the Supreme Court under article 32 or to a High Court, having jurisdiction, under article 226. Thus the printer, publisher or editor of a newspaper may file a writ petition to quash an order which imposes a ban on the entry of their journal in a State or other local area[4] or which requires it to submit its issues or particular matters for the scrutiny of the government.[5] In such a petition, the petitioner may also challenge the constitutional validity of the Act or Rule under which the impugned order was issued[6] or even the administra-

---

3. *The Second Press Commission Report,* Vol. I, p. 33.
4. *Romesh Thappar* v. *State of Madras* (1950) S.C.R. 594.
5. *Brij Bhusan* v. *State of Delhi* (1950) S.C.R. 605.
6. *Express Newspapers* v. *Union of India* (1959) S.C.R. 12.

tive policy,[7] the implementation of which violates the fundamental right.

Concept of Press freedom

Freedom of the Press has three important elements :
(i) freedom of publication; (ii) freedom of circulation; and
(iii) freedom of access to all sources of information.

The earliest case to enforce freedom of the Press which
came before the Supreme Court soon after the commencement
of the Constitution was *Romesh Thappar* v *State of Madras*.[8]
In that case, invoking the powers conferred by S.9 (1—A) of
the Madras Maintenance of Public Order Act, 1949, the Government of Madras prohibited the entry into, or the circulation, sale or distribution in, the State of Madras or any part
thereof of the newspaper entitled *Cross Roads*. Apart from
deciding the meaning of the expression "security of the
State," this case firmly established that freedom of speech and
expression includes freedom of publication and propagation
of ideas and that freedom is ensured by freedom of circulation. The court emphatically pointed out that without circulation, the publication would be of little value. *Brij Bhusan* v.
State of Delhi[9] was a case in which the weekly *Organiser* was
asked by the Chief Commissioner of Delhi to submit for scrutiny before publication all communal matters and news and
views about Pakistan, including photographs and cartoons.
The impugned order was passed in pursuance of the power
conferred by S.7(1)(e) of the East Punjab Public Safety Act,
1949. The Court held that pre-censorship of a journal fell
outside the scope of clause (2) of article 19 and, therefore, not
only was the order unconstitutional but also the law under
which it was made was void. In both the above cases, the question before the Supreme Court was about the constitutional
validity not only of executive action but also of the Acts under
which executive action was taken. The Supreme Court further

---

7. *Bennet Coleman* v. *Union of India* A.R.R. 1973, S.C. 106.
8. *Romesh Thappar* v. *State of Madras* (1950) S.C.R. 594.
9. *Brij Bhusan* v. *State of Delhi* (1950) S.C.R. 605.

held in the *Express Newspapers* case[10] that freedom of expression includes not only the right to propagate one's own views but also the views of others. It further held that if any law unreasonably curtails the right of circulation, it would be void.

Another important landmark on the subject is the decision in *Sakal Papers* case.[11] The question before the Supreme Court in this case was whether the restrictions imposed by the Newspaper (Price and Page) Act, 1956 are reasonable restrictions on the freedom of expression. This Act empowered the Central Government to regulate the price of newspapers in relation to their pages and sizes and also to regulate the allocation of space to be allowed for advertisement matter. The contention of the government was that this Act was passed to prevent unfair competition among newspapers, to prevent the rise of monopolistic combines and to secure full scope for the development of smaller newspapers. The Court held that it was not open to the State to curtail or infringe the right of a newspaper for promoting the general welfare of a section or group of other newspapers, unless the restrictions imposed can be justified on the grounds mentioned in clause(2) of article 19. The Court held that the restrictions imposed by the impugned Act do not come within the purview of clause (2) of article 19 and that restrictions mentioned in clauses (3) to (5) of that article are not relevant at all and cannot be called in aid to sustain a law like the impugned Act which affects freedom of expression guaranteed under clause (1) of article 19. It further held that the impugned Act would affect the circulation of newspapers and is void. Doubts have been expressed by many, including the Mathew Commission, about the correctness of this decision. In another case, *Bennet Coleman* case,[12] the newsprint policy of the government was challenged and the Court held that it sought to curtail unduly,

10. *Express Newspapers* v. *Union of India* (1959) S.C.R. 12.
11. *Sakal Papers* v. *Union of India* (1962) 3 S.C.R. 842, A.I.R. 1962, S.C. 305.
12. *Bennet Coleman* v. *Union of India*, A.I.R. 1973, S.C. 106.

though indirectly, the freedom of circulation of newspapers and is void.

From the foregoing survey of case-laws, it would be seen that freedom of the Press covers both content and circulation, because the one without the other is meaningless in practice. The Constitution does not permit placing any restriction on this freedom except to the extent permissible under a law falling within clause (2) of article 19. This is a valuable freedom and if we have to maintain the democratic structure of our Constitution and prevent it from being converted into one-party State, it must be jealously guarded not only by the parties in opposition but also by the party in power. This freedom, in its widest amplitude, is essential to each side and should not be sacrificed at any cost.

It is the function of the Press to disseminate correct news and spread the truth and also facts about the truth. To enable it to do so, it should have access to all sources of information. Unless the information it gathers is authentic, the news it disseminates will get distorted and it cannot properly explain the facts about the truth. Our constitutional law has been solicitous in protecting the printed word under the shelter of article 19(1)(a) but has not paid sufficient attention in assisting the Press to have access to the sources of information. Freedom to have access to public records is an important aspect of freedom of the Press. But the government is generally reluctant to allow the Press to have such access under the Official Secrets Act, 1923 and various rules and orders. If the Press has to rely on what the government chooses to supply it, the picture may be one-sided and distorted and may not represent the truth. While openness is essential to the functioning of a democratic society, secrecy is also necessary in certain vital matters. The extent to which the Press should have access to public records is a delicate question and we shall discuss it fully in the next chapter while dealing with Official Secrets Act, 1923.

Freedom of publication should include freedom of publication of the proceedings of Parliament and State Legisla-

tures. We shall see in Chapter 6 relating to Press and Privileges of Parliament that Parliament has power under article
105 to prohibit the publication of its proceedings, though it
does not do so except in gross cases of abuse. In 1956, the
Parliamentary Proceedings (Protection of Publication) Act
was passed which gave protection to newspapers from civil
and criminal proceedings in respect of the publication of a
substantially true report of any proceedings of Parliament,
unless the publication is proved to have been made with malice.
This Act was repealed during Internal Emergency declared
on June 25, 1975 but it has again been re-enacted. The 44th
Amendment has now inserted a new article 361A which gives
constitutional protection to newspapers from civil and criminal proceedings in respect of the publication of a substantially
true report of any proceedings of Parliament and State Legislatures, unless the publication is proved to have been made
with malice. Article 361A has made Parliamentary enactment
superfluous. We shall discuss this question more fully when
we deal with Privileges of Parliament in Chapter 6.

   Advertisements. Advertisement is a recognised mode of expression but a distinction should be drawn between an advertisement for the purpose of expressing ideas and views and
purely commercial advertisements. In *Hamdard Dawakhana's*
case[13] the Supreme Court held that an advertisement for
purely commercial purposes does not fall within the right to
freedom of speech and expression under article 19(1)(a).

No special privileges for the Press

   The Press in India does not enjoy any special rights or
privileges which cannot be claimed or exercised by an ordinary individual who is a citizen. This was the position before
our Constitution came into force. It was held by the Privy
Council that "the freedom of the journalist is an ordinary
part of the freedom of the subject; and....his privilege is no
other and no higher."[14] The same position continues under

---

13. *Hamdard Dawakhana* v. *Union of India* (1960), 2 S.C.R. 671.
14. *Arnold* v. *King Emperor* (1914) 18 C.W.N. 785 (P.C.).

the Constitution also. Since freedom of the Press is included in the freedom of speech and expression guaranteed to citizens only, the Press stands on no higher footing than any other citizen and cannot claim any privilege not exerciseable by other citizens. It follows that the Press is subject to the same laws and regulations as are applicable to other citizens, and a general law which is applicable to the Press as also to other citizens would not be unconstitutional.[15] There is a wrong notion that apart from the reasonable restrictions that could be imposed on the freedom of the Press under article 19(2), there could be no other interference in the exercise of that freedom. What article 13(2) forbids is the making of any law which has the effect of 'taking away' or 'abridging' any fundamental right. There can be no controversy when a right is completely taken away and such action would be clearly hit by article 13(2). In the case of abridgement, however, the Mathew Commission seeks to make a distinction between 'abridgement of speech' and 'abridgement of freedom of speech.' (See Second Press Commission Report, Vol. I, p. 35). What the Constitution forbids is abridgement of freedom of speech and not abridgement of speech. Difficulty may arise in the application of the term 'abridge' where a law, rule or regulation is designed to accomplish an object other than abridgement of freedom of speech and the impact of such law, rule or regulation upon freedom of speech is secondary, incidental and indirect. In such cases, the cardinal principle is that there is no abridgement of the freedom unless the 'content' of speech itself is regulated.

Economic and tax measures, legislation relating to social welfare and wages, factory laws etc. may have some effect upon freedom of the Press when applied to newspaper industries. But when the burden placed on them is the same as that borne by others engaged in different forms of activity, it does not constitute abridgement of freedom of speech and such laws would not be unconstitutional. It would not, however, be permissible to make a law to control the content of expression.

15. *Express Newspapers* v. *Union of India* (1959) S.C.R. 12.

It would not also be legitimate for the State to single out the Press for laying upon it excessive burden or special restrictions which could not be imposed on other citizens.[16] Any special law putting restrictions on the Press has to be judged by the test whether they are reasonable restrictions in the interests of the grounds specified in clause (2) of article 19. The Court has to test the reasonableness both from the substantive as also from the procedural point of view.

Whether a Corporation can enforce the right to freedom of expression

It has been held by the Supreme Court in *Sharma's*[17] case that a non-citizen running a newspaper is not entitled to claim as his fundamental right the benefit of liberty of the Press. This decision raises an important question whether a company or corporation incorporated in India which runs a newspaper can claim the benefit of freedom of speech and expression guaranteed under article 19(1)(a). In regard to this question, the position of corporations in U.S.A. and India are somewhat different.

In U.S.A., the first Amendment says : ''Congress shall make no law...abridging the freedom of speech or of the Press.'' It is clear from this provision that the right to freedom of speech and freedom of the Press are not confined to citizens only. In other words, there is no restriction as to the donees of these freedoms. Earlier decisions of the U.S. Supreme Court took the view that a corporation was not entitled to freedom of speech as that right was confined to natural persons only. But later decisions of that court make it clear that a corporation is a ''person'' and since the due process clause of the Fourteenth Amendment protects a 'person' from deprivation of free speech by the State, a corporation's freedom of speech is also protected.[18]

16. *Sakal Papers* v. *Union of India* (1962) 3 S.C.R. 842.
17. *M.S. Sharma* v. *Srikrishna Sinha*, A.I.R. 1959, S.C. 395.
18. Fourteenth Amendment reads : "No State shall make or enforce any law which shall abridge the privileges or immunities of the citizens of the United States ; nor shall any State deprive any person of life, liberty or property without due process of law."

But the position in India is different. It was held by the Supreme Court in the *State Trading Corporation* case[19] as also in the *Telco's* case[20] that Indian companies were not citizens within the meaning of article 19 and, therefore, could not get the protection of that article. The Citizenship Act, 1955 also specifically provides that corporations are not citizens. It follows that a company, even though incorporated in India, would not be entitled to complain of any invasion of freedom of expression or of the Press. It appears, therefore, that the proposition laid down in *Express Newspapers*[21] case that the decisions in U.S.A. can be usefully adopted for interpreting the provision of article 19(1)(a) may not be wholly right. It has, however, been held by the majority in *Bennet Coleman* case[22] that although a company running a newspaper is not a citizen, the individual rights of freedom of speech and expression of editors, directors and shareholders who are citizens are exercised through the newspaper and they may challenge the constitutionality of any law or order which infringes freedom of expression of such newspaper. Such a proceeding would not be vitiated because the company has been added as a co-petitioner. Even a reader of a newspaper has been held to be entitled to challenge the constitutionality of a law which reduces or is likely to reduce the circulation of a newspaper.[23] The position that emerges is that where freedom of the Press has been violated, a corporation owning the Press can obtain relief through its editor, printer or publisher and the disability of the corporation is only technical.

The correctness of the majority decision has been questioned by the Mathew Commission. It has been argued that the company has a separate entity and its rights are not the

19. *State Trading Corporation* v. *Commercial Tax Officer* (1964) 4 S.C.R. 99.
20. *Tata Engineerig and Locomotive Co. Ltd.* v. *State of Bihar* (1964), 6 S.C.R. 885.
21. *Express Newspapers* v. *Union of India* (1959) S.C.R. 12.
22. *Bennet Coleman* v. *Union of India* (1973) 2 S.C.R. 757 A.I.R. 1973 S.C. 106.
23. *Sakal Papers* v. *Union of India* (1962) 3 S.C.R. 842

same as those of the shareholders. It would not be correct to say that the rights of shareholders are necessarily affected if the rights of the company are affected. Nor would it be correct to say that the individual rights of freedom of speech and expression of editors and shareholders are exercised through the newspaper. If the company has no right to enforce freedom of expression, as *ex hypothese* it has none, no editor or shareholder would be entitled to challenge a legislative measure on the ground that it affects freedom of expression of the company.

As a company is not a citizen and cannot, therefore, claim the fundamental right under article 19, the Mathew Commission has recommended that all companies engaged in the business of communication and whose shareholders are Indian citizens should be deemed to be citizens for the purpose of the relevant clause of article 19. This is a welcome recommendation and should be accepted. Since many newspapers in our country are owned and published by companies and it is essential that their freedom of expression should be protected, necessary steps should be taken to achieve that object without entering into legal niceties whether *Bennet Coleman* case was correctly decided. Even assuming that the case was correctly decided, a company cannot directly enforce its right under article 19. It has to do so indirectly through its office-bearers; this is unsatisfactory. A law should, therefore, be enacted to make a clear provision that all Indian companies engaged in the business of communication and whose shareholders are Indian citizens shall be deemed to be 'citizens' for the purpose of clause (a) of article 19(1). This object can be achieved by a simple amendment to Section 2(1)(f) of the Citizenship Act, 1955.

Relation between freedom of expression and freedom of the Press

As freedom of the Press is derived from the freedom of expression, the interpretation put by courts on freedom of expression would have a bearing on the concept of freedom of the Press. Thus, it was held by the Supreme Court in *Maneka*

Gandhi's case[24] that though the right to travel abroad is a valuable right, it cannot be claimed as an integral part of freedom of expression guaranteed by article 19(1)(a). So a journalist cannot claim exemption from passport regulations on the ground that it would infringe his right to freedom of expression. But if a journalist wants to go abroad to carry on his profession of journalism or for studying or teaching abroad, an order refusing passport to him may violate his freedom of expression.

Relation between article 19 and articles 21-22

In earlier cases,[25] the Supreme Court took the view that article 19 and articles 21-22 are mutually exclusive and if a person is deprived of his liberty either by imprisonment (article 21) or preventive detention (article 22), he cannot exercise any fundamental right under article 19. Later decisions, however, point out that imprisonment or detention need not necessarily deprive a person of all the rights under article 19 and he may exercise such of those rights as could be physically exercised by a person behind prison bars.[26] Thus a prisoner should have the right to read newspapers or books of his choice and even contribute articles to give expression to his views subject to restrictions which would be justified under article 19(2). But a journalist who has been imprisoned cannot claim that he should be allowed to carry on his profession by collecting information and reporting them, because the freedom of his movement has necessarily been curtailed under article 21.

Review of article 19(1)(a)

The Mathew Commission has suggested that keeping in view the changed conditions of our society, article 19(1)(a) should be reviewed to enable ordinary citizens also to exercise their right of freedom of expression.† This article confers the right to freedom of expression to newspapers but does not confer on ordinary citizens any fundamental right to ex-

---

24. *Maneka Gandhi* v. *Union of India*, A.I.R. 1978 S.C. 597.
25. *Gapalan* v. *State of Madras* (1950) S.C.R. 88.
26. *Batra* v. *Delhi Administration*, A.I.R. 1978, S.C. 1675.
 † *Second Press Commission Report*, Vol. I, p. 37.

press their views through a newspaper. A newspaper is published for the consumption of the public. The freedom of the consumers or the public to give expression to their views is also equally important. The public has also a right to information. Freedom of expression in its widest amplitude includes the right to information. The public has a right to know the different trends of opinion and views operating in the country. But the newspapers generally refuse to publish news and views which are not to their liking. Everybody cannot afford publication of a newspaper under modern conditions for giving expression to his views which may be of vital interest to the community at large and he loses the opportunity to have his say, unless the Press agrees to publish his views. At present, the Press has unfettered right to decide what to publish and what not to publish. Self-censorship by the Press is as great a menace to the freedom of expression as government censorship. Our constitutional law has been solicitous in protecting an idea when it comes to the market but has been singularly indifferent in creating opportunities for its expression. A newspaper should give publicity to views which are even hostile to it. Taking these factors into consideration, the Mathew Commission says that there is no reason why the services of the Press should not be available to citizens for exercise of their fundamental right of freedom of speech and expression on non-discriminatory basis subject, of course, to availability of space and other considerations. A revised, realistic view of article 19(1)(a) should permit encouragement of expression by providing not only for its protection 'after publication' but also for its 'emergence by publication'. The Press Council should be empowered to look into the complaints of arbitrary and malafide denial of access to the Press.

This recommendation has not found favour with Sarvashri Girilal Jain, Rajendra Mathur, S. K. Mukherjea, H. K. Paranjape and Ishrat Ali Siddiqui who have recorded a minute of dissent. The author also feels that this recommendation need not be accepted for various reasons. In the first place, though the recommendation may express a noble sentiment, it is not necessary because, as a matter of fact, diverse points of view are already being reflected in the columns of all major newspapers. No newspaper worth the name can afford to shut out important news or views. Even an industrial house own- ing a newspaper does not wilfully prevent the Marxist or leftist point of view from emerging in his paper. Every news- paper has an editorial policy and it has the right to propa- gate its own views. But no newspaper should be compelled to launch a campaign in favour of ideas it does not believe in, and which its readers may not be prepared to buy. Secondly, there are practical difficulties in implementing the recommen- dation. It will be an open invitation to a large number of persons who are eager to see their names in print, though what they write may not be worth publishing. Even between scripts which may deserve publication, a choice may have to be made having regard to availability of space and various other considerations. This discretion has to be exercised by the editor, and cannot be left to the Press Council. The Press Council is hardly equipped to decide such issues. Moreover, the Press Council may be flooded with complaints from con- tributors and it may not be possible for the Press Council to deal with them. Thirdly, the recommendation of the Mathew Commission does not fit in with the scheme of article 19 and cannot be given effect to by an amendment of that article. It is important to note that freedom of the Press guaranteed under article 19 can be enforced against State action only and not against the action of private citizens. If a person feels aggrieved because a newspaper has refused to publish his views and feels that his right to freedom of expression has been violated by the newspaper, even then, he cannot claim any relief against the newspaper under article 19. A dispute be- tween a contributor and newspaper is outside the scope of article 19.

It would not be possible to give effect to the recommenda- tion of the Mathew Commission by amending article 19 and the recommendation, if accepted, will create more difficulties than solving them. What is really necessary is to create as many forums as may be necessary to give expression to different points of view rather than compelling a newspaper to publish what it does not consider worth publishing.

Pre-censorship

There can be no doubt that imposition of pre-censorship drastically curtails liberty of the Press which is an essential part of the freedom of speech and expression under article 19(1)(a). As Blackstone observes : "The liberty of the Press consists in laying no previous restraint upon publications; and not in freedom from censure for criminal matter when published. Every free man has an undoubted right to lay what sentiments he pleases before the public; to forbid this is to destroy the freedom of the Press."[27] In democratic countries, pre-censorship is never imposed except in times of war.

In U.S.A. the Constitution provides freedom of the Press in absolute terms. There is no mention of any contingency in which censorship may be imposed. Even so, it has been judicially recognised that in times of war, when the security of the nation is in jeopardy and the danger to the society from injurious publication is grave and imminent, 'previous restraint' including censorship can be constitutionally imposed.[28]

In England, censorship has not so far been imposed in times of peace. But it is acknowledged that in times of war, when the very existence of the State is in danger, the State has the power to prevent the dissemination of such information or comments as would interfere with the successful prosecution of the war. Thus, during the Second World War, Emergency Powers (Defence) Acts were passed in order to make such regulation possible and the regulations made under these Acts empowered the government to suppress a newspaper if it was persistently publishing matters calculated to foment opposition to the successful prosecution of the war e.g. to cause unrest among defence forces. The restraints imposed by these regulations were withdrawn after the termination of the war.

27. *Blackstone's Commentaries*, Vol. IV, pp. 151-52.
28. *Near* v. *Minnesota* (1931) 283 U.S. 697, *Freedman* v. *Maryland*, (1965) 380 U.S. 51.

In India, under our Constitution, article 19(2) makes no distinction between times of war and peace. When an emergency is declared under article 352 and article 19 is suspended, censorship may be imposed without interference from courts and rigorous censorship was, in fact, imposed on the Press during the nineteen months of Internal emergency from June 1975 to March, 1977. We shall discuss this aspect of the question when we consider the impact of Emergency on freedom of the Press. Even apart from Emergency, article 19(2) authorises the State to impose reasonable restrictions on the Press to preserve the interests specified therein either in the form of prior restraint like censorship or in the form of subsequent punishment. The law under which the restrictions are imposed must be proximately related to any of the grounds specified in clause (2) and the restrictions imposed by such law must be reasonable both from the substantive as also procedural point of view. The decision of the Supreme Court in *Virendra* v. *State of Punjab*[29] is a clear authority for the proposition that the pre-censorship even in times of peace is warranted in certain circumstances under article 19(2). The Supreme Court recognised that it is certainly a serious encroachment on the valuable and cherished right of freedom of expression, if a newspaper is prevented from publishing its views on what might be a burning topic of the day. But the Court held that if care is taken to see that the restrictive law in question is confined to any of the grounds specified in clause (2) of article 19 and the restrictions conform to the test of substantive and procedural reasonableness and there are adequate safeguards against the arbitrary exercise of the power of the executive, the law would not be unconstitutional. Following the decision of the Supreme Court in *Virendra's* case, the Assam High Court has recently upheld the validity of the power of the State to impose pre-censorship under the Assam Special Powers (Press) Act, 1960. The validity of certain provisions of that Act, however, were upheld with certain limitations as there were not adequate procedural safeguards.

29. *Virendra* v. *State of Punjab* (1958) S.C.R. 308 A.I.R. 1957 S.C. 896.

A question has arisen whether the power of censorship conferred on the State under article 19(2) should be retained or whether the exercise of that power should be allowed only in circumstances which justify the declaration of an emergency under article 352. The Mathew Commission has taken the view that apart from emergency provisions, the power of censorship under article 19(2) should also be retained. Dr. H. K. Paranjape, a member of the Commission, disagreeing with this view, holds that pre-censorship is justified only in times of emergency. He is further of the view that even if article 19(2) permits censorship at other times, there should be a convention that the power should not be used. Maintaining law and order is the paramount duty of a State and in an urgent situation, it might be necessary to take anticipatory action to avert a serious crisis arising out of public disorder. It is also recognised that social interest ordinarily demands a free pronouncement and interchange of ideas but circumstances may arise when the social interest in public order may require reasonable subordination of the social interest in free speech and expression. The author, therefore, agrees with the Commission that the power of pre-censorship under article 19(2) should be retained but at the same time, we think that the power should not be invoked except in cases of extreme necessity in the national interest, when the situation cannot be saved without resort to this power.

An enlightened Press may voluntarily impose certain restraints in the publication of certain matters in the interests of decorum or in the larger interests of the society or to avoid legal control. In U.K., there is a convention that the Press does not publish details about the private affairs of the Royal family. In U.S.A., a code of ethics for newspapers was laid down by the American Society of Newspaper Editors as early as 1923. Besides, leading journals have adopted certain self-denying codes in the larger interests of the society. In India, we have yet to adopt a code of conduct for the Press. When Emergency was declared in June, 1975, the Censoring Authority issued certain guidelines for the Press. These guidelines were imposed from above and cannot be said to be self-censorship. Occasions arise during communal disturbances and other circumstances when undue publicity to certain incidents may do incalculable harm to the society. The Press Council may, therefore, issue certain guidelines and a code of conduct for the Press and the Press should voluntarily refrain from publishing the details about certain matters. If such guidelines are framed and strictly followed by the Press, the question of pre-censorship by the State would not arise.

Restrictions on Freedom of the Press

Freedom of the Press as derived from freedom of expression under article 19(1)(a) is not an absolute or unfettered right. In a modern state, there cannot be absolute rights; they must be subject to social control. The American Constitution provides freedom of the Press in absolute terms leaving it to the courts to invent the doctrine of 'police power' and determine the grounds and the extent of State regulation of that freedom. In order to avoid judicial supremacy as in America and to strike a balance between freedom of the Press and social control, limitations have been placed on freedom of the Press by the Constitution itself. Freedom of the Press is subject to restrictions under clause (2) of article 19. As the Press is also an industry and a business, limitations may be placed on it under clause (6) of article 19 also. This right may also be suspended during an Emergency. Laws have been enacted to regulate the Press; there is also executive control over the Press. Freedom of the Press is also subject to privileges of Parliament and State Legislatures. We shall discuss in this chapter constitutional restraints on freedom of the Press and other limitations will be discussed in subsequent chapters.

Freedom of the Press is available to citizens and against State Action

We have already seen that freedom of the Press is available to citizens only and not to all persons. It is important to note that this right is available against State action only and not against the action of private citizens. Relief under article 19 cannot be claimed in the case of any dispute among private persons. But in order to make this right more effective, the word 'State' has been widely defined in article 12 to include not only the executive and legislative organs of the Union and States but also local authorities.

Restrictions under clause (2) of article 19

Clause (2) of article 19 specifies the limitations on the freedom of speech and expression guaranteed under article 19(1)(a). Clause (2) as originally enacted was narrow in scope and did not mention 'public order' as one of the restrictions but there was a reference to the security of the State. The Supreme Court in *Romesh Thappar's* case[30] made a distinction between security of the State and public order. An article or speech may tend to bring about public disorder but unless it takes an aggravated form, seeking to undermine the security of the State, freedom of the Press cannot be curtailed. The court held that unless a law restricting freedom of speech and expression is directed solely against undermining the security of the State or at overthrowing it, such law could not fall within the reservation of clause (2) of article 19. As a result of this decision, the First Amendment was undertaken which included 'public order' as one of the grounds in clause (2). Incidentally, it also added two other grounds, namely, friendly relations with foreign States and incitement to an offence. Disruptive forces appeared in various parts of the country and certain organisations, both in the South as well as in the North, advocated secession and carried on activities which had a tendency to endanger the sovereignty and integrity of India. To meet the situation, 16th Amendment was undertaken to include sovereignty and integrity of India as one of the grounds for imposing restrictions under clause (2) of article 19. The Constitution now empowers the State to make law imposing reasonable restrictions on the exercise of the right of freedom of speech and expression in the interest of eight matters, namely, (i) sovereignty and integrity of India; (ii) security of the State; (iii) friendly relations with foreign States; (iv) public order; (v) decency or morality;

---

30. *Romesh Thapper* v. *State of Madras*, (1950), S.C.R. 594.

(vi) contempt of court; (vii) defamation; and (viii) incitement to an offence.

Limitations are exhaustive

As eight restrictions have been specifically mentioned in clause (2) of article 19, the Supreme Court has time and again pointed out that the grounds of restriction mentioned in that clause are exhaustive and they have to be strictly construed. The courts cannot enlarge them or admit any other grounds on the theory of police power.[31] No new restrictions can also be imposed by the State except by an amendment of the Constitution. The result is that any restriction imposed on freedom of the Press becomes invalid unless it is related to any of the grounds mentioned in clause (2).

A question arises whether freedom of the Press guaranteed under article 19(1)(a) can be restricted on the grounds mentioned in clauses (3) to (5) of that article. A definitely negative answer to this question was given by the Supreme Court in *Sakal Papers'* case.[32] It has been held that the scheme of article 19 is to enumerate the different freedoms separately and then to specify the restrictions to which they may be subject and the object for securing which this could be done. Clauses (3) to (5) are not at all relevant to freedom of expression guaranteed under article 19(1)(a) and it would not be permissible to restrict that freedom by imposing restrictions mentioned in clauses (3) to (5). The Press has, however, a dual character. It is a medium of expression and it carries on business also. As it carries on business also, restrictions may be placed on the Press under clause (6) but this raises a slightly complicated question and we shall discuss it separately.

Restrictions by law

Clause (2) of article 19 empowers a State as defined in article 12 to impose restrictions on freedom of the Press. Such restrictions can be imposed only by law and not by executive

---

31.   *Romesh Thappar* v. *State of Madras,* (1950) S.C.R. 594.
32.   *Sakal Papers* v. *Union of India,* (1962) 3 S.C.R. 842.

orders. They may be imposed 'in the interests of' the grounds
mentioned in clause (2). The effect of the introduction of this
expression by the First Amendment Act, 1951 is to widen the
scope of restrictions and to narrow down the ambit of freedom
of expression. This expression has a wide connotation and "a
law may not have been designed to directly maintain public
order and yet may have been enacted in the interests of public order." As pointed out by the Supreme Court in *Ramjilal's* case,[33] the expression 'in the interests of' has introduced
the tendency test to determine the validity of a restriction
under clause (2). But this does not mean that "any remote or
fanciful connection with the grounds mentioned in clause (2)
would save the law by the expression in the interests of".

Restrictions should be reasonable and test of reasonableness

The restrictions imposed must be reasonable and the
reasonableness of the restrictions is subject to judicial review.
If the court finds that the restrictions imposed are unreasonable, it may declare the law void. The criteria or tests for
determining reasonableness of a restriction have been considered by the Supreme Court in a number of cases. In *Row's*
case the Supreme Court held : "the tests of reasonableness
should be applied to each individual statute impugned, and
no abstract standard or general pattern of reasonableness can
be laid down as applicable to all cases. The nature of the right
alleged to have been infringed, the underlying purpose of the
restrictions imposed, the extent and urgency of the evil sought
to be remedied thereby, the disproportion of the imposition,
the prevailing conditions at the time should all enter into judicial verdict."[34] All these circumstances have to be taken into
account in determining the reasonableness or otherwise of any
restriction.

Reasonableness of any restriction has also to be judged
both from the substantive as also procedural point of view.
"Legislation which arbitrarily and excessively invades the
right cannot be said to contain the quality of reasonableness

33.   *Ramjilal* v. *State of U.P.* (1957) S.C.R. 860 A.I.R. 1957 S.C. 620.
34.   *State of Madras* v. *V.G. Row*, (1952) S.C.R. 597.

and unless it strikes a proper balance between the freedom guaranteed and the social control permitted, it must be held to be wanting in that quality."[35] This may be said to be the substantive aspect of reasonableness. But in order to be reasonable, not only should the law be not excessive, but the procedure or manner of imposition must also be reasonable.[36] Broadly speaking, a procedure would be unreasonable, if it violates the principles of natural justice. If, for example, a restriction is imposed without giving the person affected an opportunity of being heard, it would be an unreasonable restriction.

Restrictions may include prohibition

A question arises whether the word 'restrictions' in clause (2) includes total prohibition or ban. The earlier cases of the Supreme Court were not clear on this point and it was felt that restrictions did not include prohibition but it is now well settled that restrictions may mean total prohibition or ban. In the case of *Narendra Kumar,* the Supreme Court reviewed all the earlier cases and held : "there can be no doubt that they (Constitution makers) intended the word 'restriction' to include prohibition also. The contention that a law prohibiting the exercise of a fundamental right is in no case saved cannot, therefore, be accepted."[37] It is, however, for the court to decide whether in a given case, having regard to the nature of the subject-matter and the circumstances of the case, restriction may reasonably include total prohibition or ban.

We have already discussed the general characteristics of the restrictions which may be imposed on freedom of the Press under clause (2) of article 19. We now propose to analyse very briefly each of those restrictions separately.

Sovereignty and integrity of India

This ground of restriction on freedom of expression was added by the 16th Amendment to enable the State to control

---

35. *Chintaman Rao* v. *State of M.P.,* (1950) S.C.R. 759.
36. *Gopalan* v. *State of Madras,* (1950) S.C.R. 88.
37. *Narendra Kumar* v. *Union of India,* (1960) 2 S.C.R. 375.

the activities of certain organisations such as Dravida Kazhagam in the South and the Plebiscite Front in Kashmir which were advocating secession and carrying on activities which had a tendency to endanger sovereignty and integrity of India. No independent country can tolerate any agitation on the part of any unit of its territory either to secede or form an independent State or to integrate with a foreign State. The object of this amendment was to confer on Parliament specific power to legislate on this subject and empower the State to deal with activities which might not be brought within the ambit of the expression 'security' of the State. Recently, Khalistan movement has raised its ugly head and there are ominous signs in the north-eastern region also. But no comprehensive law on this subject has yet been enacted. There are two enactments which partially deal with the subject. The Criminal Law Amendment Act, 1961 provides that whoever questions the territorial integrity or frontiers of India in a manner which is prejudicial to the interests of the safety or security of India shall be punished with imprisonment or fine or both. This Act does not, however, apply to Jammu and Kashmir. The publication of official secrets which is likely to affect the sovereignty or integrity of India is also punishable under the Official Secrets Act, 1923.

Security of the State

Equally important is the security of the State. No State can tolerate any propaganda by any organisation which seeks to undermine the security of the State or any activity which threatens to overthrow the organised government by means which are unlawful or unconstitutional. Obviously, security of the State is the very foundation on which any organised government may function. It has two aspects, external and internal. When there is external aggression or threat thereof, the State may impose restrictions on freedom of the Press, *e.g.*, by prohibiting or punishing any publication which interferes with the war efforts of the nation. It cannot allow disclosure of war measures or movement of the armed forces which may help the enemy but the right of the people to discuss the defence policy of the government or to criticise the conduct of the armed forces cannot be barred. From the internal standpoint, the Press has a right to criticise the functioning of the government formed by one party with the object of replacing it by another political party. But the State has the right to suppress an abuse of this freedom and punish the advocacy of the overthrow of the government by force or violence or unconstitutional means.

In India, the security of the State was sought to be protected by the Press (Objectionable Matter) Act, 1951 which contained restrictions upon publications which incite or encourage any person to resort to violence for the purpose of overthrowing or undermining the government established by law in India or in any State thereof. This Act expired in 1956 and was replaced by the Prevention of Publication of Objectionable Matter Act, 1976 and this Act was also repealed by the Janata Government in April, 1977. At present, there is no comprehensive enactment to protect the security of the State but there are several enactments which seek to protect this interest from different aspects :

(a) Indian Penal Code, Secs. 121-121A (abetment or conspiracy to wage war against the Government of India); S. 124A (Sedition that is, to incite disaffection against the Government established by law in India, by words which have a tendency to create public disorder); and S.131 (inciting or abetting mutiny or seduction from duty of a member of the armed forces) are intended to protect security of the State.

(b) The Official Secrets Act, 1923.

(c) Criminal Law Amendment Act, 1961.

(d) The Defence of India Act and Rules made thereunder sought to protect 'defence of India' and public security but they have expired.

(e) Secs. 3 and 8 of the Dramatic Performances Act, 1876 empower the State government to prohibit and to seize the paraphernalia required for a dramatic performance which is likely to excite feelings of disaffection against the Government of India.

(f) Section 11 of the Customs Act, 1962 empowers the Central Government to prohibit the import or export, *inter alia* of documents which are prejudicial to security of India, the maintenance of public order and standards of decency or morality.

(g) Section 3 of the Police (Incitement to Disaffection) Act, 1922 makes it an offence to do any act which causes or is likely to cause 'disaffection towards the Government established by law in India amongst the members of a police force or attempts to induce.... any member of a police force to withhold his services or to commit a breach of discipline.

Friendly relations with foreign States

This ground of restriction was added by the First Amendment. This expression has a wide connotation and will include not only libel against foreign dignitaries but also any act which imperils peaceful relations with a friendly foreign State. Any attempt on the part of citizens to imperil friendly relations with foreign States should obviously be punished. It may, however, be noted that the Foreign Relations Act, 1932 which provided penalties for the libel of foreign dignitaries has been repealed by Act 56 of 1951. At present, there is no legislation on the subject but by way of convention, the Press refrains from publishing anything which might unfavourable affect friendly relations with other States.

Public Order

It is the paramount duty of the State to maintain law and order and any speech or expression which seeks to disturb public order should be punished. 'Public order' is a term of wide import but its scope in article 19(2) has to be determined in juxtaposition with the other grounds of restrictions mentioned therein. It has to be distinguished from 'law and order' and 'security of the State'. Law and order has the widest connotation and public order is included in it. Hence, an activity which affects 'law and order' may not necessarily affect public order,[38] and an activity which is prejudicial to

38. *Bhupel* v. *Arif*, A.I.R. 1974 S.C. 255.

public order may not necessarily affect 'security of the State'.[39] The Supreme Court in *Romesh Thappar's* case[40] has drawn a distinction between public order and security of the State. An article or speech may tend to bring about public disorder but unless it takes an aggravated form, it may not seek to undermine security of the State or overthrow it. So understood, public order has been interpreted to mean 'public safety and tranquility.'

The question what constitutes public order has been the subject of consideration by the Supreme Court in a series of cases. Constraint of space would not permit us to deal with them. We shall, however, refer to some of the enactments which empower the State to put restrictions on the freedom of speech and expression in the interest of public order :

(i) *The Indian Penal Code* : Sec. 153A makes it an offence, *inter alia,* to promote enmity between different classes of citizens by words, either spoken or written, or by representation or otherwise. The preaching of communal hatred or feelings of enmity between different sections of the community may be punished and reasonable preventive measures may also be taken for the maintenance of communal harmony.[41] Secs. 295A and 298 make it an offence to utter words or to make visible representations with deliberate intent to wound the religious feelings or belief of another person or of any other class of citizens. It has been held that any person who deliberately insults or attempts to insult the religious beliefs of a class of citizens can be punished. The Supreme Court pointed out that the calculated tendency of such aggravated form of insult was to disrupt public order and was relatable to "the interests of public order."[42] Sec. 505 makes it an offence to circulate any statement, rumour or report

39. *Ram Manohar* v. *State of Bihar*, (1966) 1 S.C.R. 709.
40. *Romesh Thappar* v. *State of Madras*, (1950) S.C.R. 594.
41. *Virendra* v. *State of Punjab*, A.I.R. 1957 S.C. 896.
42. *Ramjilal* v. *State of U.P.*, (1957) S.C.R. 860.
   Kedarnath v. *State of Bihar*, A.I.R. 1962 S.C. 955.

with intent to cause mutiny or failure of duty by members of the armed forces or with intent to cause alarm to any section of the public whereby any person may be induced to commit an offence against the State or public tranquility or with intent to incite any class or community to commit any offence against any other class or community.

(ii) *The Indian Telegraph Act, 1885* and *the Post Office Act, 1898.*

(iii) *The Police (Incitement to Disaffection) Act, 1922.*

The Indian Penal Code also provides for the punishment for abetment of an offence and says that a person abets the commission of an offence, if he instigates any person to commit it.

Decency or morality

Article 19(2) enables the State to impose restrictions on freedom of expression in the interests of decency or morality. It cannot be denied that it is important in the interests of society to suppress obscenity, though it might be difficult to define it. There is some difference between obscenity and pornography but both are offensive to decency and morality. The answer to the question what is obscene has varied from country to country, from age to age and from person to person. What constitutes obscenity depends as much on the moods of the people as upon individuals constituting the society. It is always a question of degree.

Secs. 292, 293 and 294 of the Indian Penal Code are the main provisions against obscenity in the general law of this country. The validity of Sec. 293 which provides punishment for sale of obscene objects came up for consideration before the Supreme Court in *Ranjit* v. *State of Maharashtra.*[43] The main point for consideration in that case was whether 'Lady Chatterley's Lover' by D. H. Lawrence is an obscene book and the Supreme Court declared it to be so. At that time, there was no definition of the word 'obscene' in the Indian Penal

43. *Ranjit* v. *State of Maharasthra*, A I.R. 1965 S.C. 881.

Code and the Supreme Court had to decide what is obscene and in this process, it accepted the definition of the term by Cockburn C. J. in *Hicklin's* case[44] where the Judge said :

"I think, the test of obscenity is this, whether the tendency of the mattter charged as obscenity is to deprave and corrupt those whose minds are open to immoral influences and into whose hands a publication of this sort may fall....it is quite certain that it would suggest to the minds of the young of either sex or even to persons of more advanced years thoughts of a most impure and libidinous character."

The important question is whether this test of obscenity squares with the freedom of expression guaranteed under our Constitution. The Supreme Court held that what Sec. 293 I.P.C. seeks to punish is such "libidinous writings of high erotic effect unredeemed by anything literary or artistic and intended to arouse sexual feelings." The Court pointed out that "treating with sex and nudity in art or literature cannot be regarded as evidence of obscenity without something more", thereby keeping artistic works outside the purview of Section 293 I.P.C. The Court came to the definite conclusion that "the test to adopt in our country is that obscenity without a preponderating social purpose or profit cannot have the constitutional protection of free speech and expression and obscenity is treating with sex in a manner appealing to the carnal side of human nature or having that tendency. Such a treating with sex is offensive to modesty and decency but the extent of such appeal in a book etc. are matters for consideration in each individual case."

Realising the difficulties of deciding what is obscene and for giving effect to judicial decisions on the subject, Section 292 I.P.C. was amended by Act 36 of 1969 to define the word 'obscene'. A book, pamphlet etc. shall be deemed to be obscene if it is lascivious or appeals to the prurient interest or if its effect is such as to tend to deprave and corrupt persons who are likely to read, see or hear the matter contained in it. Practical difficulties will still arise in applying this definition to

44. *Hicklin's Case*, (1868) 3 Q.B. (371 .

the facts of a particular case and the test of obscenity laid down by the Supreme Court in Lady Chatterley Lover's case will still hold the field.

Apart from the general provisions of Secs. 292 to 294 I.P.C., there are several enactments regulating freedom of expression in the interests of decency or morality :

(1) Section 3 of the Dramatic Performances Act, 1876

(2) Section 11 of the Customs Act, 1962

(3) Section 20 of the Post Office Act, 1898

(4) The Cinematograph Act, 1952

(5) Drugs and Magic (Objectionable Advertisement) Act, 1956

(6) The Young Persons (Harmful Publications) Act, 1956

(7) The Criminal Procedure Code, 1973 seeks to make the law against obscene publications more severe and empowers the State Government to forfeit, search for and seize obscene publications coming under Sections 292 and 293 I.P.C.

Contempt of Court and defamation

Restrictions on freedom of speech and expression may be imposed on the grounds of contempt of court and defamation. These two grounds deserve more detailed consideration and will be discussed in the subsequent chapters.

Incitement to an offence

This ground was added by the First Amendment. The Constitution, however, does not define what constitutes an offence. Under the General Clauses Act, 'an offence shall mean any act or omission made punishable by any law for the time being in force.' What constitutes an incitement to an offence has to be determined by the court with particular reference to the facts of each case. Chapter V of the Indian Penal Code deals with abetment of offence and Sections 107 and 108 lay down that a person abets the commission of an offence, if he instigates any person to commit it.

Restrictions under clause (6) of article 19

The Press has a dual role. It is not only a medium of expression but is also an industry carrying on business with profit motive. The right to carry on any business has been conferred on citizens under article 19(1)(g) but reasonable restrictions can be placed on this right under clause (6) in the interests of the general public. Clause (6) also permits a State to make a law relating to (i) qualifications necessary for carrying on any trade or business; and (ii) the carrying on any trade, business, industry or service by the State or by a corporation owned or controlled by the State to the exclusion, complete or partial, of citizens.

Reasonable restrictions in the interests of the general public may be imposed under clause (6) to regulate the business activity of the Press. These are permissible restrictions under the Constitution and the Press cannot complain. But in regulating the economic and business aspects of a newspaper, the State cannot impose restrictions which would affect freedom of expression guaranteed to the Press under article 19(1)(a) by curtailing its circulation or freedom of discussion. It has been held by the Supreme Court in *Sakal Papers'* case[45] that article 19 does not prefer one freedom to another. A citizen is entitled to enjoy each and every one of the freedoms specified therein together, and the State cannot restrict one of those freedoms for the better enjoyment of another. Hence, the State cannot *directly* restrict one freedom by placing an otherwise permissible restriction of another freedom. Thus freedom of expression guaranteed under clause (1)(a) cannot be directly curtailed by imposing restrictions in the interests of the general public authorised in relation to the freedom of business guaranteed under clause (1)(g).

Since grounds mentioned in clause (2) and clause (6) are different, the exercise of power by the State under both the clauses may lead to anomaly or conflict and the Supreme Court has tried to remove this anomaly by evolving the doctrine of 'direct impact'. If a law regulating the business

---

45. *Sakal Papers* v. *Union of India*, (1962) 3 S.C.R. 842.

aspect of the Press imposes a restriction which *directly* affects volume of circulation of a newspaper or its freedom of discussion or otherwise affects freedom of expression, such a law would be unconstitutional. On the other hand, if a law is directly aimed at regulating the business aspect of the Press but as a result of the operation of such law, freedom of expression of a newspaper is *indirectly or remotely* affected depending on contingencies which may or may not happen, the law cannot be declared invalid as violative of article 19(1)(a).

Express Newspapers case[46] is an authority for the proposition that a law regulating the business aspect of newspaper industry would not be invalid merely because there are possibilities that the law may indirectly affect freedom of expression of newspapers. In that case, the constitutional validity of the Working Journalists (Conditions of Service and Miscellaneous Provisions) Act, 1955 was under consideration. That Act was enacted for the purpose of 'the amelioration of conditions of workmen in the newspaper industry' and provided for, among other things, the constitution of a Wage Board for fixing the rates of wages for different classes of employees. It was argued on behalf of the newspaper employers that the scales of wages fixed by the Wage Board are much higher than the contractual rates and this would put too heavy a financial burden on the Press which many newspapers would not be able to bear and they may have to close down their establishments and this would cause an abridgement of freedom of the Press. It was further argued that even those who may survive may have to seek financial assistance from government and other sources and would be subjected to external pressure and in the process, independence of the Press would be affected and freedom of discussion and volume of circulation may also be curtailed. The Supreme Court conceded that there are incidental disadvantages which may manifest themselves in the future working of the industry. Those employers who are favourably situated may not feel the strain at all while those of them who are marginally situated may

46. *Express Newspapers* v. *Union of India*, (1959) S.C.R. 12

not be able to bear the strain and may in conceivable cases have to disappear after closing their establishments. But the Court held that the impugned Act is a beneficent legislation to regulate the conditions of service of working journalists and is not directed against freedom of the Press. Apprehension about the consequences which may flow from the working of the Act are only contingent; they may or may not take place. Unless the alleged consequences are the *direct* and inevitable consequences of the legislation, it would not be possible to strike it down. The impugned Act has no direct impact on freedom of the Press and cannot be declared invalid as violative of article 19(1)(a).

On the other hand, *Bennet Coleman* case[47] is an authority for the proposition that a policy of the government regulating newspaper industry would be invalid, if it substantially curtails freedom of the Press. In this case, the newsprint policy of the Government of India under the News Print Control Order was under consideration. Government imposed restrictions upon the import and distribution of newsprint in view of its scarcity and provided that if a newspaper sought to obtain its quota of newsprint from the government, it would have to comply with the conditions laid down in the Control Order. The Court conceded that in view of the scarcity of newsprint, Government had the plenary power to control the supply and use of newsprint but the Court struck down the News Print Control Order as the conditions laid down under that Order put unreasonable restrictions on freedom of the Press guaranteed by article 19(1)(a).

In the first place, the Court held that the newsprint policy of the government discriminates against big newspapers. The quota allotted to a big newspaper was not in proportion to its size and if it has to curtail its size, it would, in its turn, affect its circulation also. The contention of the Government was that its newsprint policy was intended to eliminate unfair competition between big and small newspapers and to promote the growth of the latter. Elimination

47. *Bennet Coleman* v. *Union of India*, A.I.R. 1973 S.C. 106.

of unfair competition may be justified in "the interests of
the general public" which is a permissible ground in clause
(6) of article 19. But this cannot be a ground for restricting
freedom of the Press as it is not one of the grounds specified
in clause (2) of that article. In regulating the business activity of a newspaper under article 19(6), the State is not competent to substantially curtail freedom of the Press guaranteed under article 19(1)(a). Secondly, when there is a group
of newspapers under common ownership, quota of newsprint
was allotted to each newspaper separately and a condition was
laid down that the owner could not transfer the quota allotted
to one unit to any other unit either completely or even partially. The definite stand of the government was that this bar
was imposed to prevent growth of monopoly in the Press. The
question arose whether government could curb the growth of
monopoly in the Press through a system of control of the
newsprint. The Court held that it was open to the government to make a general law to curb monopolies in business
and if the Press was also subjected to such general law, the
Press had little to complain. But the Press could not be singled out for purpose of controlling monopolies. The condition
imposed affects freedom of the Press and is not protected by
clause (2) of article 19.

Thirdly, a question arose whether in allotting newsprint
to a newspaper, a restriction may be imposed by fixing the
maximum number of pages it would be permitted to publish.
The Court held that it would not be open to the government
to impose any restriction on the use of newsprint, subsequent
to its allotment, because in order to ensure its freedom of
expression, a newspaper was entitled to utilise its quota in any
manner it liked and that the curb on its size was a direct curtailment of its circulation. Taking all factors into account,
the Court held that the newsprint policy of the government
as also the News Print Control Order have a direct impact
on freedom of the Press and are invalid.

The doctrine of direct impact was explained by the
Supreme Court in a later case also, in *Maneka Gandhi's* case.[48]

48.   *Maneka Gandhi* v. *Union of India*, A.I.R. 1978 S.C. 597

The Court held that the right to go abroad flows from article 21 and is not guaranteed by any of the provisions of article 19(1). Hence, a law impounding a citizen's passport cannot be challenged as violative of article 19(1)(a). But an order issued under such law restraining a person from going abroad may be held to be invalid as violative of article 19(1)(a) or article 19(1)(g), if it can be shown that the petitioner intended to go abroad to exercise her freedom of expression or to carry on her profession as a journalist there and that "the direct and inevitable consequences of the impugned order was to impede the exercise of freedom of speech and expression or of her right to carry on her profession."

We have just discussed the application of the doctrine of 'direct impact' to restrictions which may be imposed to regulate commercial activities of the Press under clause (6) of article 19. The same principle applies to general laws not specifically directed against the Press. Laws of taxation, factory laws and general laws regulating industrial relations, criminal laws intended to maintain public order, security of the State and to suppress obscenity may have some effect on freedom of the Press, when applied to newspaper industry We have already discussed this question earlier in this Chapter under the sub-head that the Press has no special privileges. The same theory of direct impact applies to general laws also. If any law or restriction not protected by clause (2) of article 19 directly and substantially curtails freedom of expression, the law or restriction would be unconstitutional. But if the effect of such law or restriction on freedom of expression is indirect and remote, the law would not be vitiated and would not be violative of article 19(1)(a).

Impact of Emergency on freedom of the Press

Earlier in this Chapter, we discussed the question of censorship in times of peace, when there is no declaration of Emergency. A declaration of Emergency under article 352 has far-reaching effects on fundamental rights under articles 358 and 359. These provisions were substantially amended by the 44th amendment and the constitutional changes are intended to restrict the scope and effect of the declaration of Emergency. Under article 352 as originally enacted, Emergency could be declared on the grounds of war or external aggression or internal disturbance. The words 'internal disturbance' have been substituted by the words 'armed rebellion.' Under article 358 as originally enacted, there was automatic suspension of the fundamental rights guaranteed to citizens by article 19 when an Emergency was declared. It has now been provided that such automatic suspension will take place only when the Proclamation is issued either on the ground of war or external aggression. This means that article 358 will not be attracted when Emergency is declared on the ground of armed rebellion but in such a case, it will be possible to suspend the enforcement of the fundamental rights under article 19 by issuing a Presidential Order under article 359. There is a further provision that when article 19 is suspended either under article 358 or by a Presidential Order under article 359, the suspension of article 19 does not have automatic effect but will depend on a recital in a particular law to the effect that such law relates to the Proclamation of Emergency. In the absence of any such declaration in the law itself, neither the law nor any executive action taken thereunder shall have any immunity from attack on the ground of contravention of article 19. The position that emerges is that when article 19 is suspended on the ground of war or external aggression under article 358 or by a Presidential Order under article 359 on the ground of armed rebellion, Government will be free to impose pre-censorship without any interference from court.

Three Proclamations of Emergency have so far been issued under acticle 352. The first Proclamation was issued on 26th October, 1962 in the wake of Chinese aggression; the second was issued on December 3, 1975 when Pakistan launched an undeclared war against India; and the third Proclamation was issued on June 25, 1975 on the ground of 'internal disturbance.'' Government did not take recourse to pre-censorship when emergency was declared on the ground of external agression by the first two Proclamations but rigorous censorship was imposed during the nineteen months of emergency from June 25, 1975 to March 21, 1977 declared on the ground of internal disturbance.

Immediately after the Third Proclamation of Emergency, Government of India issued a notification imposing pre-censorship under Part V of the Defence of India Rules against publication of prejudicial matter. The Censorship Authority was empowered to prohibit the publication of any matter prejudicial to (i) defence of India; (ii) civil defence; (iii) public safety; (iv) maintenance of public order; and (v) efficient conduct of military operations. The Censoring Authority issued certain guidelines for the Press to follow during emergency and it appears that in most of the States, the Press voluntarily followed the guidelines and the question of censorship did not arise. Occasions, however, did arise when the Censoring Authority censured even innocent passages which were not directly related to prejudicial matter. But in such cases also, the Press did not fight for its right to freedom of expression; it meekly submitted to the whims of censoring authority. For the sorry state of affairs that existed during the period of internal Emergency, the Press is equally to blame. Imposition of pre-censorship is in the nature of an exception in the history of the Press in free India but it has taught us some lessons which may be of help during any future Emergency.

CHAPTER IV

Law on the Press and Executive Control

I. LAW ON THE PRESS

We have discussed in Chapter I the role of the Press and the need for its freedom. A free Press is indispensable to a democratic society. But the freedom guaranteed to the Press has certain inherent dangers, if it does not function with a sense of social responsibility. It may do incalculable harm and cause mischief by abusing its powers. People are generally prone to believe the printed word, even when it is not honest. It is this gullibility of the average reader which gives a tremendous power to the Press. It may abuse its powers in various ways. The foremost danger arises from monopolistic control of the Press. Since the Press is the most potent instrument of mass communication, powerful parties, financial groups or big industrial houses seek to control the Press to further their private interests to the detriment of the public, the result of which is that there is no "free market of ideas." Moreover, goaded by commercial motive to earn profit, many newspapers indulge in stunts to pander to the vulgar instincts of human beings, such as blackmailing, yellow journalism, horror-comics, veiled pornography and the like.

Though it is recognised that the Press in our country sometimes abuses its power, the remedy of this serious problem is not so easy. It has 'some disagreeable result but the wholesome ones are greater and more numerous' as Bryce put it. Freedom of the Press is a necessary evil and a proper balance has to be found between its freedom on the one hand

and the restrictions which may be put on such freedom to keep its abuses under control. Restrictions may be put on freedom of the Press under clause (2) of article 19 and we have discussed this question in the previous chapter.

Apart from constitutional restraints, there are laws in our country relating to the Press which seek to put statutory curbs on freedom of the Press. The number of such laws is fairly large and the Mathew Commission has dealt with some of them. We now propose to discuss some of the important laws on the Press including those considered by the Mathew Commission. A distinction should be made between Press laws which are special laws solely directed against the Press and laws on the Press which are general laws applicable to all citizens including the Press.

Central Press Laws

At present, there is no Central Act specifically directed to control the Press. The Indian Press (Emergency Powers) Act, 1931 of the pre-Independence era was repealed and it was replaced by the Press (Objectionable Matter) Act, 1951 "to provide against the printing and publication of incitement to crime and other objectionable matter." This was a temporary Act and provided certain safeguards against the publication of objectionable matters. But there was a lot of opposition against this enactment because the very idea of a special law imposing prior restrictions upon the publication of certain matters, instead of leaving them to be punished under the general law for specific offences was considered a retrograde step. This Act was allowed to lapse. For sometime there was no Central Press law but the Government of India had been feeling that the Press was abusing its freedom and the Prevention of Publication of Objectionable Matter Act, 1976 was enacted during the Emergency declared on the ground of internal disturbance. This Act was also repealed in April, 1977 by the Prevention of Publication of Objectionable Matter (Repeal) Act, 1977. Since then, there has been no Central Press law directly imposing restrictions on freedom of the Press. But the government made attempts to regulate the price of newspapers. It enacted the Newspaper (Price and Page) Act, 1956 which empowered the Central Government to regulate the price of newspapers in relation to their pages and sizes and also to regulate the allocation of space to be allowed for advertisement. In pursuance of this Act, the Daily Newspaper (Price & Page) Order, 1962 was issued which fixed (i) the maximum number of pages which a newspaper would be entitled to print; and (ii) a *minimum* price which a newspaper must charge, according to the number of pages which it is entitled to publish under the law. If the newspaper wanted to increase the volume of its publication or issue a supplement in excess of the number of pages fixed for it, the permission of the governnment would be required and price had to be increased correspondingly. This order laid down a price-scale varying with the number of pages printed. Though the Act had a laudable object of preventing unfair competition among newspapers and of securing full scope for the development of smaller newspapers, the Act and the Order made thereunder were struck down by the Supreme Court in *Sakal Papers* case[1] as it would affect circulation of newspapers. Thereafter the government enacted the Newspaper (Price Control) Act, 1972 which empowered the government to fix *maximum* price which may be charged by a newspaper or class of newspapers. The main purpose of the Act was to secure availability of newspapers at fair prices. This was a temporary Act for a period of two years and it has expired.

Among laws dealing directly with the Press, there is the Press and Registration of Books Act, 1867. It is a regulatory measure and is not intended to put any restrictions on Press freedom. There are also beneficent measures like the Working Journalists Act, but at present, there is no Central Press law which seeks to impose, either directly or indirectly, any restrictions on freedom of the Press.

The monopolistic control and the ownership pattern   of

---

1. *Sakal Papers* v. *Union of India*, (1962) 3 S.C.R. 842, A.I.R. 1962 S.C. 305.

the Press raise important issues which shall be discussed later in Chapter 9.

We shall now discuss some of the important laws on the Press which are of general application and affect the Press also.

(1) Law of Defamation

Law of defamation has an important bearing on freedom of expression. A journalist may make a defamatory statement only at his peril. He may have to face a criminal charge and also a civil action for damages. An intimate knowledge of the law of defamation is essential to every journalist and publisher of a newspaper. Defamation is an injury to a man's reputation. The law of defamation has been described as 'a tale of two interests'. On the one hand, every person is entitled to his good name. The reputation of a person is his asset and any injury to it is actionable. On the other hand, freedom of expression is necessary in the interests of society. A proper balance has to be found between these two conflicting interests. Our Constitution, therefore, allows under article 19(2) the imposition, by law, of reasonable restrictions on freedom of expression in the interests of defamation.

Defamation is a tort. A civil action for damages will lie for defamation. It is also an offence under the Indian Penal Code. There is, however, some distinction between the criminal law and civil law relating to defamation. There is a large volume of case laws on the subject and the law has become complex. While examining this law, the Mathew Commission was greatly influenced by the British Defamation Act, 1952 and has made a number of recommendations to amend our law in the light of the British Act. For a proper appreciation of these recommendations, it is proposed to examine briefly the existing provisions of our law and then take up the recommendations for consideration.

Criminal Law of Defamation

Section 499 I.P.C. defines defamation and Section 500 provides punishment for that offence. Section 499 says :

"whoever, by words either spoken or intended to be read, or by signs or visible representations, makes or publishes any imputation concerning any person intending to harm, or having reason to believe that such imputation will harm, the reputation of such person, is said, except in the cases hereinafter excepted, to defame that person''. There are four explanations and ten exceptions to the general rule enunciated by this section. In order to constitute the offence of defamation, there are three essential ingredients : (i) making or publishing any imputation concerning any person; (ii) such imputation must have been made by words,, either spoken or intended to be read or by signs or visible representations; and (iii) such imputation must have been made with the intention of harming or with knowledge that it will harm the reputation of the person concerned. It is of the essence of this offence that the impugned matter must be communicated to a third person and such communication has been made with the intention or knowledge that it will harm the reputation of the person concerning whom it is made. In considering whether a statement is defamatory, the entire statement has to be read and not merely isolated passages, and the test would be whether the statement would lower the complainant in the estimation of right-thinking members of the society in general. Once an imputation is proved to be defamatory, it is for the accused to show that he is protected by any of the Exceptions to Sec. 499. While the prosecution must prove its case beyond any reasonable doubt, the accused would succeed in substantiating his plea under any of the Exceptions, if he can prove a preponderance of probability as in a civil proceeding.

As for criminal liability, the exceptions mentioned in Sec. 499 I.P.C. are exhaustive and the Court cannot add to them. Imputation of truth for public good is a defence under the first Exception. In a criminal proceeding, truth, by itself, is not a complete defence but it has also to be proved that the publication was made for public benefit. Fair comment respecting public servant and public questions can be pleaded as defence to the charge of defamation. It is not defamation to publish a substantially true report of the proceedings of a court or to express in good faith any opinion on the merits of a decided case or conduct of witnesses and others concerned. It is not also defamation to express in good faith any opinion on the merits of a public performance. It is not also defamation if a person having lawful authority passes, in good faith, censure on another in matters to which such lawful authority relates. Under the 8th Exception, accusation made in good faith to a person in authority is not defamation. The defamatory accusation should be made in good faith and it should be made to a person having lawful authority over the person defamed. Thus accusation made in good faith to a master regarding the conduct of his servant or accusation made under law before a Magistrate would not be defamation. Under the 9th Exception, it is no defamation, if the imputation on the character of another is made in good faith and for the protection of the person making it or of any other person or for public good. Thus, if in reply to a legal claim, the accused sends a reply to the claimant making an imputation against the claimant which, if true, would be a defence to his claim. Under the 10th Exception, caution conveyed to a person intended for his good or public good would not be defamation. Thus a warning to an employer against employing a particular person because of his dishonesty may come under the exception, provided the warning has been given in good faith. 'Good faith' is a common requirement in most of the Exceptions. This expression has been defined in Section 52 I.P.C. as follows : "Nothing is said to be done or believed in good faith which is done or believed without due care and attention." Hence, in considering whether the accused acted in good faith, what is to be considered is whether he acted with 'due care and attention.'

Persons competent to lodge complaint for defamation and persons who would be liable

Under Section 199(1) of the Criminal Procedure Code, 1973, a complaint for the offence of defamation may be made only by a person aggrieved. An exception to this general rule was made in sub-Section (2) of that Section. When a defamation is alleged to have been committed against the President of India, Vice-President of India, Governor of a State, a Minister of the Union or State or a public servant in respect of his conduct in the discharge of his public functions, the Public Prosecutor has been authorised to file a complaint direct to a Court of Session. Experience has shown that even when defamatory statements appear in the Press against a Minister or a public servant, he is reluctant to go to a court of law and there remains a suspicion in the mind of the public that there may be some truth in the imputation made. This lingering suspicion should be removed. If the imputation is unjustified, the newspaper which publishes it should be punished; if on the other hand, it is found to be correct, the Minister or the public servant, as the case may be, should take the consequences. This sub-section was intended to put a curb on yellow journalism. But the power vested in the Public Prosecutor has not generally been exercised.

A complaint for the offence of defamation may be made not only against the person making the imputation but also against the publisher and printer of the newspaper which publishes the defamatory statement. The words 'makes or publishes' are wide enough to include both the printer and publisher. One of the important ingredients of the offence of defamation is that there must be intention, knowledge or reasonable belief that the publication would hurt the reputation of the complainant. It is presumed that the printer or publisher had such knowledge. Applying this test, the editor of a newspaper would also be liable unless it is shown that he had no control over the selection of the matter to be published. The proprietor of a newspaper would not be ordinarily liable, unless his responsibility for the publication of the defamatory matter is established.

Punishment for Defamation

Section 500 I.P.C. which provides punishment for defamation reads : "Whoever defames another shall be punished with simple imprisonment for a term which may extend to two years, or with fine, or with both."

The Law Commission in its 42nd report suggested addition of two more clauses to this section and the Mathew Commission approved that recommendation and Section 500 I.P.C. as amended will read as follows :

(1) Whoever defames another shall be punished with simple imprisonment for a term which may extend to two years, or with fine, or with both.

(2) Where the offence has been committed by publishing an imputation in a newspaper, the Court convicting the offender may further order that the judgment shall be published, in whole or in part, in such newspaper as it may specify.

(3) The costs of such publication shall be recoverable from the convicted person as a fine.

This is a welcome amendment and may be accepted.

Civil Law of Defamation

The civil law relating to defamation is to be distinguished from criminal law of defamation. The reputation of a person is considered as his property and any injury to his reputation constitutes an actionable wrong and gives rise to the civil remedy of damages. Unlike the criminal law of defamation, the civil law has not yet been codified and the courts have to apply rules of English common law in so far they are consistent with the principles of justice, equity and good conscience. † The civil law of defamation has been evolved through case laws.

In order to constitute defamation as a civil wrong, the essential ingredients are : (i) the statement must be defamatory; (ii) the statement must refer to the plaintiff; (iii) the statement must be published by the defendent; and (iv) the statement must be false. A statement is defamatory when it has a tendency to injure a person's reputation. The test is whether reasonable men or "the right thinking members of the society generally" to whom the publication is made would be likely to understand it in a libellous sense. In every action

† *Gulabchand* v. *State of Gujarat*, A.I.R. 1970 Guj. 171

for defamation, the plaintiff must prove that it refers to him. It is not necessary that the plaintiff's name should appear in the statement. The test is whether any person to whom the statement was published reasonably thought that the plaintiff was the person referred to.[2] Publication is the gist of the wrong of defamation. No action for defamation would lie, if the defamatory words were spoken to the plaintiff only. There must be communication at least to one third person.

In a civil action for defamation, intention of the defendant is, in general, immaterial and it is no defence in a civil action that the defendant did not intend to defame the plaintiff. In a criminal case, on the other hand, intention is an essential ingredient of the offence of defamation under Section 499 I.P.C. It has to be shown that the accused intended to harm the reputation of the complainant or that he had knowledge or reasonable belief that the imputation will harm the reputation of the complainant. Good faith on the part of the accused is a good defence in a criminal prosecution but not so in a civil action for damages.

A question arises whether unintentional defamation and intentional defamation should be put on the same footing. The Porter Committee in England considered this question and suggested that while lack of intention to defame should not constitute a complete defence, but in the case of unintentional defamation, all reasonable steps should be taken to clear the reputation of the injured person by correction and apology which should be given proper publicity. On the basis of this recommendation, Section 4 of the British Defamation Act, 1952 was enacted. It provides that in a case where a publisher establishes that he unintentionally published words complained of and that he exercised all reasonable care in relation to the publication, he may make an offer to the claimant which would include a suitable correction and apology. If the offer is accepted, proceedings in respect of the publication are barred. If the offer is rejected, the publisher can plead the rejection of the offer as a defence. The Mathew Commis-

---

2. *Hulton* v. *Jones*, (1910) A.C. 20

sion recommended that the provisions of Section 4 of the British Defamation Act should be introduced in India. Unintentional defamation should be distinguished from intentional defamation and the recommendation of the Commission may be accepted.

Defences to an action for defamation

In a criminal case, when the offence of defamation is proved, the accused has no defence except to show that he is protected by any of the Exceptions mentioned in Section 499 I.P.C. In a civil action for defamation, on the other hand, apart from general defences applicable to all torts, there are three special defences available to the defendant : (i) truth of the imputations made; (ii) fair comment; and (iii) privilege.

Truth as a defence

Truth of the defamatory statement is a complete defence to a civil action for defamation. The principle is that "the law will not permit a man to recover damages in respect of an injury to his character which he either does not possess or cannot be said to possess." Malicious motive of the defendant has nothing to do with the merits of the charge. It is enough if the statement turns out to be true. In a criminal proceeding, on the other hand, truth, by itself, is not a complete defence, but the publication should be for public benefit. The Mathew Commission examined the question whether in a civil action for damages also, truth should be accompanied by public interest. It felt that the requirement of public benefit would be adding too much of a burden on journalists and there is no reason for any departure from the present position.

Though the broad theory that truth is a complete defence in an action for defamation need not be questioned, difficulties arise when some of the statements are found to be true, while others are not. It appears that it would be unjust and improper to hold the defendant liable for damages when most of the facts stated are true but some minor, unimportant facts could not be proved to be true. The Porter Committee in England, therefore, recommended in 1948 that the plaintiff should not be entitled to recover damages, if the defendant proves that the gist of the libel is true even though he fails to prove the truth of some minor charge, provided that such minor charge does not add appreciably to the injury of the plaintiff's reputation. This led to the enactment of section 5 of the British Defamation Act, 1952. But this Section as drafted was found to be defective, as it failed to give full effect to the recommendation of the Porter Committee. This question was later examined by the Faulks Committee as also by the Australian Law Reforms Commission. The views expressed by them do not differ substantially from the recommendation of the Porter Committee, though the Australian Reforms Commission has tried to introduce certain refinements in its recommendation. It is now generally agreed that it should be a defence to the publication of defamatory matter that the matter complained of is substantially true. It should not matter if the statement is incorrect in some unimportant details. In determining the effect of the publication for the purpose of assessing damages, the court should have regard to the whole of the publication and the extent to which the defendant proves the truth of the matter concerning the plaintiff in the publication.

The Mathew Commission recommends that the principles underlying the above proposition should be incorporated in our law by suitable legislation and this recommendation may be accepted.

Fair Comment

Comments upon a man's character or work could be as harmful to his reputation as making false allegations against him and such comments may be the basis of an action for defamation. There is, however, a special defence of fair comment in this area, viz. that the statement complained of was fair comment made in good faith and upon a matter of public interest. To succeed in this defence, the defendant must establish that the view he expressed on the plaintiff or his conduct was one which he honestly held. He must further establish that the comment was made on a matter of public interest. What is fair is not capable of precise definition. But the comment must be honest and relevant to the facts involving public interest and must be a reasonable inference based on those facts.

Comment must be distinguished from facts. It is an expression of opinion, an inference from facts. Comment being a matter of opinion, he who expresses it is not required by law to prove that it is true but it must be fair and honest, though others may disagree with it.

Comments must be based on facts and the facts stated have to be proved to be true. The plea of fair comment would be available only when comments and facts are separable. But where comments and facts are mixed up and it is not possible to separate them, the entire statement has to be justified as a statement of fact. As to the truth of the facts stated on the basis of which the plea of fair comment is claimed, the common law rule was very stringent. Any minute deviation from truth in facts stated would deprive the defendant of the defence of fair comment.[3] Section 6 of the British Defamation Act, 1952 has changed the law in England and it reads as follows :

"In an action for libel or slander in respect of words consisting partly of allegation of facts and partly of expression of opinion, a defence of fair comment shall not fail by reason only that the truth of every allegation of fact is not proved, if the expression of opinion is fair comment having regard to such of the facts alleged or referred to in the words complained of as are proved".

The Mathew Commission has recommended the adoption of the principle underlying the section in our law of defamation by the enactment of suitable legislation. This may be accepted.

3. *Merivale* v. *Carson*, 1887 20 Q.B.D. 275.

Privilege

The third special defence is that of privilege. In certain circumstances, even defamatory statements are privileged and a person making such a statement shall not incur any liability, if he can successfully raise the plea of privilege. Privilege is of two kinds : absolute and qualified. Absolute privilege arises on grounds of public policy. In cases of absolute privilege, no action lies, even if the statement is false and the question of malice is entirely irrelevant in these cases. Qualified privilege, on the other hand, exists when the defendant is exempted not absolutely but conditionally, in the absence of malice. If the plaintiff can prove that the defendant was actuated by actual malice, the defence of qualified privilege will fail.

Absolute privilege

Cases of absolute privilege arise in parliamentary proceedings, judicial proceedings and official communications. No member of Parliament is liable to any proceedings in any court in respect of anything said or any vote given by him in Parliament or in any committee thereof. This privilege extends to members of the State legislatures also. In India, absolute immunity has been given not only to anything said by a member of the Legislature within the House but also to anything published under the authority of the Legislature under articles 105(2) and 194(2) of the Constitution.

In regard to judicial proceedings, absolute immunity is given to judges, counsels, witnesses and parties for anything written or spoken in the course of any proceeding, even though the words were spoken or written maliciously and without justification. But newspapers in India do not have absolute privilege in respect of report of judicial proceedings. A fair and substantially correct report of judicial proceedings enjoys only a qualified privilege. In England, on the other hand, a fair and accurate report of judicial proceedings in a newspaper has been given absolute immunity under Section 8 of the British Defamation Act, 1952 but it does not authorise the publication of any blasphemous or indecent matter. The

Mathew Commission has recommended that newspapers in India should also be given absolute immunity in respect of fair and accurate report of judicial proceedings and no exception need be made in regard to 'blasphemous or indecent matter'. This recommendation may also be accepted.

Further, communications relating to affairs of State made by one officer to another in the course of duty are also absolutely privileged on the ground of public policy.

Qualified Privilege

A person may claim qualified privilege in a variety of cases. Thus, he may claim qualified privilege when he makes a statement in performance of a duty, legal, social or moral. Qualified privilege may also be claimed when statements are made to protect an interest. Such statements are protected for the convenience and welfare of society. Fair and accurate reports of judicial proceedings enjoy only a qualified privilege at present but absolute immunity will be given to them, if the recommendation of the Mathew Commission is accepted. Reports of parliamentary proceedings are protected by the Parliamentary Proceedings (Protection of Publication) Act, 1977 as also by article 361A of the Constitution inserted by the 44th Amendment Act in 1978.

A question arises whether reports of public meetings should have qualified privilege. The law in India does not appear to be well-settled. In England, the British Defamation Act has extended the principle of qualified privilege to a fair and accurate report of any public meeting. The Mathew Commission feels that it would not be desirable to introduce this provision in India. The question is debatable. But taking into account how public meetings are conducted in our country and how irresponsible speeches are often made, the author is inclined to agree with the Mathew Commission.

Besides, the Mathew Commission has recommended in para 74 of Chapter IV of its report* that the schedule to the British Defamation Act, 1952 should be adopted in India with

---

* See *Second Press Commission Report*, Vol. I, pp. 45-46.
6—TPI

certain modifications. Part I of the Schedule gives statements having qualified privileges without explanation or contradiction and Part II gives statements privileged subject to explanation or contradiction. The entries with the modifications would read briefly as follows :

Part I—Statements privileged without explanation or contradiction

1. A fair and accurate report of any proceedings in public :

   (a) of the legislature of any foreign country;

   (b) of an international organisation of which India is a member;

   (c) of an international court; and

   (d) of a court of any foreign country.

2. Extracts from any register kept in pursuance of any Central or State Act which is open to inspection by the public.

3. A notice or advertisement published by or under the authority of any court, tribunal or commission of Inquiry.

Part II.—Statements privileged subject to explanation or contradiction

1. A fair and accurate report of the findings or decisions of any of the following associations :

   (a) an association formed in India for the purpose of promoting or encouraging the exercise of, or interest in, any art, science, religion or learning; and

   (b) an association formed in India for the purpose of promoting or safeguarding the interests of any game, sport or pastime to the playing of which members of the public are invited or admitted.

2. A fair and accurate report of the proceedings or any meeting of :

   (a) any local authority;

(b) any body acting otherwise than as a court exercising judicial authority;

(c) any commission, tribunal, committee or person appointed for the purpose of any inquiry under a Central Act or State Act;

(d) any person appointed by a local authority to hold local inquiry in pursuance of any Central or State Act; and

(e) any other tribunal, board, committee constituted by or under the authority of a Central or a State Act, not being a proceeding to which admission is denied to representatives of newspapers or other members of the public.

3. A fair and accurate report of the proceedings of a general meeting of a company constituted by or under a Central or State Act, not being a private company.

4. Any notice or other matter issued for the information of the public by or on behalf of any Government Department.

These are detailed and innocuous recommendations and may be accepted.

Right of reply

In an action for defamation, courts in India, in common with courts in England, award damages to redress the wrong done. It makes no use of *recompense* (droit de reponse) or the right of reply which is an important remedy in the continental legal system. In France and West Germany, a person who claims to have been defamed or injured by untruthful or inaccurate statements has the statutory right of compelling the editor and publisher of the offending newspaper to publish in its next issue or as soon as possible a counter-statement or a reply sent by him. The reply should receive the same prominence as the offending statement. Refusal to publish a counter-statement or reply is a criminal offence. It is, no doubt, desirable to provide a right of reply as, in our country, it is very difficult and cumbersome at present to pursue a case of defamation. The purpose of providing a right of reply is that the public should not be misled and should know the real position. Non-publication of a reply may be indicative of malice on the part of the newspaper and the plaintiff can attribute it in defamation proceedings while its publication will be a mitigating factor in the matter of awarding damages for defamation. The Mathew Commission suggests that for the present such a limited right of reply should be recognised by convention as a part of professional ethics and complaints alleging denial of the right should be looked into by the Press Council as it is already doing.

The problem of multiple publication

A defamatory statement may be communicated to different persons by the same defamer and it may also appear in different newspapers. Under the law of torts, each act of publication constitutes a separate wrong and gives rise to a distinct cause of action. The sale or delivery of every copy of the newspaper or book is technically a distinct publication and gives rise to a separate cause of action. It is open to the plaintiff to file different suits for different publications. In such a case, the defendant is put to undue harassment and the Faulks Committee in England said that it was a "tiresome application" of the law. The problem of multiple publications has been considered by the Faulks Committee, Australian Law Reforms Commission and other bodies. Considering all aspects of the question, the Mathew Commission feels that one action would normally be quite sufficient to protect the plaintiff's reputation in relation to all technically separate publications. The multiple publication of one material should give rise to one cause of action only, but in such an action, the plaintiff should have relief appropriate to all publications. The Commission suggests that a single publication rule should be adopted.

This broad statement has, however, one snag. The plaintiff may not be aware of all the publications but the defendant would, however, know the extent of the publication. The defendant should be under an obligation to disclose before the court all the publications made to enable the court to award appropriate relief. If it is found later that the defendant has not disclosed all the publications or the defamatory matter has been published after the trial, this would give rise to a fresh cause of action. This proposal would give certainty to the parties and is equitable. This proposal may be adopted in our law by suitable legislation.

Who may sue and be sued

Any person who has been defamed is entitled to sue for damages. But as defamation is a personal action, an heir or other legal representative cannot sue after the death of the person defamed, except where the libel against the dead man defames the heir also.

A corporation, being a fictitious person, has no personal reputation and cannot, therefore, sue for defamation affecting personal reputation only. But it can sue for defamation when it affects its business or property.

In an action for defamation, the person making the imputation as also the publisher would be primarily liable. The editor of a newspaper, book or other printed matter is presumed to know what is being published and would be liable, though the defamatory statement might have been made by another. The proprietor of a newspaper is also vicariously liable for whatever is published in his newspaper. A corporation is liable for libel published by its servants or agents within the scope of their employment, according to the general principles of agency.

In an action for defamation, the liability of distributors, vendors, printers and translators stands on a slightly different footing. Distributors, vendors and printers are also technically liable but in an action for defamation, they are not generally impleaded. Distributors and vendors do not generally have knowledge of the content of the publication and even if they are impleaded, book-sellers, newsagents and vendors enjoy the special defence of innocent dissemination which is not available to publishers. The printers are presumed to know what is being printed and under the existing law, they are liable in an action for defamation. But in practice, the printers print the materials given to them mechanically without trying to analyse their content. The Faulks Committee which dealt extensively with this question recommended that the above defence of innocent dissemination should be extended to printers also as in the case of vendors and news agents. As regards translators, the Faulks Committee recommended that protection should be given to translators but not to the publication of offending matter in translation. The publishers of translation may, however, claim qualified privilege.

The Mathew Commission suggests that the recommendations of the Faulks Committee with regard to the liability of distributors, vendors, printers and translators should be accepted and incorported into our law.

Joint and several liability

In an action for defamation, the defamer, publisher, editor, proprietor and printer are jointly and severally liable and may be sued as such. But it is open to the plaintiff to sue any one of them singly, but he cannot recover more than one decree for a single defamatory statement for which several persons are jointly and severally liable. In a joint action against several defendants, where the plea of qualified privilege is raised by way of defence, malice on the part of any one of the persons jointly responsible is sufficient to defeat the plea of qualified privilege as to render all the defendants jointly liable to the plaintiff. This is the position under the existing Indian law, as pointed out by the Mathew Commission. In England, however, the position has undergone a change by a decision of the Court of Appeal[4] where it has been held that those against whom malice is not proved cannot be vicariously tainted with malice and their plea of privilege, if otherwise proved, should prevail.

The Mathew Commission feels that the existing Indian law causes unnecessary hardship and suggests that the plea of qualified privilege should fail only against those who are found

4. See *Egger* v. *Chelmsford*, (1965) 1 Q.B. 248 (C.A.).

to be malicious and they should be liable to the plaintiff while others should not be vicariously tainted with malice and their plea of privilege should prevail. The Mathew Commission recommends that this principle should be incorporated in our law. The effect of the incorporation of this principle in our law would mean that a publisher of a newspaper :

(i) will continue to be vicariously responsible for the malice of his agent;

(ii) will not be vicariously responsible for the malice of an independent contributor;

(iii) will not be vicariously responsible for the malice of an unsolicited correspondent, whether anonymous or otherwise.

Codification

The civil law relating to defamation has not been codified in our country. From the foregoing brief survey, it would be seen that the law is complex because it is based on case laws. It has become particularly complex because courts in India have to apply the corresponding rules of English Common law in so far as they are consistent with the principles of justice, equity and good conscience. Because of this complexity, neither the plaintiff nor the defendant is sure of his legal rights and liabilities. Moreover, we, in India, are generally used to codified laws. It is suggested, therefore, that for the sake of clarity and certainty, the law of civil defamation should be codified by taking into consideration the various suggestions made by the Mathew Commission and others. The task is not easy. It might be useful to appoint a new committee for the purpose or entrust the Law Commission with the task of drafting the law.

(2) Official Secrets Act, 1923

In a democratic society, it is imperative that the people should be kept well informed about current affairs and broad issues, political, social and economic, to enable them to discharge their necessary functions. They must "arm themselves with power which knowledge gives" as James Madison said.

Neither the right to elect periodically their representatives to the legislative bodies nor their accountability to the people at the end of their period of stewardship is of much avail, unless the representatives are made responsible to public opinion when they decide public issues. The necessary condition of an enlightened public opinion is the existence of a well-informed citizenry. To keep the people well-informed free exchange of ideas and free debate are essential. To fulfil this duty, the people must have the necessary information, for they cannot carry on a discussion in the void. It is this duty which generates the right to know. Right to information is a basic right which is included within the freedom of expression in its widest amplitude.

Need for access to public records

In a modern welfare state, the government is involved in an ever-increasing variety of functions and services and regulates the political, social and economic life of the citizens in diverse ways. There is hardly any phase in the life of a citizen which is not affected by the manifold activities of the government. In order to carry out these activities, government has to collect all necessary information relating to public problems. As a result, government has become perhaps the most important single institutional repository of information about our society and its political, social and economic problems. In some areas, the government is virtually the only significant source of information.

If it is the function of the Press to keep the people well-informed, to disseminate correct news and spread the truth, it must have access to the sources of information. No investigative reporting on any policy of the government, whether it is economic policy, foreign policy or defence policy, is possible unless the Press has access to public records. People must know not only the decisions arrived at by the government but also the decision-making process. They must know the background of the decisions, why a decision was taken or not taken. "A constant vigil by the people of the decision-making process of public authorities would make them arrive at the decision in an objective and impartial manner."[5] If the Press has to rely solely on what the Press Information Bureau chooses to supply to it, the picture may be one-sided and distorted and may not represent the truth. The Press should, therefore, have access to public records.

But secrecy is inherent in bureaucracy. It arose out of functional necessity. The secrecy which begins as a means to achieve organisational efficiency becomes an end in itself and is sought as a result of conscious desire on the part of bureaucracy to insulate inself from effective outside control. On the other hand, open government is the basis of democracy. As against the necessity for an open government, we have to acknowledge the imperative need for keeping certain affairs of the State as secret. National security, foreign affairs, cabinet proceedings, intelligence, information relating to detection of crimes, personal privacy, trade secrets and information volunteered by people in confidence are some of the items which a government will have to keep secret. There is an inherent conflict between the democratic needs of openness and requirements of secrecy and "this tension", as the Franks Committee observed "has been increasing in recent years." It is necessary, therefore, to draw a proper balance between these two conflicting claims.

An in-depth study of this question was undertaken by the Indian Law Institute at the request of the Press Council. It says that while the two wings of the government, namely, the legislature and the judiciary function in the open, the executive does its business in its secret chambers to which the public have hardly any access. There is an inherent danger that the vast powers of the executive may not always be used for public welfare but used for private gain or with corrupt motives or arbitrarily and capriciously. It is essential, therefore, for the public to know what the government is doing. The study group, therefore, recommends that in drawing a balance between the needs of openness and the requirements of secrecy, this balance has to be tilted more in favour of open-

5. *Press Law*, Mudholkar, J. (Tagore Law Lectures) p. 63

ness than it has been hitherto. Till now, secrecy was the rule
rather than the exception. This proposition has now to be
reversed and openness should be the rule and secrecy the exception. James Michael in his book *The Politics of Secrecy*
makes a detailed study of the question and forcefully pleads
the case for open government.

A most sensational instance of the conflict between the
needs of secrecy and of the freedom of the Press in dissemi-
nating information of public affairs was offered by the cases
which came up before the American Supreme Court[6] in relation to 'Pentagon papers'. These papers related to the American foreign policy regarding the Viet Nam war. A prayer was
made to the Court for the grant of an injunction restraining
the Press from publishing extracts of these papers. The Court
held that the First Amendment would not tolerate any 'previous restraint' against publication unless the interest of
national security was very heavy. The Court refused to grant
the injunction prayed for on the ground that there was no
impending peril to the national security by the disclosure in
1971 of the Pentagon papers which relate to the events in
1967. The Court, however, added that the Congress would have
powers to penalise publication of information which would
endanger national security. This decision was hailed in many
quarters as the triumph of freedom of the Press in America.
Whatever might be the legal position under the First Amendment, the Press should have exercised self-restraint in publishing papers which might affect national security and would
certainly undermine the honour and dignity of the nation.

Yet another sensational disclosure was made in India in
the Judges' case decided on December 30, 1981. In this case,
the question arose whether the confidential correspondence
which passed among the Chief Justice of India, Chief Justice
of the Delhi High Court and the Union Law Minister should
be made public. The government claimed privilege but the
Supreme Court overruled this plea in the interests of justice

6.   *Gravel* v. *U.S.* (1972) 408 U S. 606.   *N.Y. Times* v. *U.S.* (1971) 402
     U.S. 713

and the entire correspondence was made public. Wide publicity was given to this correspondence in all the newspapers
and this historic decision of the Supreme Court has been widely
acclaimed as it has vindicated that we live in an open society.
Here again, the author feels that the disclosure of the confidential correspondence has stripped the judiciary of much
of its aura of respectability and has damaged the image of
judiciary beyond repair. "The judiciary can never be the
same again." People will hesitate to express themselves freely
even in confidential notes and correspondence and the disclosure has done more harm than good and should have been
avoided.

On the other hand, there are many cases where the executive unnecessarily spreads the cloak of secrecy over public
records. When the author was in the Law Ministry, Mr. Gran-
ville Austin sought permission to consult Constituent Assembly papers. There was the usual objection from the office.
But the papers were innocuous except that there were some
personal references, some of which were even derogatory. Mr.
Austin was permitted to consult the Constituent Assembly
Papers on the clear understanding that he would not make
any use of derogatory personal references. As a result, Gran-
ville Austin produced an excellent treatise : *Indian Constitution : Corner Stone of a Nation.* The executive should
carefully weigh the pros and cons in each case whether it
would be against public interest to allow the public to have
access to public records under its control.

Statutory Bar against disclosure of official information

We shall now discuss the statutory bars against disclosure
of official information. The chief obstacle to the free flow of
legitimate information to the people is the existence of certain
provisions in the Official Secrets Act, 1923. There are some
other Acts also imposing ban against disclosure of information, such as the Atomic Energy Act, 1962. Under this Act, it
is an offence to communicate to any person, other than an
authorised person, any information relating to any existing
or proposed atomic energy plant. New advances in the deve-

lopment of atomic energy have both peace-time and military applications and no exception can be taken to the bar imposed against disclosure of information relating to atomic energy. Criticisms have been levelled mainly against the Official Secrets Act which was modelled on the British Act of 1920. Three sections of the Official Secrets Act, 1923 deserve special notice, namely, Sections 3, 5 and 14. Section 3 of the Act provides penalty for spying for any purpose prejudicial to the safety or interests of the State and the punishment is imprisonment which may extend to fourteen years in some cases, and to three years in other cases. In a prosecution under Section 3, it is not necessary to prove that the accused person was guilty of any particular act which showed that his purpose was prejudicial to the safety or interests of the State but this purpose may be inferred from the facts and circumstances of the case. Section 5 provides penalty for wrongful communication of any official secret and the punishment is imprisonment which may extend to three years or fine or both. As the offences committed under this Act may affect safety of the State, the court has been specifically empowered under Section 14 to exclude all or any portion of the public from any proceeding before it if the court is of opinion that the publication of any evidence would be prejudicial to the safety of the State. Obviously, under this provision, newspaper reporters may also be excluded from court proceedings in certain circumstances.

Though the Act has been sometimes severely criticised, there have not been many cases of prosecution under the Act. In one case, the accused, a captain in the Indian Army, was prosecuted under Sections 3 and 5 of the Act but the High Court granted him bail. When the matter came up before the Supreme Court,[7] it said that this was an offence of a very serious kind affecting the safety and interests of the State and the High Court should not have exercised its discretionary powers to grant bail to the accused. The highest court in the land thus upheld the stringent provisions of the Act.

7.   *State* v. *Capt. Jagjit Singh*, A I.R. 1962 S.C. 253

Section 5 is, perhaps, the most controversial provision in the Act. It says that if any person has in his possession or control any secret official code or password or any sketch, plan, model, article, note, document or information which relates to or is used in prohibited place or which is likely to assist directly or indirectly an enemy or which relates to a matter the disclosure of which is likely to affect the sovereignty and integrity of India, the security of the State or friendly relations with foreign States, he commits an offence if he wilfully communicates the same to any person who is not authorised to receive it. An offence is committed not only by the person who passes an official secret but also by the person who voluntarily receives an official secret. There is also a specific provision on the communication of secrets to a foreign government. The Official Secrets Act was amended in 1967 and a new Section 15 was inserted. The effect of this amendment is that any publication by a newspaper of an official secret would make not only the correspondent, editor, publisher and printer liable to punishment but also every director of the company which owns the newspaper, unless he can prove that the publication was made without his knowledge or that he exercised all due diligence to prevent the commission of the offence.

This is rather a bald and brief summary of the provisions of Section 5. The language of this section is so involved that even those well versed in law will have a problem in understanding the language or implications of the rigmarole that Section 5 is. The coverage of the section is very wide. The chief vice in this section is its catch-all character covering all kinds of secret official information whatever be the effect of the disclosure. The section does not define what is secret or what is an official secret. In the absence of any definition in the Act, it is for the Government to decide what it should treat as secret and what it should not. The section gives a blanket power to the executive to prosecute any person disclosing official information as also any person receiving such information.

The necessity for amending Section 5 of the Act has been

considered by several committees and commissions, such as the Press Laws Enquiry Committee in 1948, the first Press Commission in 1954, the Law Commission in 1971 and by a study group in 1977. The Law Commission recommended some changes with regard to punishment under the Act. The Press Laws Enquiry Committee and the first Press Commission did not suggest any change in the Act as they thought that the Act as a whole was being administered in an eminently reasonable manner.

The Mathew Commission, however, feels that the section as it stands can prevent any affair of government being disclosed to the public and that Section 5 should be replaced by a new section to meet the paramount need of national security and other vital matters as well as the right of the people to know the affairs of the State affecting them. The Commission thinks it essential to restrict the operation of Section 5 by prescribing the types of information which need protection from disclosure. These types of categories will necessarily be broad and it will be the task of the executive to determine whether a document falls under any of the specified categories. This will create an atmosphere in the bureaucracy that anything or everything which they consider secret would not get the protection of the Act. Even if Section 5 is replaced by a new section as proposed by the Mathew Commission, the new section will also leave a large measure of discretion to the executive to decide which document is secret and which is not. This perhaps cannot be helped. The proposed amendment will, at any rate, lay down broad guidelines for the executive to follow and may, therefore, be accepted.

As regards other provisions of the Act, the Mathew Commission suggests that an expert committee may be appointed to see which of them deserve modifications and thereafter those provisions could also be incorporated in the proposed legislation. We may have a simplified and modified version of the Official Secrets Act to suit our needs and the question of scrapping the whole Act, as has been demanded from some quarters, does not arise.

Freedom of Information Bill

The Official Secrets Act imposes a bar to the disclosure of certain official information. It is a negative law and an amendment to that law will serve only a limited purpose. What is needed is a positive law enabling the citizens to have access to public records. There is no such law in our country at present. Right to information, as we have discussed earlier, is a basic right and it is necessary to give effect to that right. We have, in our country, an Archival Policy Resolution of the government under which public records are sent to the national archives after a lapse of twenty five years and by observing the thirty-year rule, those records are throws open to public after 30 years. After a lapse of thirty years, the records acquire a historical value and benefit the research scholars. Ordinary citizens are, however, interested in current affairs and they would like to have access to current records. Several countries have enacted legislation to ensure a measure of access to the citizens to official information. Sweden was the first country to enact such legislation. Later, Finland, Denmark, Austria, France, U.S.A. and other countries enacted such legislation. Australia and Britain have also framed Bills for the purpose. It is only appropriate that we should also have a Freedom of Information Act, enacted for the purpose.

The broad scheme of the proposed legislative measure would be to give to the citizens the right to have access to official documents on the basis of an application. It is, however, obvious that in the interests of security and safety of the State, certain categories of documents should be kept secret, and they should be exempt from public access. In U.S.A. under U.S. Freedom of Information Act, 1966, various categories of documents have been exempted from public access. The scheme of exemption may vary from country to country and we have to devise our own scheme of exemption, having regard to the conditions prevailing in the country. The Bill should also provide that if the application of a citizen for having access to any document is rejected, an order

must be passed stating the reasons for the rejection and the
order should be communicated to the applicant. There should
also be a provision for review against the order of rejection.
In the British Information Bill, it has been proposed that
the complaints about the rejection of an application would lie
only to the Parliamentary Commissioner. The Mathew Commission feels that the review should not lie to the courts which
are already over-burdened with work but should lie only to a
functionary of status like the Parliamentary Commissioner in
England. This gives us an outline of the proposed Freedom
of Information Bill.

Shri K. R. Ganesh, a member of the Mathew Commission
is opposed to any legislative measure to confer the right to
information in the present situation in which the country is
faced, with internal and external threats to its stability and
security. The objections of Shri Ganesh will be met if we carefully devise a scheme of exemption having regard to the conditions facing the country, so that public does not have access
to any sensitive document. Taking all factors into account,
the suggestions of the Mathew Commission may be accepted
and early steps should be taken to confer a statutory right on
the citizens to have access to public records.

(3) The Press and Registration of Books Act, 1867

The Press and Registration of Books Act, 1867 is the
oldest surviving Press law. It is merely a procedural law and
a regulatory measure and it is not intended to put any restrictions on freedom of the Press or to establish governmental
control over newspapers. As the long title would show, it is
an Act for the regulation of printing presses and newspapers,
for the preservation of copies of books and newspapers in
India and for the registration of such books and newspapers.
Working of this Act has revealed certain defects and the
Mathew Commission has suggested a number of changes to
remove those defects. The changes suggested are procedural
in nature and do not raise any substantial question of
policy. We shall briefly examine some of the important recommendations of the Commission.

The word 'newspaper' has been defined in the Act to mean 'any printed periodical work containing public news or comments on public news.' Every copy of a newspaper shall contain the names of the printer and publisher, the place of printing as also the names of editor and owner and also the date of its publication printed clearly on such copy. Newspaper as defined comprehends not only daily newspapers but also news magazines of all periodicities under one category. This is rather confusing. The Mathew Commission suggests that a paper should be classified under three different categories, namely, daily newspapers, news-magazines and other periodicals, and there should be separate sets of provisions for the registration of these three categories of publication in three separate registers to be maintained by the Press Registrar.

The Commission also feels that the existing procedure for publication of a newspaper entails inordinate delay and inconvenience. Under the existing procedure, the intending printer or publisher of a newspaper has to appear before a magistrate either in person or through an authorised agent and make a declaration as to the title of the newspaper and other particulars. The Magistrate then refers the matter to the Press Registrar as to whether the title is free. On receiving clearance from the Press Registrar, the Magistrate authenticates the declaration and sends copies thereof to the printer or publisher and the Press Registrar and the newspaper may be published only after such authentication. The Commission suggests that the onus of getting such clearance should be thrown on the printer or publisher. The intending printer or publisher should ascertain from the Press Registrar that the title of the newspaper intended to be published is not the same as or similar to that of any other newspaper. On getting a clearance from the Press Registrar, the printer or publisher may make an affidavit to that effect. The declaration required to be made under Section 5(2) could also be in the form of an affidavit and they may be sent to the concerned magistrate by registered post and the newspaper may be published immediately thereafter, without waiting for the authentication of the Magistrate, because the Magistrate has no discretion

7—TPI

in the matter. This procedure will considerably reduce delay and avoid the inconvenience of personal attendance before a Magistrate. No exception can be taken to the above two recommendations of the Commission and they may be accepted. Necessary changes have, however, to be made in various sections of the Act.

Under Section 5(7) of the Act, where a newspaper has ceased publication for a period exceeding twelve months, the declaration made in respect thereof ceases to have effect. As the registration of a newspaper under the Act enables it to make a claim for certain facilities, such as allotment of newsprint, concessions in postal and telegraph tariffs, the Mathew Commission suggests that the time limit under Section 5(7) should be more stringent. It suggests that in the case of a daily newspaper, the declaration should cease to have effect, if the publication does not come out for a month; in all other cases, the time limit should be three months from the due date of the next issue. This provision should not apply, if the publication cannot be made owing to strike, lock-out, go-slow, power shortage or similar causes beyond the control of the publisher. There is no objection to this recommendation.

If a newspaper is published in contravention of the Act or rules, the magistrate has been empowered under Section 8B(i) to cancel the declaration. The Magistrate has been further empowered to impose a penalty of fine or imprisonment for violation of the Act or rules under Section 15(1) and under sub-Section (2) of Section 15, he has been vested with a discretion to cancel the declaration. The Mathew Commission thinks that the provisions of Sections 8B(i) and 15(2) are too drastic and should be deleted. It is difficult to agree with the suggestion of the Commission. There must be some provision in our law to cancel a declaration, if the publication is made in contravention of the Act and rules. The Magistrate exercises his discretionary powers under Section 8B(i) after giving the parties an opportunity of being heard. There is a further safeguard that an appeal lies against the order of the Magistrate to an Appellate Board under Section 8C. We, therefore, feel that the recommendation of the Commission to delete Sections 8B(i) and 15(2) should not be accepted. But we welcome the recommendation of the Commission that the Magistrate should record his reasons for cancelling a declaration. Necessary amendment may be made for the purpose.

Under Section 19E, the publisher of every newspaper is bound to furnish to the Press Registrar such returns, statistics and other information as the Press Registrar may require with regard to matters referred to in Sections 19(B)(2) and 19D. Such information should be adequate and complete; but it is not so at present. Firstly, information such as the number of persons employed in a newspaper, the capital invested and the capacity of the machinery in use are not available with the Press Registrar. The object may be achieved by a simple amendment of the Act and Rules. Secondly, techno-economic data including financial data are not available with the Press Registrar. Supply of techno-economic information by the publishers of newspapers to the Press-Registrar not only in respect of individual publication but also in respect of separate editions of the same newspaper should be made obligatory. Thirdly, it should be possible for the Press Registrar to obtain regular information about the volume of advertising revenue of newspapers from the advertising agencies operating in the country.

All these are welcome suggestions. For a study of the working of newspapers in India, all necessary information should be available with the Press Registrar. For this purpose, the Act may be suitably amended and if necessary, the Companies Act and other Acts should also be amended.

If the publisher of a newspaper refuses or neglects to furnish to the Press Registrar returns and reports as required by Sections 19E or 19D or publishes in the newspaper any particulars which he has reason to believe to be false, he commits an offence and is punishable with fine. The Mathew Commission suggests that the power to impose fine may be vested in the Press Registrar himself instead of the Magistrate by a suitable amendent. The power to impose a fine is the prerogative of a court and we do not think it proper that this power should be exercised by the Press Registrar. We think that this recommendation should not be accepted.

It was brought to the notice of the Mathew Commission that about 90,000 titles of newspapers were blocked with the Press Registrar. One of the main reasons for this state of affairs was a judgment of the Mysore High Court in the *Printers (Mysore) Pvt. Ltd.* v. *Union of India* in which the Court held that the right to publish a newspaper under a particular name is property and is subject to the ordinary law of property. The Press Registrar assumed that cancellation of a declaration does not extinguish the right of a person to the property inherent in the title of the newspaper and, therefore, the title cannot be declared to be free. In order to clear this confusion, the Commission suggests that a specific provision may be incorporated in the Act to provide that the title of a newspaper becomes free whenever a declaration in respect of that newspaper ceases to have effect or becomes void or is cancelled under any provision of the Act. Any intending publisher can file a declaration claiming that title. The Commission, however, suggests that in the case of cessation of publication of a newspaper, its title should not be available to a new claimant before the expiry of a period of one year from the date of cessation of its publication.

We have discussed all the recommendations of the Mathew Commission which deserve notice. They do not raise important questions of policy nor would they affect freedom of the Press. But they have important bearing on the functioning of the Press Registrar.

(4) Post and Telegraph Acts

Section 5(2) of Indian Telegraph Act, 1885 empowers the government or an authorised officer to intercept, detain or withhold any telegraphic message. On the face of it, this is a drastic power and a serious invasion of freedom of expression. Although there are legislative provisions in U.K. and U.S.A. for interception of postal packages, there is no provision in those countries for interception of telegraphic messages. Section 5 of our Act has been subjected to criticism both in the Press and Parliament. It is necessary, therefore, to examine closely the provisions of Section 5(2) which reads as follows :

5(2) : "On the occurrence of any public emergency or in the interest of public safety, the Central Government or a State Government or any officer specially authorised in this behalf by the Central Government or a State Government may, if satisfied that it is necessary or expedient so to do in the interests of the sovereignty and integrity of India, the security of the State, friendly relations with foreign States or public order or for preventing incitement to the commission of an offence, for reasons to be recorded in writing, by order, direct that any message or class of messages to or from any person or class of persons, or relating to any particular subject, brought for transmission by or transmitted or received by any telegraph, shall not be transmitted, or shall be intercepted or detained, or shall be disclosed to the Government making the order or an officer thereof mentioned in the Order :

Provided that press messages intended to be published in India of correspondents accredited to the Central Government or a State Government shall not be intercepted or detained, unless their transmission has been prohibited under this sub-section".

A perusal of the above sub-section would show that the power vested in the Government is not unfettered; it is subject to various safeguards. In the first place, this power can be exercised only on the occurrence of a public emergency or in the interests of public safety. Public emergency mentioned in this sub-section need not be confined to national emergency declared under article 352 on the grounds of war or external aggression or armed rebellion. An emergency may arise in a locality, such as communal disturbance, which is likely to have its repercussions in other parts of the country. There can be no doubt that circulation of false rumours or exaggerated statements concerning certain incidents may cause public disturbances which may spread to other areas.

Secondly, the power can be exercised only by the Government or an authorised officer in the interests of certain grounds specified in the sub-section itself. These grounds like sovereignty and integrity of India, security of the State etc. are all covered by article 19(2). The provisions of this sub-section do not, therefore, violate freedom of expression guaranteed under article 19(1)(a). Thirdly, the power is to be exercised by an order for reasons to be recorded in writing. Lastly, this sub-section does not apply to press messages sent by accredited press correspondents, unless their transmission has been specifically prohibited. These are important safeguards against abuse of power.

The facility of telegraphic communication is widely used in India for transmission of messages meant for publication in newspapers. It is not possible to ignore the fact that false or distorted news has been transmitted through telegraphic messages in several cases. No newspaper can claim access to, or the right to publish, news which is likely to endanger the safety of the community at large. The Mathew Commission, therefore, feels that the power of interception provided in Section 5 should not be taken away. This power must be vested in the government to be exercised in appropriate cases in the interest of maintaining and ensuring public safety.

At the same time, it cannot be denied that this power may be misused and has been misused in some cases. In order to reduce the chances of its misuse, the Mathew Commission has made a few suggestions. It may be noticed that the occurrence of public emergency is not an objective fact. Its existence has to be determined on the subjective satisfaction of some public functionary. The Mathew Commission suggests that the appropriate government should declare the existence of public emergency by a notification and this power should not be delegated. It is only after the issue of such notification that the power under Section 5(2) would be exercisable. But when the power of interception has to be exercised in the interest of public safety, it may not be possible to issue a previous notification. The Minister concerned may issue an order relating to public safety or he may delegate his power to the district magistrate. The delegation of power must be for short periods only and clear instructions should be given to the delegated authorities to prevent misuse of power. Such prior notification or order would only warrant the exercise of power under Section 5(2) and this power can be exercised only so long as such notification or order remains in force.

In exercising powers under Section 5(28), if the principal officer of a telegraph office comes across any objectionable telegram, he should submit it to the District Magistrate with his recommendation for withholding the telegram. Thereupon, the District Magistrate should pass an order in writing, withholding or allowing the transmission of the telegram. If an order is passed by the District Magistrate withholding the transmission of a telegraphic message, he should give reasons therefor and the order should be communicated to the government and also to the sender and addressee of the telegram. The text of the order should be placed on the table of the legislature after a period, say three months. The Commission further suggests that the telegraph office as also the District Magistrate should maintain registers noting therein all the necessary particulars regarding objectionable telegrams. The procedure suggested is long and time-consuming but in view of drastic power vested under Section 5(2), the suggestions of the Commission may be followed.

Tapping of Telephones

Complaints are heard not infrequently that the Press in general and its editorial staff in particular have to suffer tapping of telephones. Some members of Parliament also complain that their telephones are tapped. Tapping of telephones is a serious invasion of privacy. If Press telephones are tapped, people will be reluctant to supply confidential information to the Press and this may result in constraints on freedom of information and consequential drying up of its source. But the Indian Telegraph Act, 1885 does not provide for tapping. Tapping cannot also be regarded as a tort because the law as it stands today does not know of any general right to privacy. This is hardly a satisfactory situation.

The Mathew Commission, therefore, recommends that telephones should not normally be tapped except in the interest of national security, public order, investigation of crime and similar objectives. There should be a   specific order in this behalf by the Minister concerned or by an officer of rank to whom the power may be delegated warranting tapping of particular telephones. The order should disclose reasons and should not continue for more than three months at a time. The Commission further suggests that the order should come up for review before a Board constituted on the lines prescribed in statutes providing for preventive detention. The Board should decide whether tapping should continue any longer. It is further suggested that the Telegraph Act should be suitably amended to give effect to the above recommendation. This recommendation may be accepted but we are not sure whether it would be practicable to constitute a Board for review of the order made by the Minister or his delegated authority.

Indian Post Office Act, 1898

Section 26 of the Indian Post Office Act empowers the government or an authorised officer to intercept or detain a postal article or dispose of the same in such manner as may be directed on the occurrence of any public emergency or in the interests of the public safety or tranquility. This is rather a bald section and does not specify the grounds on which this power may be exercised. The Mathew Commission recommends that the words "in the interests of the sovereignty and integrity of India, the security of the State, friendly relations with foreign States or public order or for preventing incitement to the commission of an offence", which find place in Section 5(2) of the Telegraph Act should be incorporated in Section 26 of the Post Office Act also. This is absolutely necessary to put Section 26 beyond challenge on the ground of violating article 19(1)(a).

The Mathew Commission further suggests that its recommendation with regard to the exercise of powers under Section

5(2) of the Telegraph Act should be made applicable to the exercise of power under Section 26 of the Post Office Act. In other words, there should be a prior order of the competent authority warranting the exercise of power under Section 26 and the procedure suggested for the exercise of power under the Telegraph Act should apply to the exercise of power under Section 26 of the Post Office Act. These recommendations may be accepted.

Section 27B of the Act

Under this section, power is given to certain officers of the post office to detain any newspaper or other postal article in the course of transmission by post where such officer suspects that the newspaper or postal article contains any seditous matter. This section gives wide powers to officers of post office but in view of the circumstances prevailing in the country, no exception can be taken to the provisions of this section.

(5) Industries (Development and Regulation) Act, 1951

This Act gives the Central Government power to take over industrial undertakings included in the First Schedule to the Act without investigation under certain circumstances. An amendment to the Act in 1979 included a number of additional industries in the First Schedule and among them was "printing including litho printing industry". The Mathew Commission recommends that printing presses used mainly for printing newspapers should not be taken over by the government under any circumstances and the Act should be suitably amended to make this position clear beyond any doubt.

(6) The Copyright Act, 1957

Copyright is the right which a person acquires in a work which is the result of his intellectual labour. What a man produces by the application of his labour, intellect or skill is his property. The law of copyright creates a further statutory right of property in respect of a man's original literary, dramatic, musical and artistic works. In order to be protected by the Copyright Act, 1957 the work must be 'original', in the sense of not being entirely copies of another similar work. In other words, it must originate from the author who claims copyright. The primary function of the law of copyright is to protect from annexation by other people of the fruits of a man's work, labour or skill.

It has been held that there is no copyright in ideas, subject-matter, theme, plot or historical facts, because they are common property. What the law of copyright protects is not the originality of one's ideas, thought or information but the originality of his expression of such idea, thought or information in a particular form. The defendant would be liable for infringement of copyright, only if he makes a substantial use of this form and reproduces the work or any substantial part thereof in any material form.

Section 45 of the Act provides for the registration of copyright but this is only an enabling provision. It does not lay down that registration is obligatory. But the Madhya Pradesh High Court took the view that no copyright could be claimed unless the work was registered.[8] This view is obviously wrong because there is no provision in the Act making it obligatory for the author to get his copyright registered. The correct view has been taken by other High Courts. Copyright accrues to the author of a work under Section 13(1)(a) and registration is not necessary either to give him title or to enforce his rights against infringement.[9]

Section 14 of the Act defines the ingredients of copyright; Section 51 enumerates the acts which constitute infringement of a copyright; and Section 52 enumerates certain acts which are exceptions and cannot, therefore, be actionable as infringement. It is not proposed to make a detailed study of these provisions but we shall merely deal with the broad effect of these provisions. The combined effect of Sections 51 and 52

8. *Mishra Bandhu* v. *Koshal*, A.I.R. 1970, M.P. 261.
9. See *Satsang* v. *Kiran*, A.I.R. 1972 Cal 533 ; *Manoj Productions* v. *Sundaresan*, A.I.R. 1976 Mad. 22

read together is that a person shall be liable for infringement
of copyright if he reproduces a copyrighted work in any material form, but it would not be an infringement of copyright
if the reproduction is made by way of 'fair dealing' for any
of the purposes mentioned in Section 52(a) or 52(b). It would
also be an infringement of copyright, if the defendant makes
a cinematograph film by reproducing or converting a substantial portion of the plaintiff's novel or drama. Reproduction of material in which a person has copyright will not be
an infringement of the copyright, if the reproduction is made
for the purposes of research or private study or for criticism
or review of that work. Fair quotations, extracts from comments and criticism, *bona fide* abridgements are held to be
fair dealing and do not infringe the copyright law. What is
fair dealing depends on the circumstances of each case. To
succeed, the plaintiff must show that the reproduction has
been made of a substantial part of the infringed work. It is,
however, always difficult to draw a line of demarcation between fair use which is permitted and that which is forbid-
den. But if the extracts made are so profuse as to supersede
the original work or to such an extent that the review becomes
a substitute for the book, such extracts exceed the limits set
by law. The test laid down by courts is whether the matter ex-
tracted would materially reduce the demand for the original
work. Again, it is an infringement of the copyright, if the
abridgement or any version thereof amounts to adaptation as
defined in Section 2(a) of the Act. On the other hand, if there
is only a brief synopsis given by way of review or criticism,
it is fair use of the copyrighted work.

It may be noted here that the law provides certain special
exceptions in favour of newspapers, obviously in public interest. Thus, reproduction of a literary, dramatic, musical or
artistic work in a newspaper, magazine or similar periodical
work would not be an infringement of copyright, if it constitutes fair dealing and has been done for the purpose of reporting current events [52(1)(b((i)]. But if a newspaper publishes an article of another newspaper verbatim without the

permission of the author, such reproduction would not be justified on the plea of fair dealing. So also, reproduction in a
newspaper or other periodical of an article on current economic, political, social or religious topics would not constitute
an infringement, unless the author of such article has expressly reserved to himself the right of such reproduction [S.52
(1)(m)]. Similarly, the publication in a newspaper, magazine
or other periodical of a report of a lecture delivered in public does not amount to infringement of the copyright [S.52
(1)(n)]. It follows that if the lecture was delivered in private, its reproduction would constitute an infringement of
copyright. It should be pointed out that the special mention
of certain privileges of newspapers under sub-clauses (b)(i),
(m) or (n) of Section 52 would not debar them from availing themselves of any other exception specified in the other
sub-clauses of the same section which are available to all members of the public.

There are some exceptions available to all citizens. Thus,
it does not amount to infringement, if the reproduction is of
any literary, dramatic or other work in a certified copy made
or supplied in accordance with any law for the time being in
force [Sec. 52(1)(b)(c)]. It is not an infringement to repro-
duce or publish any matter which has been published in the
Official Gazette, exception being an Act of the Legislature
unless it is published with comments thereon. So also, there
would be no infringement of copyright in the reproduction
or publication of :

(i) the report of any Committee, Commission, Council,
Board or other like body appointed by the government if such report has been laid on the table of
the Legislature, unless the reproduction or publication of such report is prohibited by the government;

(ii) any judgment or order of a court, tribunal or other
judicial authority, unless the reproduction or publication of such judgment or order is prohibited by
the court, the tribunal or other judicial authority,
as the case may be.

(7) Criminal Law Amendment Act, 1961

The Criminal Law Amendment Act, 1961 was passed to stop certain activities prejudicial to the safety and security of India which had been taking place in the areas bordering on Pakistan and China for sometime.. It supplements the criminal law and seeks to punish any person who may question the territorial integrity or the frontiers of India.

Section 2 of the Act provides that whoever by words, either spoken or written, or by signs or by visible representation or otherwise questions the territorial integrity or frontiers of India in a manner which is, or is likely to be, prejudicial to the interests of the safety or security of India, shall be punishable with imprisonment for a term which may extend to three years or with fine or with both. Section 3 of the Act empowers the Central Government to declare any area adjoining the frontiers of India to be a notified area, if it considers that in the interests of the safety or security of India or in the public interests, it is necessary or expedient to do so. This section further provides that whoever makes, publishes or circulates in any notified area any statement, rumour or report which is, or is likely to be, prejudicial to the maintenance of public order or essential supplies and services in the said area or to the interests of the safety or security of India shall be punishable with imprisonment for a term which may extend to three years or with fine or with both. Where any newspaper or any other document wherever printed appears to the State Government to contain any matter the publication of which is punishable under Section 2 or Section 3, the State Government may declare every copy of the issue of the newspaper containing such matter and every copy of such book or document to be forfeited to the government.

The provisions of this Act are no doubt somewhat sweeping in their nature but the need for enacting such a law cannot be over-emphasised. The territorial integrity and frontiers of India have to be guarded at all costs. It must, however, be said to the credit of State Governments that they have not used the provisions of this Act to stifle freedom of speech and expression. Even when occasions arose for taking action against any newspaper, the State Governments did not file complaints before a Criminal Court; instead, they lodged complaints with the Press Council where the procedure is simpler and disposal of cases much quicker than in courts. Newspapers could not also complain that they had been harassed by being dragged into criminal courts.

(8) The Young Persons (Harmful Publications) Act, 1956

This is an Act to prevent dissemination of certain publications harmful to young persons. A harmful publication is defined to mean "any book, magazine, pamphlet, leaflet, newspaper or other like publication which consists of stories told with the aid of pictures or without the aid of pictures or wholly in pictures, being stories portraying wholly or mainly:

(i) the commission of offences; or

(ii) acts of violence or cruelty; or

(iii) incidents of a repulsive or horrible nature;

in such a way that the publication as a whole would tend to corrupt a young person into whose hands it might fall, whether by inciting or encouraging him to commit offences or acts of violence or cruelty or in any other manner whatsoever." Section 3 provides penalties where such harmful publication is advertised, sold, distributed or possessed and empowers the court to order the destruction of all the copies of harmful publication in respect of which the conviction was made. Section 4 empowers the State Government, in the manner described therein, that every copy of such harmful publication shall be forfeited to the government and where such an order is passed, a police officer can seize the same wherever found. Section 6 of the Act confers on a police officer power to seize and destroy harmful publications.

(9) The Delivery of Books and Newspapers (Public Libraries) Act, 1954

This Act defines a newspaper to mean any printed periodical work containing public news or comments on public news published in conformity with the provisions of Section 5 of the Press & Registration of Books Act, 1867. Section 3A enjoins upon the publisher of every newspaper to deliver at his own expense one copy of each issue of such newspaper as soon as it is published to each such public library as may be notified by the Central Government. Contravention of any provision of this Act becomes punishable with fine up to rupees fifty.

(10) The Police (Incitement to Disaffection) Act, 1922

This Act penalises any act which causes or is likely to cause disaffection towards the Government among the members of a police force or which induces or attempts to induce any member of a police force to withhold his services or to commit a breach of discipline.

(11) The Drugs and Magic Remedies (Objectionable Advertisement) Act, 1954

This Act is intended to control advertisement of certain drugs and prohibit the advertisement of remedies alleged to possess magic qualities. This Act deals not merely with matters which relate to indecency or morality but its primary object is to save innocent people from being duped to purchase harmful medicines by advertisement in eloquent terms. Objectionable advertisement in relation to certain drugs and magic remedies is punishable under Section 7 of the Act. Secs. 3 and 5 of the Act provide that 'no person shall take part in the publication' of such objectionable advertisement. These words are wide enough to include the printer and publisher of the newspaper or journal where such advertisement is published.

(12) Indian Penal Code, 1860 and Cr. P.C., 1973

We have so far dealt with specific laws which put some restrictions on the freedom of expression of a newspaper. The Indian Penal Code also contains certain provisions which create offences and provide for punishment of a person who commits such offence by printing, publishing or circulating an objectionable matter. Thus under Section 124A, whoever preaches sedition is punishable under that section. Under Section 153A, whoever promotes enmity between different groups on grounds of religion, race, place of birth, residence, language etc. and does any act prejudicial to maintenance of harmony is punishable under that section. So also, imputations or assertions prejudicial to sovereignty and integrity of India are punishable under Section 153B. Section 292 deals with obscene matters which we have already discussed. Deliberate and malicious acts intended to outrage religious feelings of any class by insulting its religion or religious beliefs is an offence under Section 295A. In certain sensitive areas of the country, there are still to be found communal forces which, in the name of Press freedom, frequently make attempts to rouse communal hatred among peaceful neighbours. Section 295A seeks to deal with such cases.

Criminal Procedure Code (Cr.P.C.)

Section 95 of the Cr.P.C. 1973 provides that if it appears to the State Government that any newspaper, book or document contains any matter the publication of which is punishable under certain specified offences of the I.P.C., the State Government may declare that every copy of such newspaper, book or document shall be forfeited to Government. The specified offences are Secs. 124A, 153A, 153B, 292, 293 and 295A of the I.P.C. Upon such declaration of the State Government, any police officer may seize any copy of the offending publication and a magistrate may authorise any police officer not below the rank of a Sub-Inspector to enter upon and search any premises where any such copy may reasonably be suspected to exist. The State Government has been empowered to make such a declaration without the intervention of any court but such declaration of forfeiture may be challenged by an application to the High Court under Section 96. The executive forfeiture is thus subject to judicial review and the constitutionality of this section has been upheld as a reasonable restriction under article 19(2) of the Constitution.

II. EXECUTIVE CONTROL

Having discussed the statutory restrictions imposed by various laws, it is now proposed to examine executive control over the Press. Such control may be exercised by the Government in various ways, such as (i) through its advertising policy; (ii) through its newsprint policy; and (iii) also by extra-legal action.

Advertising Policy of Government

Advertisement revenue is a major source of revenue to a newspaper undertaking. Advertisement at present brings in roughly as much revenue to a newspaper undertaking as the amount earned by the sale of the newspaper. The financial viability of a newspaper depends, to a large extent, on its pull with advertisers. This is true of small and medium newspapers as also of the big ones. Advertisements which a newspaper can attract are vitally connected with its circulation. Newspapers, therefore, generally aim at keeping the selling price as low as possible to gain higher circulation which results in higher advertisement rates and revenue.

Reliable statistics are not available but a survey conducted in the early seventies for 50 undertakings shows that revenue from advertisement in the case of big newspaper undertakings accounts for 47.11 per cent of the total revenue, while in the case of medium undertakings, advertisement revenue was 38.74 per cent of the total. A later survey in 1981 shows that advertisement revenue varies from 45 per cent to 55 per cent of the total revenue.

Expenditure on advertisement has grown over the years. The Indian News and Feature Alliance Year Books would show that the total amount spent on advertisement was Rs. 60 crores in 1971-72. It rose to Rs. 103 crores during 1979 and it has risen to about 218 crores in 1981. Out of the total of Rs. 103 crores of advertisement revenue in 1979, the share of Central and State Governments (excluding public sector undertakings) accounted for 10.80 crores or roughly 10 per cent. Public sector undertakings are estimated to be spending around Rs. 20 crores on advertising a year. If these figures are added up, it would appear that about 30 per cent of the Press advertising is directly or indirectly controlled by the State. The amount spent on advertising by the Supreme Court,

8—TPI

High Courts and local bodies would account for about 3 per cent of the total amount spent on press advertising. Advertising from public funds would thus account for about one-third of the total advertisement revenue. Advertisement from public funds is, therefore, of public concern and, sometimes, of controversy.

At the Central level, the Directorate of Advertising and Visual Publicity (DAVP) handles both display and classified advertisements of the Government of India, except Railways. DAVP has at present about 2000 newspapers on its media list. It releases advertisements directly to newspapers and not through private agencies and secures 15 per cent agency commission from newspapers. A number of public sector undertakings also make use of D.A.V.P's services.

There is a general feeling, however, that advertising is used by Government not merely as a means of communication but also as a means of financial assistance to small papers and sometimes also as an instrument of patronage or for punishing a newspaper for its policy. The Mathew Commission points out that there have been instances where patronage has been extended to a newspaper or withdrawn from it depending upon the political complexion of the Government in office and the line followed by the newspaper. A recent instance of advertising policy being utilised for purposes other than communication of information to the public is in the move in certain States to reduce the advertising rates of newspapers which have not implemented the Palekar award.

A question has arisen whether government advertisements should be used only as a means of communication or should also be a means for financial support to small and medium newspapers. This is a debatable question and different views have been expressed by different persons. The Mathew Commission feels that government advertisements should not be used for giving financial support to small and medium newspapers and they should be considered only as a means of communication. For giving financial and technical support to small and medium newspapers, the Commission has recommended the setting up of a Newspaper Development Commission which will help small and medium newspapers to improve their standards and to come up. We shall discuss this question later but we agree with the Commission that advertisements should be considered as a means of communication only and not for other purposes.

Taking note of the misuse of government advertisements, the Mathew Commission has made two recommendations. In the first place, government should announce its advertising policy each year and adhere to it. Copies of the advertising policy should be placed before the Legislatures. Secondly, to avoid bias in the choice of newspapers for placing government advertisements, D.A.V.P. should be split up and its function of handling government advertisements should be entrusted to an autonomous corporation in the public sector. The Directorate should, however, retain its other functions relating to government publicity. While the government may lay down the overall policy of releasing advertisements, it should not interfere in the day-to-day affairs of the corporation. Further, public sector undertakings should not be compelled to release their advertisements through the corporation.

Is is now proposed to examine closely whether it is at all necessary to set up an autonomous corporation for handling government advertisements. It is true that no newspaper has any right to government advertisements. Denial of advertisement by a government to a newspaper does not entail violation of the right to freedom of the Press under article 19(1) (a) of the Constitution. But the government should not be as free as an individual in selecting recipients for its advertisements. A democratic government cannot lay down arbitrary or capricious standards in the matter of selection of newspapers for issue of its advertisement. The funds set apart for advertisements have to be used in a reasonable manner. The object of government advertisement is generally to inform the people about its activities or to educate them or to promote its policies. The object sought to be achieved through the advertisement should be the main guiding principle in the matter of selection of the media. The guidelines should be rational, relevant and non-discriminatory.

Now, the government has an advertising policy which is published from time to time. The advertising policy of the Government of India effective from October 1, 1980 clearly states that the primary objective of the government advertising is to secure widest possible coverage through newspapers and standard journals on science, art, literature, sports, films, cultural affairs etc. While giving advertisements, political affiliations or editorial policies of the publications concerned are not to be taken into account. It further says that advertisements should not be issued to newspapers and journals which incite or tend to incite communal passions, preach violence, offend the sovereignty and integrity of India or socially accepted norms of public decency or morals. It also gives some policy guidelines and lays down that government advertisements are not intended to be a measure of financial assistance to newspapers or journals and further some appropriate weightage or consideration may be given to :

(a) small and medium newspapers;

(b) specialised scientific and technical journals;

(c) language newspapers and journals; and

(d) newspapers and journals published especially in backward, remote and border areas.

Small, medium and big newspapers and journals have been categorised, having regard to their circulation :

(a) Small—up to a circulation of 15,000 copies per issue.

(b) Medium—circulation between 15,000 and 50,000 copies per issue.

(c) Big—circulation above 50,000 copies per issue.

In selecting newspaper for issue of advertisement, certain further considerations have been laid down.

No exception can be taken to the policy statement in so far as it goes. It is rational, relevant and non-discriminatory. The Mathew Commission, however, feels that despite the advertising policy of the government, D.A.V.P. has in actual practice misused its powers in the past which has caused dissatisfaction among newspapers and has, therefore, recommended the setting up of an autonomous corporation to apply the guidelines in a fair and objective manner. But the evidence produced before the Commission does not justify the conclusion that D.A.V.P. has grossly abused its powers. Having regard to the limited funds available to D.A.V.P., it has necessarily to exercise some discretion in selecting newspapers for issue of advertisement. The exercise of such discretionary powers cannot obviously · please everybody and some dissatisfaction is bound to remain among newspapers. Such dissatisfaction cannot be avoided whether selection of newspapers is made either through D.A.V.P. or through an autonomous corporation. Moreover, though the government may not be as free as an individual in selecting newspapers for the issue of its advertisements, it should have some discretion in the matter. Furthermore, it is doubtful whether the proposed autonomous corporation would be economically viable, particularly if public sector undertakings are not permitted to avail of the services of the corporation. Taking all the factors into consideration, we do not think it necessary to set up an autonomous corporation for handling government advertisements or to disturb the existing arrangements.

But we have a few suggestions to offer to make the existing arrangement function more satisfactorily and to cause less dissatisfaction among newspapers. Firstly, the advertising policy of the government should be published every year and a copy of the statement should be laid on the table of Parliament and copies thereof should be made available to newspapers and journals. Secondly, the policy statement should spell out in greater details the criteria which will make newspapers and journals eligible for government advertisements as also the ground for denial of advertisement to them. The grounds for denial of advertisement to newspapers and journals should have a reasonable nexus with the interests sought to be protected under article 19(2) of the Constitution or the provisions of any law, e.g., the Indian Penal Code or the unwritten code of journalistic ethics. The government should keep this principle in view while laying down guidelines for issue of government advertisements. To cite an example, Andhra Pradesh Government spelt out eight grounds for withholding advertisement to a newspaper. These grounds were considered by the Andhra Pradesh High Court in *Ushodaya Publications* v. *Government of Andhra Pradesh* and they were generally upheld except that a few of them were struck down as violative of art. 14 of the Constitution. Such a detailed policy statement will restrict the scope of discretionary powers of D.A.V.P. Thirdly, it is proposed that an expert committee should be appointed to oversee the functioning of D.A.V.P. and to ensure that the guidelines laid down by the government are being applied in a fair and objective manner. This Committee may consist of representatives of the government and also representatives of appropriate professional organisations. Fourthly, there should be a provision for an appeal by an aggrieved newspaper against denial of government advertisement to it and the appellate body may be constituted by the Press Council. The Mathew Commission does not consider it necessary to provide for an appellate body as an aggrieved newspaper can always approach a court or the Press Council. But court proceedings are always dilatory and the court may not do justice to the case, as the question involved is not one of legality but one of propriety. Moreover the very existence of an appellate body would act as a restraint on D.A.V.P. from functioning arbitrarily or capriciously. Dr. Paranjape, a member of the Mathew Commission, is also of view that there is need for an appellate body to go into disputes between government advertisers and newspapers and we strongly endorse that view. Finally, we are of the view that what is done with public money should be within public knowledge and there should be no secrecy about the newspapers to whom advertisements are given. We suggest that the government should lay on the Table of Parliament each year a list of newspapers in which their advertisements, as well as those of public sector undertakings and other bodies under them, were placed and the value of advertisements placed in each paper along with its circulation figure. With the various safeguards we have suggested, we are of the view that it is not necessary to set up an autonomous corporation and D.A.V.P. may continue to handle government advertisements.

It may be noted that the current advertising policy of the Central Government specifies that small and medium newspapers, particularly those published in regional languages will be given more consideration. There have been complaints that smaller newspapers are favoured with government advertisements at the cost of bigger newspapers. In considering this question, it has to be borne in mind that the policy statement also lays down that government advertisements are not intended to be a measure of financial assistance to newspapers and that the primary objective of government advertising is to secure widest possible coverage. In selecting a newspaper for a particular advertisement, the primary concern should be to reach the largest audience for which the advertisement is meant. The Mathew Commission undertook a study of this question and came to the conclusion that newspapers in the small category have a fairly high share in the display advertisements, released through D.A.V.P. but in the classified advertisements category, the share of smaller newspapers is much less. The Commission further stresses the growing importance of rural market and suggests that in order to reach the rural audience more effectively, it will be necessary to make greater utilisation of newspapers in Indian languages. No exception can be taken to the policy so far pursued in distributing advertisements between smaller and bigger newspapers.

Government Advertising Rates

Till the mid-seventies, there was no fixed yardstick at the Centre for settling advertising rates for various types of newspapers. Every case was decided on its merits based on the paper's circulation, format, production, standards, standing and media value. To streamline the procedure, a Committee was set up in 1976 and it evolved a formula based on the cost of production of a newspaper. The formula had a built-in provision for helping small and medium newspapers. The rate structure provided for special weightage in certain cases. This rate structure came into force from 1st February, 1977. When Janata Government came to power, the rate structure was slightly modified and the modified rate structure came into force from 1st May, 1977. The rate structure was further

modified in October, 1978 by introducing equality of rates between English and Indian language newspapers in the same
circulation range.

A complaint has been voiced by both big and small newspapers that the rates offered by D.A.V.P. are very low, much
lower than the lowest commercial rates. Several newspapers
do not even accept government advertisements as the rates
offered are very low. But it has to be realised that government
advertisements are messages to the public and are not inspired
by profit motive and government advertising rates cannot be
equated with commercial rates. The Mathew Commission recognises that government advertisements stand on a different
footing from commercial advertisements. But at the same time,
it suggests that rates for government advertisements should
be fixed on a realistic and fair basis. It suggests that there
should be an expert committee consisting of representatives
of government and also representatives of appropriate professional organisations to advise D.A.V.P. on advertisement
rates. The rates fixed for government advertisements should
not be made applicable to the advertisements of public sector
undertakings. The Calcutta High Court also observed in a
recent judgment on the *Statesman's* petition against D.A.V.P.
that the rates offered by D.A.V.P. are meant for government
advertisements only and not for public sector undertakings.
The Commission further suggests that there should be no
secrecy about the rates offered to different newspapers and a
list showing the rates offered to different newspapers should
be placed on the Table of Parliament. These suggestions may
be accepted.

Newsprint Policy of Government

Newsprint is the most crucial input for daily newspapers
and accounts for more than 50 per cent of the cost of production. The demand for consumption of newsprint has been
steadily increasing on account of the growth of population,
higher literacy rates, increasing political consciousness and
other factors. There has been five-fold increase in the consumption of newsprint during the last two and a half decades, from

about 78,000 tonnes in 1957-58 to 3,70,000 tonnes in 1980-81. But the supply of newsprint is extremely limited. Indigenous production accounts for only about one-eighth of the total requirements. The rest has to be imported, but owing to our limited foreign exchange resources, import of newsprint has also to be made on a restricted scale.

The prices of both domestic and imported newsprint have been going up over the years. Imported newsprint which cost Rs. 735 a tonne in 1953 rose to Rs. 5,425 a tonne in 1981. Apart from this, an import duty ranging from 5 per cent in the case of medium newspapers to 15 per cent in the case of big newspapers was imposed during the financial year 1981-82. The price of indigenous newsprint which is of inferior quality compared to imported newsprint has risen to Rs. 4,700 per tonne. Not only has the price of newsprint gone up but the average page level of dailies, especially those of English language, has gone up substantially and these factors have been responsible for the hike in the share of newsprint in the cost of production.

Allocation of Newsprint

Allocation of newsprint is one of the non-statutory functions of the Press Registrar. With the limited supply of newsprint and an ever increasing demand for it, the Press Registrar has an unenviable task. He is not in a position to allocate newsprint to all newspapers. In 1979-80, out of 17,168 newspapers registered with the Press Registrar, only 2039 newspapers actually obtained allocation of newsprint. The policy of newsprint allocation has varied from time to time.

The newsprint policy for 1981-82 makes only dailies and periodicals, and not books, eligible for allotment. But some journals are specifically excluded from the eligible category, such as journals published to promote sale of goods or services, fiction, newspapers or periodicals with regularity of less than 50 per cent in a year etc. The Mathew Commission feels that while specialised journals and sports journals should continue to get newsprint, it recommends that cinema and sex magazines should not. Sarvashri Girilal Jain, Rajendra Mathur, H. K. Paranjape and S. K. Mukherjee have reservations about this recommendation. Whatever might be the position in regard to sex magazines, we fail to see why cinema magazines should not continue to get newsprint as before.

Under the newsprint policy, new publications are at present allowed an initial quota for the first four months on the basis of their average circulation up to a maximum of 10,000 copies of eight standard pages in the case of dailies and 16 standard pages in the case of periodicals. The Mathew Commission suggests that the present system of allocation of newsprint to new newspapers should continue with certain minor modifications.

The policy for allocation of newsprint for 1981-82 is based on the average number of pages published in 1979. It provides for an increase over the basic entitlement, on application, of 5 per cent in the case of big newspapers and 7 per cent or the actual percentage increase in circulation between 1979 and 1980, whichever is higher, in the case of medium and small newspapers. It also provides for upward revision once during the year on the basis of actual increase in circulation.

The limiting of the number of pages to the 1979 level for the purpose of allocation of newsprint is designed to conserve newsprint. The problem which faces the country is not merely to conserve newsprint but also to increase indigenous production. Previously, there was only one factory producing newsprint, namely, the National Newsprint and Paper Mills Ltd. Two more newsprint plants have come up, namely, the Mysore Paper Mills in Karnataka and a unit of Hindusthan Paper Corporation in Kerala. It is understood that these plants have also gone into production. The total newsprint production capacity in the country may go up to 2,20,000 tonnes a year if all the plants go into full production. Steps have to be taken to facilitate the production of these three plants and also to improve the quality of newsprint.

When all the three newsprint plants go into production, newsprint position will no doubt considerably improve but indigenous production will still fall far short of our total requirements and our dependence on newsprint import will continue. Every possible step should, therefore, be taken to conserve newsprint. Firstly, spurious publications which do not come out regularly should not get any allocation of newsprint. At present, newspapers with a regularity of less than 50 per cent a year are excluded from allocation of newsprint. The Mathew Commission suggests that the requirement of regularity should be increased from the present 50 to 90 per cent in the case of dailies and two-thirds in the case of weeklies and other periodicals. However, allowance should be made for failure to publish on account of strikes or lockout, prolonged power cuts or other circumstances beyond the control of the publisher. Secondly, newsprint should not be allocated for publication of image building and other wasteful advertisements. It is recognised that classified advertisements relating to employment, matrimony, housing and the like serve a useful function, but a considerable part of display advertising is prodigal and has to be curtailed.

Having regard to the foreign exchange position in our country, it is recognised that only a limited amount of foreign exchange can be allocated for import of newsprint. But newsprint is used by an industry which is in the nature of public utility. Newspapers play an important role in educating the people by providing the raw material for thought. Cutting down newsprint import would not, therefore, be proper as it is not a large drain on our foreign exchange resources. It accounted for only 1.3 per cent of the value of total imports in 1980-81. The Mathew Commission recommends that as far as possible a liberal allocation of foreign exchange should be made for newsprint imports to meet the growing demand for readership.

For conservation of foreign exchange and newsprint, the Mathew Commission considered a number of alternative proposals such as excise duty on copies of newspapers, tax on advertisement, progressive import duty on newsprint and the like. Keeping the various considerations in mind, the Commission has recommended that newspapers should be given newsprint free of import duty or excise duty up to the level of 12 pages. Above that level, as long as the newsprint availability position continues to be difficult, there should be a progressively increasing rate of duty so that the tendency to increase the number of pages to accommodate more and more advertisements with a view to earn higher profits is rendered uneconomical. Government should work out the rates of duty above the level of 12 pages from time to time in accordance with the prevailing circumstances.

All the four dissenting members of the Commission S/Shri Girilal Jain, Rajendra Mathur, S. K. Mukherjee and H. K. Paranjape have opposed the above recommendation. They would rather prefer to have a tax on advertisement.

It is necessary to examine the recommendation of the Commission which raises questions of legality as also of propriety. So long as the decision of the Supreme Court in *Bennet Coleman's* case[10] remains the declared law, the constitutional validity of the proposed recommendation is not free from doubt. In that case, the Newsprint Control Order made allowance for newsprint consumption only to the extent of 10 pages per issue of a daily newspaper. This limitation as well as the differential growth rates allowed for different categories of newspapers were struck down by the Supreme Court. The Court agreed that in view of the scarcity of newsprint, Government had the plenary power to control the supply and use of such newsprint, the majority nevertheless annulled the Import Policy and the Newsprint Control Order on the ground, among others, that it would affect circulation of newspapers and is an unreasonable restriction on freedom of the Press. Newsprint control could not be turned into an instrument of newspaper control and that it could not be used for promoting small newspapers, making unequal paper equal by giving the weaker papers a fairer opportunity and promoting a more competitive market of ideas. The proposed recommendation is somewhat different from the Newsprint Control Order which was under consideration in *Bennet Cole-*

---

10. *Bennet Coleman* v. *Union of India*, A.I.R. 1973 S.C. 106.

man's case, but nonetheless, the constitutional validity of the recommendation should be thoroughly examined.

On merits also, the proposed recommendation is not acceptable. In 1981-82, an import duty was imposed on newsprint which operated at 5 per cent in the case of medium newspapers and 15 per cent in the case of big newspapers. In 1982-83, this duty has been replaced by a specific duty of Rs. 825 per tonne for big newspapers and Rs. 275 per tonne for medium newspapers. The Mathew Commission now suggests that for the sake of conservation of newsprint, a penal import duty on newsprint may be imposed on newspapers when their page level exceeds the prescribed limit of 12 pages. We find that the page level in 1979 of the *Times of India* (Bombay) was 18.21; of Hindu, 17.48; of Hindustan Times, 14.78; and of the Statesman 14.17. The number of such newspapers is small and the amount of newsprint consumed by them in respect of pages exceeding the prescribed level would be negligible. The recommendation of the Commission would not have any appreciable effect on conservation of newsprint but it may create difficulties for our quality papers. They may have either to reduce their pages or increase the price. In either case, the volume of their circulation may be curtailed and the import policy may be struck down. Newsprint policy should not be used for controlling pages of newspapers. Newspapers being a public utility, we agree with the dissenting members that import duty on newsprint should altogether be abolished and the recommendation of the Commission should not be accepted.

Agency for Import of Newsprint

At present, the newsprint is imported through the agency of the State Trading Corporation. The Chief Controller of Imports and Exports issues licences in favour of S.T.C. based on allocations made to newspapers by the Press Registrar. But newspapers of all categories expressed dissatisfaction with S.T.C's role in importing newsprint and distributing it among newspapers. In view of such dissatisfaction, the Mathew Commission recommends that newspapers of all categories should come together to form a cooperative to handle news-print imports. It would no doubt be a very good move, if such a co-operative can be formed. Even if this suggestion cannot be implemented, those newspapers who want to avail of S.T.C's services may do so, but those who do not want to do so may be permitted to import newsprint direct. The Chief Controller of Imports and Exports may issue licences in favour of newspapers based on allocation made to them by the Press Registrar and they may import newsprint directly.

Extra-legal Action of Government

Government enjoys vast powers of distributing patronage as also of harassing unfriendly newspapers in diverse ways, by its acts of omission and commission. A newspaper may feel aggrieved by government action but it can hardly expect any relief. The Mathew Commission has cited various instances of harassment of newspapers by government, particularly by State Governments. During the *gherao* of Bangalore news-papers in September, 1980, there was an outbreak of mob violence against the newspaper offices and staff but the govern-ment took no action. There are instances of the exercise of extra-legal methods of coercion employed by governments to silence or tame unfriendly sections of the Press. The *Tribune* complained to the Press Council that taxis and delivery vans carrying copies of the newspapers to various towns in Har-yana and to Delhi had been impounded on flimsy technical grounds. The Press Council held : ''We have found that the checking of the transport vehicles at Ambala and Rohtak was part of the plan of the government to impede the circulation of the *Tribune* and cause it material loss.'' The Press Coun-cil also upheld two other allegations, namely, stoppage of advertisements to the *Tribune* and stoppage of subscription to the paper by municipal authorities in Haryana, in retalia-tion to the editorial policy of the newspaper. Another very common device to harass a newspaper is to cut off electric supply to it. This happened to *Hind Samachar* group of papers in Punjab in 1974 and it has also happened to many other newspapers not only during Emergency but also in normal times.

There has also been criticism of the manner in which accredition facilities are conferred or withheld, specially by the State Governments, as a reward or punishment. Government also offers various inducements to journalists which would undermine the independence of the Press. One such inducement is to offer government accommodation to journalists on concessional terms and then not to bother even to collect such concessional rent. Journalists should be cautious in accepting such favours, if they want to retain their independence.

Instances have also come to notice of selective invocation of provisions of various laws. It was alleged by the Indian Express Group of Newspapers that the Inquiry Order of 2nd December, 1975 under M.R.T.P. Act, which was later withdrawn, was politically motivated. Another instance that was cited was the show-cause notice for the appointment of government directors which was issued to the *Statesman* towards the close of 1975 and which was withdrawn after about a year. The Associated Journals, Lucknow, publishers of *National Herald* and allied publications, complained that the Janata Government harassed them in various ways, including obstructions in the way of letting out portions of the premises owned by the newspaper undertakinng, and initiation of proceedings under the Employees' State Insurance Act and Industries (Development and Regulation) Act.

Partisan and politically motivated invocation of the provisions of laws hardly promotes respect for the rule of law. But there is no simple remedy against extra-legal action of the government. What is necessary is to create an enlightened public opinion against the misuse of the powers of the Government. It should be realised that fair and even-handed implementation of laws is essential for the independence of newspapers.

CHAPTER V

The Press and Contempt of Court

"The Press" writes Lord Denning, "plays a vital part in the administration of justice. It is the watchdog to see that every trial is conducted fairly, openly and above board. Any misconduct in the trial is sure to receive notice in the Press and subsequent condemnation by public opinion. The Press is itself liable to make mistakes. The watchdog may sometimes break loose and have to be punished for misbehaviour."[1] This is the reason for the law of contempt of court as applied to the Press.

In India, there was no codified law of contempt of Courts prior to 1926. The High Courts, were however, courts of record and had inherent powers to punish summarily for their own contempt. Under the Constitution, article 129 declares the Supreme Court to be a court of record and that it shall have "all the powers of such a court including the powers to punish for contempt for itself." A similar declaration is made in respect of High Courts under article 215. While leaving intact the powers of a High Court to punish for its own contempt, the Contempt of Courts Act, 1926 was passed to remove the controversy as regards the power of a High Court to punish for contempt of a subordinate court. The Act of 1926 was replaced by the Act of 1952. The working of the 1952 Act revealed that it needed changes and a Special Com-

---

1. A Denning, *The Road to Justice*, p. 78.

mittee was appointed under the Chairmanship of Shri H. N. Sanyal, the then Additional Solicitor General, to examine the entire law on the subject and on the recommendation of that Committee, the Contempt of Courts Act, 1971 was enacted.

The Act of 1971 was passed, as the long title would show, 'to define and limit the powers of certain courts in punishing contempts of courts'. It is a fairly comprehensive measure and the expressions used in it have to be understood in the sense in which they have been so far understood by our courts with the aid of English law, where necessary. This Act, for the first time, seeks to define 'contempt of court' by codifying the results of judicial decisions. There are two categories of contempt, civil and criminal. Disobedience of judicial decrees, orders and the like constitute civil contempt. Section 2(c) deals with criminal contempt and this is the category to which the Press generally becomes answerable.

Section 2(c) which defines criminal contempt reads as follows :

'Criminal Contempt' means the publication (whether by words, spoken or written, or by signs or by visible representations, or otherwise) of any matter or the doing of any other act whatsoever which —

(i) scandalises or tends to scandalise, or lowers or tends to lower the authority of, any court; or

(ii) prejudices, or interferes or tends to interfere with, the due course of any judicial proceedings; or

(iii) interferes or tends to interfere with, or obstructs the administration of justice in any other manner.'

Criminal contempt covers two types of cases : (i) scandalisation of any court; and (ii) interference with, or obstruction in the administration of justice in pending proceedings.

Scandalisation of a Court

The purpose of the law of contempt is to clothe the court with necessary sanctions to protect itself and the administration of justice against scurrilous allegations. The scandali-

sation may be of the judiciary as a whole or of the court as
an institution or of an individual judge or judges thereof[2]
but in either case, it would constitute contempt only if the
scurrilous attack is made with reference to the administration of justice.[3] The very concept of contempt of court is that
the public should be protected from any obstruction to public
justice and that there will be such obstruction if the autho-
city of the court or the confidence of the public therein is undermined or impaired. In other words, the object of contempt
proceedings is not to afford protection to judges personally
from imputations to which they may be exposed as individuals
but to give protection to the public whose interests would very
much be affected if by the act or conduct of any party, the
authority of the court is lowered and the sense of confidence
which people have in the administration of justice is weak-
ened.[4] Fair and reasonable criticism of a judicial act in the
interest of public good does not amount to contempt. As Lord
Atkin observed : "No wrong is done by any member of the
public who exercises the ordinary right of criticising, in good
faith, in public or private, the public act done in a seat of
justice.... provided that the members of the public abstain
from imputing improper motives to those taking part in the
administration of justice. Justice is not a cloistered virtue;
she may be allowed to suffer the scrutiny and respectful, even
though outspoken, comments of ordinary men.[5] But when
allegations of ability, integrity or impartiality are made against
a judge, it is a wrong done to the public because such allegations would undermine their confidence in the system of
administration of justice of which the particular judge is a
limb. If the offending matter consists of the vilification of a
Judge, the question which the court dealing with contempt
proceedings should consider is whether the vilification is of
the Judge as a Judge or of the Judge as an individual. In

2. *Brahma Prakash* v. *State of U.P.* (1953) S.C.R. 1169.
3. *Barada Kanta* v. *Chief Justice*, A.I.R. 1974 S.C. 710.
4. *Brahma Prakash* v. *State of U.P.* Ibid.
5. *Ambard* v. *Attorney General for Trinidad and Tobago*, (1936) A.C.
    322 P.C.

the latter case, the Judge would be left to his private remedy and it would not be contempt of court. But if the vilification is of the judge as a judge, it becomes public mischief punishable for contempt, if it substantially affectts administration of justice.[6] In another case, the Supreme Court held the editor, printer and publisher of the *Times of India* guilty of gross contempt for having published an article, 'A disturbing decision,' criticising a decision of the Supreme Court in which it was stated among other things that "politics and policies have no place in the pure region of law; and courts of law would serve the country and the Constitution better by discarding all extraneous considerations and uncompromisingly observing divine detachment which is the glory of law and the guarantee of justice." The Court, though it dropped further proceedings in view of the unconditional apology tendered by the respondents, observed : "No objection could have been taken to the article had it merely preached to the courts of law the sermon of divine detachment. But when it proceeded to attribute improper motives to the judges, it had not only transgressed the limits of fair and *bona fide* criticism, but had a clear tendency to affect the dignity and prestige of this court. The article in question was thus a gross contempt of court. It is obvious that if an impression is created in the minds of the public that the judges of the highest court in the land act on extraneous considerations in deciding cases, the confidence of the whole community in the administration of justice is bound to be undermined and no greater mischief than that can possibly be imagined."[7] The criticism may be outspoken but should be respectful and should not impute improper motives to those taking part in the administration of justice and should be devoid of malice. Mere truthfulness of the material published is no defence, if there is malice or imputation of improper motive.

Interference with or obstruction of pending proceedings

Under Section 2(c)(ii) and (iii) of the Act of 1971, a

---

6.   *Barada Kanta* v. *Chief Justice*, Ibid.
7.   *Aswini Kumar Ghose* v. *Arabinda Bose*, A.I.R. 1953 S.C. 75.

newspaper becomes liable for contempt of court, if it publishes any matter which prejudices, or interferes with the due course of any judicial proceeding. A fair trial conducted free from prejudice and in which the court tries the case impartially after considering all the available evidence which has been properly submitted is the very foundation of the administration of justice in our country. Any interference with the fair trial of a person constitutes contempt of court. This provision is controlled by Sections 3 and 13. There will be no liability, unless the contemptuous publication is made at a time when the proceeding is 'pending' before a court. The explanation to Section 3 clearly specifies when a particular kind of judicial proceeding is said to be pending. Before the Act of 1971, criminal contempt could be committed not only from the point of time when a civil or criminal proceeding was instituted and could be said to be pending but also from before that point of time when it could be said to be 'imminent'. It has now been clearly laid down that there will be absolute immunity if the proceeding in relation to which the offending publication is made is not 'pending'. It follows that no publication at the stage of police investigation can be brought within the mischief of Section 2(c)(ii). Further, even if the judicial proceeding is pending, the contemner will have immunity if he can show that at the time when he made the publication, he had no reasonable grounds for believing that the proceeding was pending. Furthermore, though every interference with or obstruction of justice would technically constitute 'contempt', Section 13 lays down that the court should not impose any punishment unless it substantially interferes or tends substantially to interfere with the due course of justice.

The reason why a court should intervene and punish the publication of any matter which causes prejudice to a pending proceeding is to keep the stream of justice clear and pure so that parties may proceed with safety both to themselves and to their character. It is, however, sometimes difficult to determine what causes 'prejudice' to a pending proceeding.

'Prejudice' has been held to mean 'to obtain a result of legal proceedings different from that which would follow in the ordinary course.'[8] Prejudice may be caused in various ways. It may arise by a discussion of the merits of the case or of the evidence to be adduced at the trial.[9] If the comment is one which is likely in some way or other to bring pressure to bear upon one or other of the parties to the action in a manner which would prevent that party from prosecuting or defending the action or encourage that party to submit to terms which he otherwise might not have been prepared to entertain, the comment will amount to contempt. If the publication is likely to interfere with the proper adducing of evidence by discouraging witnesses from coming forward or by influencing them in some other way, such publication will amount to contempt. Any comments on the character of the accused or other party to litigation will also amount to contempt.

Any publication which tends to interfere with the administration of justice would constitute contempt, provided it is substantial, even if the court might not have been actually influenced. In the case of *Hiralal*, the Supreme Court had to deal with a case, involving contempt of that court itself. A party to a pending appeal in the supreme court in which the State of Uttar Pradesh was the respondent distributed in the court a leaflet which contained a strong denunciation of the State of Uttar Pradesh regarding the matter under consideration of the court and also contained, among other things, the following passage : "The public has full and firm faith in the Supreme Court, but knowledgeable sources say that the Government acts with partiality in the matter of appointment of those Hon'ble Judges as Ambassadors, Governors, High Commissioners etc. who give judgments against the government, but this has so far not made any difference in the firmness and justice of the Hon'ble Judges." The Supreme Court held the writer of the leaflet guilty of contempt on two grounds, (i)

8. *Ludlow Charities, re* (1837) 2 My & Cr. 316.
9. *A.G.* v. *Times Newspapers*, (1973) 3 ALL E.R. 54.

for an attempt to prejudice the Court against the State, one of the parties before the Court; and (ii) for an attempt to interfere with the proper administration of justice. Das, J. (as he then was) observed : "it is not necessary that there should in fact be an actual interference with the course of administration of justice,....it is enough if the offending publication is likely or if it tends in any way to interfere with the proper administration of law. Such imputations as are implicit in the passage in question are derogatory to the dignity of the Court and are calculated to undermine the confidence of the people in the integrity of the Judges."[10] In cases, where contempt of court is alleged, courts would not impose any punishment unless it is shown that there has been substantial interference with the course of justice and that there is a "real risk as opposed to a remote possibility that the article was calculated to prejudice a fair hearing." "The test must always be, whether or not in the circumstances of the particular case what has happened is something which is likely to prejudice the fair trial of the action, and the risk that it will prejudice the fair trial of the action must be a real risk."[11]

There is a conflict of public interest in the area of publications relating to pending proceedings. Important issues may be involved in a pending judicial proceeding and public interest may demand public discussion of those issues. Such freedom of expression is very important for a free society but no less important is another freedom, namely, administration of justice without interference from outside. Public policy generally requires a balancing of interests which might conflict. Freedom of speech ought not to be limited to any greater extent than is necessary but if there is real prejudice to the administration of justice, freedom of speech has to give in. The conflict between freedom of speech and administration of justice came into sharp relief in the *Times News-*

10. *Hiralal Dixit* v. *State of Uttar Pradesh*, (1955) 1 S.C.R. 677.
11. *Vine Products* v. *Greem*, (1966) 1 Ch. 484.

papers[12] case where the Divisional Court, the Court of Appeal and the House of Lords applied different tests to determine whether the publication in the newspaper amounted to contempt. In this case, a company manufactured and marketed a drug containing thalidomide. About 450 children were born with gross deformities to mothers who had taken the drug during pregnancy. Certain actions against the company were compromised by lumpsum payment of compensation. Other complaints followed. The company made a proposal to set up a charitable trust fund for the benefit of deformed children involved which was conditional on all the parents accepting the proposal. Some parents refused. A newspaper published the first of a series of articles to draw attention to the plight of thalidomide children. The Company complained that the article was contempt of court because litigation against them by some parents was still pending. The *Times* sent another article in draft to the Attorney General and the Company for comment for which it claimed complete factual accuracy. The Divisional Court granted an injunction restraining the publication of the article on the ground that it would be contempt of court. While the case was pending, the thalidomide tragedy was debated in Parliament and there was a national campaign in the Press and among the general public directed to bring pressure on the company to make a better offer to the children and their parents. While the Divisional Court held that the publication of the article would be a clear case of contempt, the Court of Appeal held that there was no contempt of court in the case. The House of Lords reversed the decision of the Court of Appeal and upheld the decision of the Divisional Court. But the tests applied were different. According to the Divisional Court in the *Times Newspapers* case, the test was whether the words complained of created a serious risk that the course of justice may be interfered with. The House of Lords, on the other hand, applied the test of 'pre-judgment.' It held that the publication of the material could amount to contempt because there was a serious danger that it would

12. *A.G.* v. *Times Newspapers*, Ibid.

produce public prejudgment of the issue before the court, viz., whether or not the company had been negligent.

The decision in the above case attracted lively reaction from the Phillimore Committee in U.K. The Committee noted that the greatest criticism of the law of contempt lay in its uncertainty as it affected the Press. Many different definitions of contempt by publication had been propounded by the courts over the years. The application of the test of contempt in any given case was, however, difficult. In this context, the Committee tried to frame a test of general application to mitigate the difficulties of the Press. According to the Committee, the test of 'pre-judgment' laid down by the House of Lords would make for greater certainty, provided a satisfactory definition of pre-judgment could be found. It was difficult to determine at what point a discussion or expression of opinion ceased to be legitimate and qualified as pre-judgment. The scope and precise meaning of the words 'pre-judge' or 'pre-judgment' were not easier to determine than the phrase 'risk of prejudice'. The Committee concluded that the tests to be applied should have direct reference to the mischief which the law of contempt was designed to prevent, namely, the risk of prejudice to the due administration of justice. What the law aims at is prejudice and obstruction. The law should aim at preventing serious prejudice. The test suggested by the Committee is : "The test of contempt is whether the publication complained of creates a risk that the course of justice will be seriously impeded or prejudiced." This test also will not remove all uncertainties. It is not obviously possible to lay down any rigid, inflexible or invariable rule which should govern all cases of contempt.

One of the most common forms of prejudicing the due course of justice in a pending case is the trial of the case by newspapers. Where a newspaper conducts a trial, the party is deprived of the right to reply or cross-examine witnesses and there is no question of the rules of evidence being applied. The newspapers usurp the function which properly belongs to the court and thus deny the basic right of the individual to have a fair trial. A trial by newspaper constitutes an interference with the proper administration of justice in many ways :

  (a) It is likely to affect the mind of those who may later become witnesses;

  (b) It might, from fear of public dislike, cause a plaintiff to discontinue his action or the defendant to come to a compromise which he otherwise might not have entertained;

  (c) If the issues are pre-judged by the public as a reaction to the newspaper publication, unpopular causes would fare very badly; and

  (d) Finally, it would undermine the confidence not only of the parties to particular litigation but also of the public as potential suitors in the due administration of justice by the established courts of law.

Report of Crimes

Publication of reports of crimes is a regular feature of the news. Such items are clearly matters of public interest. But there are dangers in such publication, particularly where the circumstances of a crime seem to lay suspicion on a particular person. It is also clear that a trial for the commission of these crimes will probably follow sooner or later. A report of the crime may contain a statement of fact which is likely to be hotly disputed at the trial. In order to compile a report, it is usually necessary to interview witnesses who may later be witnesses at the trial. Even the publication of photograph of an accused is a question of extreme delicacy, as in many criminal trials, identification of an accused person is a vitally important issue. Such publication may jeopardise the accused. On the other hand, photographs of wanted men are published at the request of the police either to assist the police in their apprehension or to warn the public against them, or both. It must, therefore, necessarily be a question of fact and circumstances whether a publication in any particular case offends against the law.

Journalists sometimes investigate suspected crimes, malpractices and abuses and collect evidence. Publication of such material is often in the public interest and also helps in boosting the circulation of the newspaper. The law of contempt does not hinder the publication of such accumulated evidence before the accused is arrested and charged. But when once judicial proceedings are set in motion, the Press should not publish the evidence. When a person is being tried for an offence, if the Press has evidence that some other person is guilty of the crime, propriety would demand that the evidence in possession of the Press be placed before the court. By adopting such a course, it will get credit for its investigative effort, though the advantage of increased circulation through publication exclusively in its columns would be lost.

Report of Judicial Proceedings

Publication of a fair and accurate report of a pending judicial proceeding is protected under Section 4 of the Act, provided it is not prohibited under Section 7. Section 7 prohibits such publication where it is prohibited by a statute or by the court on certain grounds such as security of the State, public order and the like. To claim the protection under Section 4, the report must be fair and accurate. Misrepresentation or misreporting of court proceedings may amount to contempt, if it can be shown that further proceedings are likely to be prejudiced by such misreporting. No civil or criminal action will lie against a newspaper for publishing a faithful and fair report of proceedings of a court, though it may contain matter disparaging to the character of an individual. This is saved by Exception 4 to Section 499 I.P.C. which says : "it is not defamation to publish a substantially true report of the proceedings of a court of justice or the result of such proceedings." The principle involved here is that the advantage of publicity to the community at large outweighs any private injury resulting from the publication.

Publication of a fair criticism of a judicial act including a judicial decision is protected under Section 5 because the public has an interest in the proper administration of justice.

This provision is founded on the principles stated in *Gray's* case. "Judges and courts are alike open to criticism, and if reasonable argument is offered against any judicial act as contrary to law or public good, no court could or would treat that as contempt of court."[13] The immunity on the ground of fair comment is an adjustment between the public interest in freedom of expression and the public interest in the free flow of justice.

Difficulty, however, arises in determining what is fair comment. It cannot be precisely defined. It would depend on the facts and circumstances of each case, the situation in which the comment was made, the language employed, the context in which the criticism was offered, the people for whose benefit the exercise was taken, and the effect it will produce on the litigants and the society in relation to courts and the administration of justice.[14] It would not be a contempt to comment on the correctness of a judicial decision or to point out the inequality of sentences in different cases, without imputing an improper motive.[15] But a comment ceases to be fair, if the critic imputes improper motive to the judge or lack of impartiality or that he acted 'officiously, arbitrarily and illegally.'' The judgment may be the subject of criticism but not the Judge. The plea of fair comment on a judgment cannot be availed of if comment is made before the case is heard and finally decided. From Explanation (a) to Section 3, it would be evident that a case cannot be said to have been finally decided until the period of limitation for preferring appeal or revision against the decision commented upon has expired, or if any appeal or revision has been filed, the appeal or revision too has been heard and finally decided.

The Act has introduced yet another important safeguard in contempt proceedings under Section 20. This section, for the first time, prescribes a period of limitation of one year for initiating a proceeding for contempt. This bar will apply

13. *R. V. Gray*, (1900) 2 Q.B. 36.
14. *Ram Dayal* v. *State of M.P.* A.I.R. 1978 S.C. 621.
15. *Ambard* v. *A.G. of Trinidad*, Ibid.

not only to cases on motion reference but also where the Court acts *suo moto*. No notice can be issued to the contemner, in any case, if one year has expired from the date on which the contempt is alleged to have been committed. The starting point of limitation is the date of the act by which the alleged contempt was committed, irrespective of the date of knowledge of the complainant of that contempt.[16]

Procedure in contempt cases

It has been held by judicial decisions that the proceedings in contempt, though not criminal are of a quasi-criminal nature[17] and that, therefore, in the case of criminal contempt, if there is any reasonable doubt, the person charged with contempt is entitled to the benefit of doubt. In cases of civil contempt also, it has been held that, as the liberty of the subject is involved, the charge must be proved beyond reasonable doubt and the alleged contemner should have the benefit of doubt. Neither the Act of 1926 nor the Act of 1952 laid down the procedure to be followed in contempt cases. The Supreme Court held that the power of the High Court to institute proceedings for contempt and punish where necessary is a ''special jurisdiction'' which is inherent in all courts of record and the Code of Criminal Procedure does not apply in matters of contempt triable by High Court.[18] The Act of 1971 has, however, laid down the procedure for contempt cases under Sections 14, 15, 17, 18 and 19. Under Section 14, when it appears to the Supreme Court or a High Court that a person has committed contempt in its presence or hearing, *in facie curiae*, the court may proceed against that person. The proceeding is summary but the procedure laid down in Section 14 is generally in conformity with the principles of natural justice so that the alleged contemner cannot be punished without furnishing him with a charge in writing, affording him an opportunity to make his defence to the charge and

---

16. *Venkataramanappa* v. *Naikar*, A.I.R. 1978, KNT 57.
17. *Weston* v. *Editor, Printer etc. of the 'Bengolee'* (1911) 15 C.W.N. 771. *State* v. *Jagannath*, (1977) Cr. L.J. (NOC) 253.
18. *Sukhdev Singh* v. *Chief Justice*, A.I.R. 1954 S.C. 186.

after taking all evidence on such charge. In case of contempt *in facie curiae* before a judge, the judge himself may proceed to try the case and he becomes not only the judge but also prosecutor and witness in these proceedings. We should bear in mind the oft-quoted maxim that justice must not only be done but must also be seen to be done, particularly by an accused person. The Supreme Court, therefore expressed an opinion in *Sukhdev Singh's* case[18] that an accused person "should always be given, as far as that is hunanly possible, a feeling of confidence that he will receive a fair, just and impartial trial by judges who have no personal interest or concern in his case." This opinion of the Supreme Court has been recognised in Section 14 which provides that if the person charged with contempt applies to have the charge against him tried by some judge other than the judge in whose presence or hearing the offence is alleged to have been committed, the matter will be placed before the Chief Justice for such directions as he may think fit to issue as respects the trial thereof. In the case of indirect or constructive contempt, the procedure has been laid down in Sections 15, 17, 18 and 19. In these cases also, the proceeding is summary but the procedure laid down is in conformity with the principles of natural justice. Every case of criminal contempt under Section 15 shall be heard and determined by a Bench of not less than two judges. Further, where a High Court has heard the case, an appeal shall lie as of right from any order or decision of the High Court in the exercise of its jurisdiction to punish for contempt. Such right to appeal under Section 19, however, depends on the condition that such order or decision has been made "in the exercise of its jurisdiction to punish for contempt." If the High Court finds the alleged contemner guilty and punishes him, he would be entitled as of right to file an appeal. As regards interlocutory orders, it is clear that no appeal can as of right lie under Section 19, for every interlocutory order cannot be said to have been made in the exercise of the power to punish; it can come under Section 19 only

18. *Sukhdev Singh* v. *Chief Justice*, A.I.R. 1954 S.C. 186.

if it decides any contention raised by the alleged contemner
which relates to the jurisdiction of the court to punish for
contempt, e.g., an order deciding any contention raised by
him that the proceeding be dropped.[19] As regards interlocutory
order, the Supreme Court may, however, be moved under article 136 of the Constitution for special leave to appeal. Under
Section 19, the appellate court has been given all the powers
which are vested in an appellate court, including the power
to hear the appeal notwithstanding that the appellant has not
purged his contempt. Prior to 1971, courts in India followed
the principle that a contemner should not be heard in appeal
until he purged himself of contempt. The Sanyal Committee,
however, noted that appeals before the Privy Council and the
Supreme Court in contempt cases had more often succeeded
than not and, therefore, the contemner should have an appeal
as of right and such appeal should be heard notwithstanding
the fact that the appellant has not purged himself of the contempt. Section 19 gives effect to this recommendation.

Courts, both in England and India are aware that the
summary jurisdiction exercised by superior courts in punishing contempt is arbitrary. In *Hiralal's* case[20] the Supreme
Court observed that "this is certainly an extraordinary power
which must be sparingly exercised." Time and again the
Supreme Court has warned that the summary jurisdiction
which the courts exercise in regard to contempt matters
has to be exercised with scrupulous care and only when the
case is clear and beyond reasonable doubt. This question
attracted the attention of the Phillimore Committee in U.K.
as also of the Mathew Commission. The Mathew Commission
thinks that it is not necessary to adopt the summary procedure in vogue for dealing with all cases of contempt. In the
summary contempt procedure, judges sit as judges in their
own cause and the defendant cannot lay claim to all the safeguards provided under the normal procedural law. It is only
where the offensive conduct or offending imputations are made

19.   *Purushottam* v. *Dhillon*, A.I.R. 1978 S.C. 1014.
20.   *Hiralal Dixit* v. *State of U.P.*, Ibid.

in the face of the court or they relate to particular proceedings which are in progress and give rise to a risk of prejudice to the proceedings on hand that the application of the summary procedure would be justified on the ground of urgency. The Mathew Commission, therefore, recommends that the application of summary procedure should be restricted to such cases only and a new criminal offence should be created to take care of all other cases of contempt. Such an offence should be triable only on prosecution. As the offence would be one which would strike generally at the administration of justice, prosecution should be only at the instance of the Attorney General or Advocate General. As regards defence of the new offence, Mathew Commission agrees with the view of the Phillimore Committee that if the defendant can prove the truth of his allegations and also show that its publication was for public benefit, he should be entitled to an acquittal. The Mathew Commission is of the view that the creation of the new offence with the defence suggested would go a long way in removing the complaint that the summary procedure adopted for trying contempt cases inhibits honest and truthful criticism of the administration of justice in public interest.[21]

The Press does have the right, which is also its professional function, to criticise and advocate. The whole gamut of public affairs including the administration of justice is the domain for fearless and critical comment. But the public function which belongs to the Press makes it an obligation of honour to exercise this function only with the fullest sense of responsibility. Without such a lively sense of responsibility, a free Press might readily become an instrument of injustice. The competing claims of the court to maintain its authority and of the freedom of the Press to comment on matters of public interest must be reconciled. Without a free Press there can be no free society. Freedom of the Press, however, is not an end in itself but a means to an end of a free society. The independence of the judiciary is no less a means to the end of a free society and in fact, the proper functioning of an

---

21. *Second Press Commission Report*, Vol. I. Ch. IV, para 88, p. 49.

independent judiciary puts the freedom of the Press in its proper perspective. A free Press is not to be preferred to an independent judiciary, nor an independent judiciary to a free Press either. No judge fit to be one is likely to be influenced except by what he sees and hears in court and by what is judi cially appropriate for the deliberation. However, judges are human. There is the powerful pull of the unconscious. Since judges, however stalwart, are human, the delicate task of administering justice ought not to be made unduly difficult by irresponsible publication.

It has, therefore, been suggested by the Mathew Commission that the Press must at all times act in a responsible manner. The Press should eschew use of immoderate language, the tendency to give a slant to the copy and sensationalising events with a view to increasing circulation or satisfying the sadistic curiosity of the public.

CHAPTER VI

The Press and Privileges of Parliament

Parliamentary privilege is one of the most sensitive areas in which a journalist has to tread warily and his task has become more complex because of the uncertainties created by judicial decisions from time to time. Yet a free Press and strong public opinion are indispensable to a parliamentary democracy. People must know what their representatives in Parliament are doing and Parliament also, while deciding grave public issues, should know the trends in public opinion. The Press provides the necessary link between the Government, Parliament and the public interpreting each section to the other and, at times, urging its own views on both. But the Press is often reluctant to make a critical analysis of the functioning of Parliament for fear of the breach of its privileges which hangs over the heads of journalists like the sword of Damocles. This question has assumed considerable importance in our country in recent years on account of the increasing number of privilege motions against the Press and the wide variety of causes for which notices of such motions have been given. It is necessary, therefore, to have a clear understanding of the rights of the Press and the limitations which may be imposed on it by the privileges of Parliament.

'Privilege' means a right, advantage or immunity granted to, or enjoyed by, a person or class of persons beyond the common advantage of others. Erskine May has defined parliamentary privilege as follows :

145

"The sum of the peculiar rights enjoyed by each House collectively as a constituent part of the High Court of Parliament and by members of each House individually, without which they could not discharge their functions and which exceed those possessed by other bodies or individuals. Thus privilege, though part of the law of the land, is to a certain extent an exception from the ordinary law."[1]

May then quotes from Redlich to define the peculiar privileges of the Commons as "the sum of fundamental rights of the House and of its individual members as against the prerogatives of the Crown, the authority of the ordinary courts of land and the special rights of the House of Lords."[2] According to Halsbury's *Laws of England*,[3] any act or omission which obstructs or impedes any member or officer of the House in the discharge of his duties, or which has a tendency to produce such a result would constitute contempt of legislature. Viewed in this light, our legislatures enjoy certain privileges, that is to say, certain rights, advantages and immunities which are not enjoyed by others. They have been enshrined in article 105 in respect of Parliament and in article 194 in respect of State Legislatures. The provisions of these two articles are identical in terms with this difference that under clause (3) of article 105 the power to make laws with respect to privileges of Parliament is conferred on Parliament while under clause (3) of article 194, this power is conferred on the State Legislatures.

No Special Privilege for the Press

No such special rights or privileges have been conferred on the Press. The Press derives whatever rights it has from article 19(1)(a) of the Constitution in common with all citizens and it has no special privileges of its own. Prior to the coming into force of the Constitution, it was held by the Privy Council that "the freedom of the journalist is an ordi-

1. Erskine May, *Parliamentary Practice*, 16th Edn. Chap. III p. 47.
2. *Ibid.*
3. Halsbury, *Laws of England*, 3rd Edn., p. 465.

nary part of the freedom of the subject, and to whatever lengths the subject in general may go, so also may the journalist, but apart from statute law, his privilege is no other and no higher. No privilege attaches to his position.''[4] The Constitution does not seek to alter the position in any way. Unlike U.S.A., where the First Amendment specifically refers to the freedom of speech and of the Press, there is no such specific reference in our Constitution to freedom of the Press. But the Supreme Court has held in a number of cases that freedom of expression guaranteed to citizens is a wide term and includes freedom of the Press. This question has been considered by the Supreme Court in the cases of *Romesh Thappar,*[5] *Brij Bhusan,*[6] *Express Newspapers,*[7] *Bennet Coleman*[8] and various other cases and it has been held that freedom of the Press includes not only the right to propagate one's own views but also the views of others and that this freedom is ensured by freedom of circulation. As freedom of the Press flows from freedom of expression guaranteed to citizens, it follows that the Press does not enjoy any rights which other citizens do not have and no privilege attaches to the Press as such.

The Press not only does not have any special rights but it suffers from a disability. A non-citizen running a newspaper is not entitled to the benefit guaranteed under article 19(1)(a). Under the Citizenship Act, 1955, a corporation is not a citizen and it has been held by the Supreme Court in the *State Trading Corporation's* case[9] as also in *Telco's* case[10] that a corporation is not a citizen for the purposes of article 19. Most of our newspapers are owned by corporations and even when the freedom of expression of a particular news-

4. *Arnold* v. *King Emperor*, (1914) 26 M.L.J. 621.
5. *Romesh Thappar* v. *State of Madras*, (1950) S.C.R. 594.
6. *Brij Bhusan* v. *State of Delhi*, (1950) S.C.R. 605.
7. *Express Newspapers* v. *Union of India* (1959) S.C.R. 12.
8. *Bennet Coleman* v. *Union of India*, A.I.R. 1973 S.C. 106.
9. *State Trading Corporation* v. *Commercial Tax Officer*, (1964) S.C.R. 99.
10. *Tata Engineering & Locomotive Co. Ltd.*, v. *State of Bihar* (1964) S.C.R. 885.

paper is invaded by the State, the Corporation owning that newspaper cannot bring a proceeding under article 32 or 226 of the Constitution. This difficulty was to a great extent removed by the Supreme Court in the *Bennet Coleman's* case[11] where it was held that though the corporation owning a newspaper cannot obtain relief directly, it can do so through its shareholders or office-bearers like the editor or printer. The disability of the corporation is, therefore, only technical. But the Mathew Commission has argued that there is a fundamental difference between the corporation seeking relief directly and the office-bearers of the corporation seeking such relief. The Commission has, therefore, recommended that "all Indian Companies engaged in the business of communication and whose shareholders are citizens should be deemed to be citizens for the purpose of the relevant clause of article 19."* This recommendation should be accepted and the object may be achieved by a simple amendment of the Citizenship Act.

Privileges of Parliament

Turning to parliamentary privileges, clauses (1) and (2) of article 105 expressly confer privileges in respect of two matters only, namely, (i) freedom of speech in Parliament; and (ii) immunity in respect of publication of proceedings, report, paper etc. of a House by or under the authority of that House. Clause (1) confers freedom of speech in Parliament and clause (2) gives complete immunity to a member of Parliament from any action in any court in respect of anything said or done in Parliament or any committee thereof. Reading clauses (1) and (2) together, it is plain that freedom of speech in Parliament is absolute and unfettered. This view has been upheld in Sharma's case[12] and confirmed in *Special Reference No. 1* of 1964.[13] It has been held that freedom of speech in Parliament is not subject to article 19(1)(a) but it is subject only to those provisions of the Constitution which

11.   *Bennet Coleman* v. *Union of India*, A.I.R. 1973 S. C. 106.
      Second Press Commission Report, Vol. I, p. 34.
12.   *M.S. Sharma* v. *Shri Krishna Sinha*, A.I.R. 1959 S.C. 395.
18.   *Special Reference No. I of 1964* A.I.R. 1965 S. C. 745.

regulate the procedure of Parliament such as article 118 or article 121. Freedom of speech in Parliament does not, however, affect the Press. In regard to the publication of the proceedings of a House of Parliament, immunity has been given only when the publication is made by or under the authority of that House. The implication is that even a true newspaper report of the proceedings of a House is not protected under this clause.

Clause (3) of article 105, as originally enacted, provided that *in other respects,* the powers, privileges and immunities of each House of Parliament and of the members thereof shall be such as may from time to time be defined by Parliament by law, and until so defined, shall be those of the British House of Commons and of its members at the commencement of this Constitution. This clause was amended by the 42nd Amendment but that amendment was never brought into force. This clause was again amended by the 44th Amendment which provides that until Parliament codifies its own privileges, the powers, privileges and immunities of each House and of its members and committees "shall be those of that House and of its members and committees immediately before the coming into force" of this amendment. This amendment has made some verbal changes omitting reference to the House of Commons but the substance of the clause remains the same. The position that emerges is that until Parliament codifies its own privileges, its powers and privileges other than those specified in clauses (1) and (2) of article 105 shall be the same as those of the British House of Commons as they existed on 26th January, 1950.

Privileges of the House of Commons

The powers, privileges and immunities of the House of Commons in England are nowhere definned. They are an organic growth which the Commons had to win after a fierce and prolonged struggle waged through the centuries against the prerogatives of the Crown, against the authority of the courts of law and against the special rights of the House of Lords. They are a part of the common law of England and have to be pieced together from numerous precedents. Historically speaking, the King of England claimed all the privileges and they were enjoyed by his servants who acted in his name. In course of time, the people wrested those rights from the King by claiming them for the House of Commons. The real trouble between Parliament and the Courts arose in the days of the Stuart Kings. Punishment for contumacious or insulting conduct towards the House of Commons was frequent and lawyers and judges were punished for contempt of the House of Commons. The House of Commons claimed to be the sole judge of the nature, the existence and the extent of privileges. The courts in England did not concede this right. As Erskine May says : "The decisions of the courts are not accepted as binding by the House in matters of privilege, nor the decisions of the House by the Courts. Thus the old dualism remains unsolved."[14] Examples of this dualism may be seen in the cases of *Ashby* v. *White*,[15] *Stockdale* v. *Hansard*,[16] *Sheriff of Middlesex*[17] and *Bradlaugh* v. *Gosset*.[18] This daulism which rudely disturbed public life during the 17th, 18th and 19th centuries is now a matter of history and an equilibrium has been reached amid rival claim of privileges and the House of Commons and the courts now seldom encroach on the sphere of the other. "The commons used the privileges against the King in the 17th century and in the next century exercised them against the people themselves somewhat arbitrarily."[19]

The list of privileges claimed by the House of Commons in early days was a long and formidable one. In course of time, however, many of them have fallen into disuse and faded out of existence and some were controlled by legislation. The privileges which the House of Commons enjoy may be collected from May's *Parliamentary Practice* and the classic

14.   Erskine May, *Parliamentary Practice*, 16th Edn., p. 172.
15.   *Ashby* v. *White*, 1 Sm. L.C. 263
16.   *Stockdale* v. *Hansard*, 9 A. E. 1.
17.   *The Case of Sheriff of Middlesex*, 11 A. E. 273.
18.   *Bradlaugh* v. *Gosset*, Q. B.D. 281·
19.   Holdsworth, *History of English Law*, Book 4, Part 1.

Annotated Constitution of the Australian Commonwealth by Quick and Garran also contains a fairly exhaustive list of the powers, privileges and immunities of the British Houses of Parliament. But even then, the privileges of the Commons are not readily ascertainable. As Anson in his book *Law and Custom of the Constitution* points out :

"The rules of which they (the privileges) consist are not readily ascertainable, for they obtain only legal definition when they are cast in statutory form, or when a conflict between the House and the court has resulted in some questions of privilege being settled by judicial decisions."

Nevertheless, the major privileges which the House of Commons enjoys are fairly well known. They fall into two broad groups. In the first group are those privileges which are demanded of the Crown by the Speaker of the House of Commons at the commencement of each Parliament and granted as a matter of course. They are (a) freedom of speech, (b) freedom from arrest, (c) the right of having the most favourable construction placed upon its proceedings, (d) the right of access to the Crown as well as other rights and immunities which have come to be recognised as part of the law and custom of Parliament and are thus law of the land. In the second group are the rights claimed by the House in its corporate capacity. They comprise (i) the right to provide for the due composition of its body; (ii) the right to regulate its own proceedings; (iii) the right to exclude strangers; (iv) the right to prohibit publication of its debates; and (v) the right to exercise penal jurisdiction and to punish breaches of its privileges and for contempt.

Privileges affecting freedom of the Press

Under article 105(3) of the Constitution, the privileges of our Parliament are identical with those of the House of Commons as they existed on 26th January, 1950. But the Supreme Court has held in *Special Reference No. 1 of 1964* that the privileges available to our Parliament are only those powers of the House of Commons which were not only in existence at the relevant time but were also recognised by the British Courts. The court further held that Parliament cannot claim all the powers and privileges which were possessed by the House of Commons at the relevant time. Parliament can exercise only those powers of the House of Commons which are incidental to legislative functions and not those powers which are exercised by the House of Commons as a superior court of record. We shall discuss this question later. Though Parliament enjoys a number of privileges, we are concerned only with such of those powers as would impinge upon freedom of the Press. They are : (i) the right to exclude strangers from Parliament; (ii) the right to prohibit publication of its proceedings by a newspaper; and (iii) the right to punish breaches of privileges and for contempt. These privileges have been justified on the grounds of "necessity, practice and universal acquiescence."[20] The executive exercises its rights through a process of law and the violation of its rights is punished by law. "But the representative bodies must necessarily vindicate their authority by means of their own, and these means lie in the process of committal for contempt."[21] They are also justified as a legal incident of their legislative authority.

The right to exclude strangers

The first privilege claimed is the right of Parliament to exclude strangers. Under the rules of the Houses of Parliament, the Speaker or the Chairman, as the case may be, may, whenever he thinks fit, order the withdrawal of strangers from any part of the House, including representatives of the Press. This right has not been exercised by the House of Commons except for imperative reasons, for example, in times of war. In India, this right has not so far been exercised. If on any occasion—and such occasions are bound to be rare—Parliament holds a secret session, the Press correspondents may be excluded from the House.

20.   *Stockdale* v. *Hansard* 9 A.E.I.
21.   *The Case of Sheriff of Middlesex*, 11 A.E. 273.

Even in normal sitting of a House, the entry to the Visitors' Gallery is regulated by passes and only accredited newspaper Correspondents are admitted to the Press Gallery. The Lok Sabha exercises this privilege in consultation with a nominated Press Gallery Committee of Journalists, but the Rajya Sabha has no such committee at all. An accredited newspaper correspondent has a fairly wide freedom of movement within the part of the House used by members. He may move freely in the lobbies and Central Hall of Parliament and interview Ministers, Members, the Speaker and Officials of the House. But the newspaper correspondents have always to be on their guard. Their cards may be withheld on account of reporting lapses, misreporting or publication of expunged proceedings of the House.

The Lok Sabha has exercised its right of withdrawing press cards twice by way of punishment. The last case was that of Mr. A. Raghavan, Special Correspondent of the *Blitz*. In his case, the news items published by him was deemed to be a breach of privilege of the House and his Press Card was withdrawn and it was not returned to him until he tendered an apology to the Speaker. The other case was that of Mr. C. L. Chandrakar, Special Correspondent of the *Hindustan*, New Delhi. A news item relating to a conflict between the Lok Sabha and Rajya Sabha was published by him in his newspaper and in that report, he criticised some officials of the Lok Sabha. The Lok Sabha Secretariat took objection to the report on the plea that it interfered with the working of Parliament and his Press card was withdrawn. The Press Gallery Committee and the Press Gallery Association took up the matter with the Speaker and after prolonged negotiations, the card was restored to him. There have been many other cases where on account of some minor lapses, the newspaper correspondents were threatened that their Press cards would be withdrawn but the situation was saved because the correspondents invariably tendered apology. It appears that Parliament sometimes becomes over-sensitive in regard to its own privileges.

Right to prohibit publication of its proceedings

The right of Parliament to prohibit publication of its proceedings, if strictly enforced, would seriously affect not only freedom of the Press but also the functioning of Parliament itself and would strike at the root of democracy. In modern times, this power is not exercised except for a limited purpose only to prevent *mala fide* publication of an inaccurate report or any report of the expunged portion of its proceedings.

In England, the struggle for recognition of the right of the Press to publish parliamentary proceedings was a long and arduous one. From the very inception, deliberations of the House of Commons were treated as secret and there was a standing order forbidding the publication of its debates and proceedings. Various devices were adopted by the Press to publish parliamentary proceedings but this often led to a conflict between the Press and Parliament. It was only after 1868 that the Press was allowed to report parliamentary proceedings. The House of Commons has, however, absolute privilege to publish its own proceedings and even if the official report contains any defamatory or other unlawful matter. neither the member who made the statement nor the officer of the House who published the official record is liable under the ordinary law. On the other hand, if such proceedings are published in a newspaper, both the member who made the speech and the newspaper which published it would be liable under the ordinary law. The common law, however, offers the protection of a 'qualified privilege' to such a publication. To claim such qualified privilege, the report published must be fair and accurate and must have been made in good faith and without malice. This was based on the decision in *Wason* v. *Walter*[22] where it was held that a faithful report in a public newspaper of a debate in Parliament containing matter disparaging to the character of an individual which had been spoken in the course of a debate was not actionable provided that the publication had been made in good faith and without

22. *Wason* v. *Walter*, (1869) 4 Q.B. 73.

malice. The principle involved here is the same as in an accurate report of proceedings in a court of law, namely, that the advantage of publicity to the community at large outweighs any private injury resulting from the publication. "Practically speaking, therefore, it is idle to say that publication of parliamentary proceedings is prohibited by Parliament." The position in England has been summarised by May in his *Parliamentary Practice* as follows :

"So long as the debates are correctly and faithfully reported, the orders which prohibit their publication are not enforced; but when they are reported *mala fide*, the publishers of newspapers are liable to punishment."

This principle has now been given statutory recognition in the British Defamation Act, 1952. In any case, where it is proposed to take action against a newspaper for alleged misrepresentation, it has been the practice to call attention to the report as an infringement of the order of the House, and then to complain of the misrepresentation as an aggravation of the offence.

In India, there is no rule or standing order of Parliament prohibiting the publication of its proceedings. But it has been well established by judicial decisions that Parliament does possess this right. In the case of *Sharma* v. *Shrikrishna Sinha*,[23] the question arose whether publication of expunged portions of the proceedings of a legislature amounted to contempt of the legislature. A notice was issued to the Editor of *Searchlight*, a daily newspaper, to show cause why he should not be punished for contempt of the legislature for publishing portions of a speech which were expunged by the Speaker. The Editor moved the Supreme Court on the ground that the issue of the notice amounted to contravention of articles 19 (1)(a) and 21. The question that fell for consideration was whether the privilege claimed by the legislature was a subsisting privilege in England and what was the impact of the above articles on article 194(3). The majority held that "the

---

23. *M.S.M. Sharma* v. *Shri Krishna Sinha*, A.I.R. 1959 S.C. 395.

House of Commons had at the commencement of our Constitution the power or privilege of prohibiting even a true and faithful report of the debates or proceedings that take place within the House. *A fortiori* the House at the relevant time had the power or privilege of prohibiting the publication of an inaccurate or garbled version of such debates or proceedings.'' The Court, therefore, held that articles 105(3) and 194(3) confer all those powers and privileges on Parliament and State legislatures.

On the further question whether privileges of Parliament and State legislatures under articles 105 and 194 prevail over the fundamental right of freedom of speech and expression guaranteed to the Press under article 19(1)(a), the court pointed out that the provisions of articles 105(3) and 194(3) were constitutional laws and not ordinary laws made by legislatures. On the principle of harmonious construction, the Court held that the provisions of article 19(1)(a) which were general had to yield to the special provisions of articles 105(3) and 194(3). The decision on this point is well-settled and has been reiterated in *Special Reference No. 1 of 1964.*[24]

Experience, however, shows that our Parliament, like the House of Commons, does not exercise these powers except in gross cases. It fully appreciates the benefit of publicity and accords all necessary facilities to the reporters and encourages the publication of reports of its debates and proceedings. But when a newspaper publishes the proceedings of Parliament which contain defamatory statement, the Press becomes liable for action. It may be that the statement was privileged when made in the House but there is no immunity to a newspaper publishing the statement, even if the publication is substantially true and faithful. Immunity has been given under article 105(2) only to the reports published by or under the authority of Parliament. In England, however, a newspaper publishing the proceedings of the House of Commons enjoys a 'qualified privilege.' In order to confer such qualified privilege on a newspaper. Parliamentary Proceedings

.24.   *Special Reference No. 1 of 1964*, A.I.R. 1965 S.C. 745.

(Protection of Publication) Act was enacted in 1956 due to the efforts of late Shri Feroze Gandhi. Under this Act, no liability, civil or criminal, attaches to the publication in a newspaper of a substantially true report of any proceedings of either House of Parliament, unless it is proved to have been made with malice. If the publication is for public good, then, too, it is protected. This Act was repealed in December, 1975 during Emergency but was re-enacted in 1977. Now the law on this point has been incorporated in the Constitution itself by a new article 361A which has been inserted by the 44th Amendment Act, 1978. The protection conferred by this article extends to news agency reports containing material for publication in a newspaper. It should be mentioned, however, that while the Parliamentary Act as also article 361A of the Constitution give protection to newspapers from civil and criminal proceedings in a court of law, they do not give protection to a newspaper from punishment by Parliament for breach of its privileges. It is, however, inconceivable to think that having enacted such a law and in view also of the constitutional provision, Parliament would proceed against a newspaper for publishing a true and faithful account of its proceedings.

The Press is, however, often tempted to publish expunged portion of parliamentary proceedings for its news value. But it should not do so, as the expunged portion does not really form part of the proceedings and its publication is not saved by article 361A. Dr. H. K. Paranjape, a member of the Mathew Commission, is, however, of the view that a newspaper should have the right to publish even those portions which have been expunged, because the citizens have the right to be informed of the activities of their representatives. In Australia, the right of newspapers to report whatever happens in their Parliament is not questioned. If a portion of the proceedings is expunged or if a remark made by a member is held to be unparliamentary or offensive and is retracted, a newspaper may give a full report of the episode, publishing the expunged portion as also the expressions used and retracted. The position in U.K. is, however, different. A publication of an expunged portion of the proceedings of the House of Commons is recognised as a breach of privilege and it should be so in India in view of clause (3) of articles 105 and 194.

It has become almost a matter of habit with some presiding officers to expunge parts of the proceedings. The Press Gallery Committee in a resolution had to draw attention to this evil which was fast developing. It has been pointed out that a problem arises when certain portions of the proceedings of the House are expunged by the Chair without making it clear on the spot what exactly is expunged and the expunged portions are published by the newspapers without knowing that they have been expunged. It is not also completely unknown that presiding officers sometimes expunge statements from official records not at the time when the statement is made but at some subsequent stage. In order to overcome these difficulties, the Mathew Commission has recommended that "unintentional and unavoidable transgressions of the rulings of the Chair such as publication of the proceedings of the legislature before the order of the presiding officer expunging those proceedings reaches the newspaper offices should not be regarded as a breach of the privileges of the House."[25] This recommendation should be accepted.

It is not an easy task for a journalist to report parliamentary proceedings. It requires a good deal of skill and also a sense of responsibility. It is neither possible nor desirable to give a verbatim account of Parliament's proceedings. The task of the journalist is to make a selection of passages from various speeches to give a clear and balanced account of the entire proceedings, and then to clothe the debates with vividness, wit and shrewdness. The bare words of the debate do not convey any meaning, unless the reader is given the "atmosphere of the discussion." If an agitated member removes the mace from the Speaker's table or disobeys Speaker's orders, every newspaper would describe the event at great length and with colourful description. But if a journalist

25. *The Second Press Commission Report*, Chapter IV, para 129.

oversteps the limits of fair comment or says something light-hearted or humorous, he may have to face a charge of contempt. Thus, as Mudholkar J. points out "the present state of law has placed a very harsh restriction on his right to comment on the conduct of members and the way in which proceedings have been conducted in Parliament."[26]

Power to punish for contempt

The most important privilege claimed by our Parliament is the power to commit for contempt. "The power of commitment," says May, "is truly described as the keystone of Parliamentary privilege." It is this punitive power possessed by each House which tends to bring the Press into conflict with Parliament. This power of Parliament being identical with that of the House of Commons, it is necessary to ascertain the punitive powers enjoyed by that House and then to consider how far they are available in India. The House of Commons acquired its privileges in a militant way after a fierce struggle for about 400 years until some kind of equilibrium was reached in the 19th century. It is now well-settled that the House of Commons in England possesses powers "akin in nature and origin to the powers possessed by the courts of justice to punish for contempt."[27] It has powers not only to punish the offender for breach of its privileges but also for offences against its authority, such as disobedience to its legitimate commands or libels upon itself or against its officers and members and it has exclusive right to exercise those powers analogous to the rights enjoyed by a superior court to punish for contempt of court.

In India, the power to punish for contempt was not available to the legislatures under the Government of India Act, 1919. Under the Government of India Act, 1935, certain privileges were conferred on the legislatures and they were also empowered to define their privileges but under Section 28, the status of a court was not conferred on them and they were

26. Mudholkar, J. *Press Law*, (Tagore Law Lectures) p. 90.
27. May. *Parliamentary Practice*, 16th Edn., p. 91.

not authorised to punish any person for contempt. Under the
Indian Independence Act, 1947, the members of the Dominion
legislature could claim the privileges enjoyed by the members of the House of Commons before the establishment of the
Dominion, but the Provincial legislatures could not do so.
Under the Constitution, the powers of the House of Commons
were expressly conferred on Parliament and State Legislatures under articles 105(3) and 194(3). The scope and effect
of these articles came to be considered by the Supreme Court
in several cases and the judicial decisions have raised some
controversy with which we shall deal later. A contempt may
be committed in the presence of the House which is *ex facie* or
'direct' contempt. But the Press generally becomes subject to
indirect contempt. There is, however, no dispute on the main
question that Parliament has power to punish not only for
contempt which is committed in its presence but also for contempt committed by any one outside its four walls.

The question which arises for consideration is whether
the existence of this punitive power of Parliament seriously
affects freedom of the Press. It would be well to bear in mind
in this connection the distinction between the existence of a
power and the exercise of that power. In England, during
medieval times, British Parliament sometimes used this power
in a manner which would shock everybody, but during the last
100 years or more, the House of Commons has ceased to be
oversensitive and it exercises this power with commendable
restraint. Even as early as 1887, when the question of privilege arose in respect of an article in the *Times*, the Speaker
of the House of Commons observed :

> "It has been the practice of this House to restrain
> privilege under great limitations and conditions. The
> rule is that, when imputations are made, in order to
> raise a case of privilege, the imputation must refer to
> the action of honourable members in the discharge of
> their duties in the actual transaction of the business
> of this House."

The House of Commons not only tolerates public criticisms

but recognises the absolute necessity of the freedom of comment. Speaking in the House of Commons in 1888, Gladstone observed :

> "Indeed, it is absolutely necessary that there should be freedom of comment. That freedom of comment may, of course, be occasionally abused; but I do not think that it is becoming the dignity of the House to notice that abuse of it."

In India also, following the traditions of the House of Commons, it has been the practice of each House to restrain privilege under great limitations and conditions. When the question of privilege was raised in respect of a reported speech of Shri C. Rajagopalachari in which he said the Congress "representatives in the legislatures were such people whom any first-class Magistrate would round up," the Speaker of the Lok Sabha referred to the case of the *Times* in England and refused his consent to the motion. In 1958, Shri Namboodiripad, the then Chief Minister of Kerala, in a telegram to the Home Minister said that "some members of Parliament tried to slander the State Government in the name of explanation." The matter was referred to the Committee of Privileges but the Committee found that the matter did not involve any breach of privilege. The Committee also endorsed the following observation made by the Prime Minister in his speech in the Lok Sabha on the 27th November, 1958.

> "There are things said, often enough, which are not desirable and things said in the heat of the moment which a person thinking more coolly would not have said. If it was a deliberate flouting of the dignity of Parliament or of any individual member of Parliament, then, of course, there can be no doubt that that challenge has to be met. But where in other contexts, in the heat of the moment or in a controversy, something is said, I would prefer personally this House not to take too much notice of it."

In 1959, a question of privilege was raised in respect of the letter written by Shri M. O. Mathai to the Prime Minister and

11—TPI

the matter was referred to the Committee of Privileges. The Committee of Privileges came to the conclusion that the remarks made by Shri Mathai would amount to breach of privilege of the House, but felt that it would not be consistent with the dignity of the House to take notice of every such statement which might technically constitute contempt of the House. In 1954, a question of privilege was raised in the Rajya Sabha in respect of a reported speech of Shri N. C. Chatterjee in which he said that "the Upper House seemed to be behaving irresponsibly like a pack of urchins." Even in regard to this matter, the House did not take any action when he expressed his regret. In the *Blitz* case, the editor of the newspaper was reprimanded by the Lok Sabha, but the Privilege Committee recognised the right of fair comment and observed as follows :

> "Nobody would deny the members or, as a matter of fact, any citizen, the right of fair comment. But if the comments contain personal attack on individual members of Parliament on account of their conduct in Parliament, or if the language of the comment is vulgar or abusive, they cannot be deemed to come within the bounds of fair comment or justifiable criticism."

These illustrations have been cited to show the manner in which Parliament is exercising its punitive power. It does not take action against anybody for making legitimate criticism or fair comment on Parliament or its members. It is only when criticism ceases to be legitimate and comments are not fair, when reflections or imputations of *mala fides* are made or when vulgar or abusive language is used or when the object of comment or criticism is to lower Parliament in the estimation of the public, Parliament takes penal action against the offender.

But of late, there has been an increase in the number of privilege motions and the Privileges Digests from October, 1979 to October, 1981 would show that in course of two years, there have been 56 such cases before Parliament. Of them, the most sensational case was that of Mrs. Gandhi in which she was imprisoned and also expelled. Mr. Hardwari Lal in his book *Myth and Law of Parliamentary Privileges* has given several instances how the privilege motion has been used as an instrument of coercion. A question, therefore, arises whether the Press has any remedy in a court of law, if Parliament misuses or abuses its powers. The jurisdiction of courts in India in cases affecting parliamentary privileges is not very clear.

In England, the history of the jurisdiction of courts over parliamentary privileges is full of contradictory precedents. But the controversy may be said to have been settled to a large extent by agreement between the judiciary and the House of Commons. It is now well settled that a committal for the contempt of the House of Commons is within its exclusive jurisdiction; it is the sole judge of the question whether any of its privileges has been infringed and the court cannot question the decision of the House of Commons. It is, however, recognised that the existence and extent of privilege can be examined by courts. It is also well-settled that if the House of Commons issues an unspeaking or general warrant, the courts would invariably treat the general warrant as conclusive and would not examine the validity of the order passed by the House. If, however, a speaking warrant is issued, it would be open to the courts to examine whether the reasons set out in the warrant amount to contempt or not. To this limited extent, the jurisdiction of the courts is recognised and whenever it becomes necessary for Parliament to justify the orders passed by it for contempt, a return has always been filed in courts. In *habeas corpus* cases, the court may entertain the petition and issue a rule. There is no question of bail before the return is filed, but if the return is not filed or is defective, the prisoner could be admitted to bail and also released.

Having outlined the scope of judicial review in England, it is necessary to enquire into its scope and extent in India. The answer to this question depends largely on the construc-

tion of article 105(3) or 194(3). In *Sharma's* case[28] the
Supreme Court had no difficulty in construing these articles
and came to the conclusion that the powers of a State legislature are identical with those of the House of Commons subsisting on January 26, 1950 and the courts can exercise only
limited jurisdiction to decide the question whether a particular privilege subsists, leaving the legislature as the sole judge
of the question whether contempt has been committed. In
Keshav Singh's case[29], however, the majority took a different
view. In this unfortunate case, one Keshav Singh was found
to have committed a breach of privilege of the U.P. legislative Assembly and was summoned to receive a reprimand at
the bar of the House. Keshav Singh wrote a disrespectful
letter to the Speaker and his behaviour in view of the House
was unseemly. For the second contempt, Keshav Singh was
sent to prison. An advocate, Solomon, filed a petition under
article 226 to the Lucknow Bench of Allahabad High Court
on behalf of Keshav Singh. The Court admitted the petition,
ordered the release of Keshav Singh on bail and issued notices
to the Speaker and others. This irritated the House which
proceeded to take action not only against Keshav Singh and
his advocate but also against the two judges who passed the
order. The matter came up before the Allahabad High Court
and when the conflict between the Legislature and the High
Court was taking an ugly turn, a reference was made to the
Supreme Court under article 143 of the Constitution.

In this case, the Supreme Court held that Parliament
cannot claim all the powers and privileges which were possessed by the House of Commons at the relevant time. They
point out that the privilege of freedom of access to the Crown
or the privilege to pass Acts of attainder and impeachments
cannot be claimed by our Parliament. But these privileges are
not applicable to India at all. Even in regard to the most
important privilege, namely, the power to commit for contempt
they point out that there is a vital difference between the

28. *M.S. Sharma* v. *Shri Krishna Sinha*, A.I.R. 1959, S.C. 395.
29. *Special Reference No. I of 1964*, A.I.R. 1965, S.C. 745.

powers of the House of Commons and of Parliament in our
country. They embarked upon a laborious historical research
into antiquities to find out if the powers enjoyed by the
House of Commons were incidents of their legislative function
and integral part of their privileges or whether they were
enjoyed as a superior court of record. They also took into
consideration the wide and unfettered powers vested in courts
under articles 32 and 226 of the Constitution and the fundamental rights guaranteed to the citizens. On these considerations, they held that the legislatures in India are not superior courts of record and they can exercise only those powers
of the House of Commons which are integral part of its privileges and which are incidental to legislative function but not
those powers which are exercised by the House of Commons
as a superior court of record or as a result of convention or
comity. The Supreme Court was, therefore, of the opinion
that the courts in India can not only examine the existence or
extent of privilege but can also examine the validity of an
order of commitment made by the legislature, whether the warrant issued is a speaking or general warrant. They also expressed doubts about the legality of issuing general warrants. They
further held that the courts have jurisdiction to make an interim order in the proceedings before it, including an order for
the grant of bail to a person who stands committed for contempt.

The main consideration which weighed with the Supreme
Court in giving its opinion was that the history of the legislatures in India shows that they did not exercise judicial functions and were not courts of record and even under the Constitution, these functions are in the exclusive jurisdiction of
courts and by a legal fiction, the legislatures cannot be vested
with powers of a superior court of record which the House
of Commons enjoys. It may be true the legislatures in India
were not courts, not to speak of courts of record. But the question is not whether these powers were historically available
in India, but whether they have been vested in the legislatures by the Constitution. This depends on the language of
the relevant articles which is plain and unambiguous **and**

leaves little scope for speculation. Sarkar J. who delivered the minority opinion in *Keshav Singh's* case observes :

"I cannot imagine more plain language than this. The language can have only one meaning and that is that it was intended to confer on the State legislature powers, privileges and immunities which the House of Commons in England had."

Moreover, it is not also true to say that the Constitution has not vested in Parliament any judicial functions whatsoever. The powers exercisable by Parliament under article 61 for impeachment of the President or for removal of judges under article 124(4) or 218 are certainly judicial in nature. It does not, therefore, stand to reason that Parliament should be denied certain privileges of the House of Commons merely because legislatures in India were not courts of record in the past.

The advisory opinion of the Supreme Court paves the way for judicial intervention in the arena of parliamentary privileges, and this the legislatures do not seem prepared to concede. The Conference of Presiding Officers, meeting in Bombay after *Keshav Singh's* case, adopted a resolution on January 12, 1965 expressing the view that the advisory opinion of the Supreme Court had the effect of reducing the legislatures to the status of inferior courts and that this was against the underlying intention of the Constitution makers who had actually meant to oust the jurisdiction of courts. The resolution also suggested that articles 105 and 194 should be amended to make it clear beyond doubt that the powers and privileges of the legislatures could not, in any case, be construed as being subject or subordinate to any other article of the Constitution. The scope of judicial review has not also been clearly laid down by the Supreme Court. If a person is punished for contempt by a House of Parliament, will the courts have jurisdiction to set aside the findings of that House or to determine the adequacy of punishment imposed ? These questions were raised in the Supreme Court but no attempt has been made to answer them.

In regard to the question whether Parliament in exercise of its punitive power can override the fundamental rights guaranteed to the Press, we have already seen that it has been held in *Sharma's* case that the general right of freedom of expression guaranteed to the Press must yield to the special power conferred on Parliament under article 105(3) but it has been held that article 21 would control article 105(3). This view has been confirmed in *Special Reference No. 1 of 1964.* It has been further held in the *Special reference* that if article 21 applies, article 20 may conceivably apply. As regards other articles including article 22, the question has been left open to be decided when occasions arise. This uncertainty about the impact of the various fundamental rights on parliamentary privileges is rather unsatisfactory.

Codification of privileges

Article 105(3) imposes a constitutional obligation on Parliament to codify its privileges but as the enactment of such a law would take some time, Parliament was vested in the transitional period with the powers of the House of Commons as they existed on the 26th January, 1950. Explaining the reasons for leaving parliamentary privileges undefined, Dr. Ambedkar said that it was not practicable to define parliamentary privileges as a part of the Constitution and the best course was to leave it to Parliament to define its privileges. Dr. Rajendra Prasad said that the provisions of article 105(3) are "only a temporary affair" and sounded a prophetic note when he said : "of course Parliament may never legislate and it is, therefore, for the members to be vigilant."[30] Shri Seervai has, however, argued that the second part of article 105(3) is not transitional.[31] The plain language of article 105(3) as also the intention of the Constitution-makers as revealed in the Constituent Assembly Debates makes it clear that it is only a transitional provision. Australia has an analogous provision under which no legislation has so far been

30. C.A. Debates, Oct. 16, 1949 p. 375.
31. H.M. Seervai, *Constitutional Law of India*, 1967, p. 849.

undertaken. An example, however, is not a complete answer. It would not also be correct to say that because, there is no time limit in articles 105 and 194 and because at any rate, Parliament cannot be compelled to pass any particular legislation, there is no obligation to define privileges. For, a constitutional directive does not depend merely on the prescription of a specific time-limit or a mode of enforcement. While we do not agree with Shri Seervai, we do not also agree with the other extreme view propounded by Subba Rao, J. that if legislation defining parliamentary privileges is not enacted within a reasonable time from the date of the commencement of the Constitution, then the transitory provision making the privileges of the House of Commons available to Indian legislatures may be construed to have lapsed. We feel that article 105(3) gives a constitutional directive to Parliament to define its privileges and Parliament must give effect to this directive.

Equating the privileges of our Parliament with those of the House of Commons has led to good deal of uncertainty. The privileges of the House of Commons are not static. Sometimes a particular rule persists in the record but falls into disuse in practice. Difficulty arises because the House of Commons seldom formally rescinds a principle, it no longer wishes to follow. Extensive research has, therefore, to be undertaken to find out if a particular privilege of the Commons subsisted on the relevant date. In 1978, when Mrs. Gandhi was found guilty of contempt of the Lok Sabha and she was expelled, to justify her expulsion, precedents were cited from the House of Commons which were 200 years old. It is doubtful if the Commons itself will follow that precedent now. With the lapse of time, it would be still more difficult to ascertain these privileges. The scope of judicial intervention in the arena of parliamentary privileges has not yet been clearly defined. There is no authoritative pronouncement on the impact of fundamental rights on parliamentary privileges except in respect of articles 19(1)(a) and 21. The question of parliamentary privileges is full of uncertainties. In this anomalous position, the Press is the worst sufferer. The Press is not sure of its rights and liabilities; Parliament is not sure of its privileges; and the courts are uncertain of their powers. It is not in the public interest to allow these uncertainties to continue and to hope that, in course of time, they would be resolved by judicial decisions and conventions. It is a tribute to the remarkable English genius for finding pragmatic *ad hoc* solutions to problems which appear to be irreconcilable by adopting the conventional method of give and take. This is not, however, possible in India. Eventual codification of privileges is implicit in our constitutional scheme and inescapable in the circumstances prevailing. It would be a transition from an incohate and nebulous uncertainty to a state of greater legislative precision and clarity.

Although between 1937 and 1947 when the privileges of the legislatures were very much restricted, there was demand by the presiding officers for express legislation to define and safeguard parliamentary privileges, but after 1950, they have consistently opposed the idea of such codification. Parliament has now been vested with nebulous and uncertain privileges of the Commons which it can adjust to suit its needs and successive Speakers have expressed the fear that a law on the subject would curtail the privileges of Parliament. But in view of the advisory opinion of the Supreme Court in *Special Reference No. 1 of 1964* which has reduced Parliament to the status of an inferior court whose decisions on contempt are subject to review by higher courts, the Conference of Presiding Officers held at Bombay on 12th January, 1965 passed a unanimous resolution recommending suitable amendments to articles 105 and 194 to make it clear that parliamentary privileges should not be subject to any other provision of the Constitution.

The main aversion to codification lies in the fact that a law of Parliament in pursuance of clause (3) of article 105 would be an ordinary law which would be open to scrutiny and review by the judiciary and would be subject to fundamental rights and would be void to the extent of repugnancy. This apprehension is justified by the observations of the Supreme Court in *Sharma's* case wherein it has been held that an ordinary law of privileges cannot be sustained, if it contravenes the peremptory provisions of article 13(2). This difficulty can easily be overcome by a suitable amendment of the Constitution.

Constitutional Amendments

It is necessary to have a clear picture of the problems before us and how we propose to solve them. We can then achieve our objective through a comprehensive law of Parliament defining its privileges and necessary constitutional amendments to safeguard such privileges. The first problem which we face is that the power to enact legislation defining privileges belongs to Parliament and State legislatures separately. This power is derived by Parliament from entry 74 of the Union List read with article 246, while the State legislature derives its power from entry 39 of the State List. These powers are mutually exclusive and if Parliament and State legislatures exercise their powers separately, we shall have multiplicity of separate enactments in respect of privileges making confusion worse confounded. If codification is to be attempted, our first task should be to amend the Constitution to provide that the powers of the State legislature to make a law on the subject should be transposed from the State List to the Concurrent List in the Seventh Schedule to the Constitution. This would enable Parliament to make a common law of privileges applicable to Parliament and State legislatures contributing to the growth of a stable system of *Lex Parliamenti.*

The next point which arises for consideration is the impact of fundamental rights on parliamentary privileges. It is now well settled that the general right of freedom of expression guaranteed to the Press must yield to special rights conferred on Parliament under article 105(3). To achieve this object, it will be necessary to amend clause (2) of article 19 which imposes several restrictions on the freedom of expression. These restrictions include a reference to 'contempt of court' and it is suggested that this clause should be suitably amended to include a reference to "contempt of Parliament and State legislatures.'' It is now settled by judicial decisions that article 21 would control article 105(3). The procedure which Parliament should follow in contempt proceedings should be in accord with article 21 and no restriction need, therefore, be placed on this article. As regards other fundamental rights including article 22, conflicts may arise between a fundamental right and a privilege of Parliament. In order to resolve such conflict, it would be necessary to undertake a proper study of the problem. While trying to safeguard the privileges of Parliament, we have also to bear in mind the rights of the Press in a modern democracy. Complete abrogation of other fundamental rights is neither necessary nor desirable and the Constitution may be amended by imposing reasonable restrictions on other fundamental rights to the extent necessary for the proper functioning of parliamentary privileges.

The next problem which raises intricate questions of some nicety is the scope of judicial intervention in cases affecting parliamentary privileges. In U.S.A. where the theory of separation of powers has coloured the functions of various organs of the State, the Congress is not armed with the power to punish for contempt and the question of judicial review does not arise. In India, where Parliament has been vested, like the House of Commons, with powers to punish for contempt, the question of judicial review has assumed considerable importance in view of the advisory opinion of the Supreme Court in *Keshav Singh's* case.[32] It is generally conceded that Parliament should be the sole judge to punish a member for contempt or a stranger who commits contempt in view of the House. But there is controversy over Parliament's power to punish a stranger, like the Press, who commits contempt outside the four walls of the House. Many feel that in respect of contempts outside Parliament, the more conspicuously fair procedure adopted by courts could, without loss of dignity, be adopted by Parliament. Sir John Quick, an eminent constitutional lawyer says that ''English procedure for punish-

32. *Special Reference No. I of 1949*, A.I.R. 1965 S.C. 745.

ment of contempt of Parliament is generally admitted to be
clumsy, ineffective and generally not consonant with modern
requirements of administration of justice" and recommended that the High Court should deal with breaches of privileges.[33] Morris-Jones also in his book *Parliament in India,*
after referring to the well-known case of *Bankstown Observer*
in Australia, expressed doubts whether the powers to punish
for contempt "ought to be exercised by a body like Parliament without even the possibility of an appeal to the ordinary
courts and an open trial."[34] But Parliament's sense of its own
dignity is too deep-rooted to permit the enactment of any law
for abdication of its jurisdiction in the matter of privileges.
No exception can, however, be taken even if Parliament is
trusted with powers which have been vested in it by the Constitution. During the last 32 years, Parliament has exercised
its punitive powers generally with restraint and there should
be no cause for apprehension that in future, in the name of
parliamentary privileges, it will stifle legitimate criticisms or
fair comments from the Press. There may have been some cases
where Parliament and State legislatures became over-sensitive
to criticisms, but such cases are not many and in relation to
the Press in particular, Parliament has acted with commendable restraint. We are also proposing some procedural safeguards in contempt proceedings. The procedure to be followed by Parliament in these proceedings should be in accordance with article 21 and principles of natural justice. With
these procedural safeguards, the chances of abuse or misuse of
Parliament's powers would be minimised.

In regard to the scope of judicial intervention in contempt proceedings, dualism which disturbed public life in
England for centuries was introduced into India by the
Supreme Court in *Keshav Singh's* case. This dualism should
not be allowed to continue and courts should have limited jurisdiction as in England and their jurisdiction should be clearly
defined. In *Sharma's* case, the Supreme Court held that courts

33.   *Australian Law Journal,* Vol. 29, p. 97.
34.   Morris-Jones, *Parliament in India.*

can exercise only limited jurisdiction to examine the existence and extent of any particular privilege, leaving the legislature as the sole judge of the question whether contempt has been committed. We may accept this view. If Parliament issues a general warrant, the courts should invariably treat the general warrant as conclusive and should not examine the validity of the order passed by Parliament. If, however, a speaking warrant is issued, the courts may examine whether the reasons set out in the warrant amount to contempt. To this limited extent, the courts may exercise jurisdiction. In a writ petition for *habeas corpus*, the courts may entertain the petition and issue a notice and Parliament should file a return. There should be no question bail before the return is filed but if the return is not filed or is defective, the prisoner could be admitted to bail and even released. All these provisions should be suitably incorporated in our Constitution.

Law of Parliament

Apart from the constitutional amendments suggested, Parliament should enact a comprehensive law to define its privileges. Definition of privileges is a complicated but not an impossible task. Privileges have been codified in South Africa and Ceylon. Bengal also drafted such a Bill in 1939. Materials for the proposed legislation may be collected from May's *Parliamentary Practice* and the classic *Annotated Constitution of the Australian Commonwealth* by Quick and Garran also gives a fairly exhaustive list of the powers, privileges and immunities of the Houses of British Parliament. A select committee appointed by the House of Commons in 1966 to review the law of parliamentary privileges made a series of recommendations. These recommendations which were approved by the Mathew Commission may also be taken into account. The Committee proposed that the term 'privilege' should be replaced by 'rights and immunities' and we should speak generally of 'penal jurisdiction of Parliament' rather than 'breach of privileges.' These are only verbal changes. The Committee was of view that the law of parliamentary privileges should not be administered in a way which would fetter or discourage free expression of opinion or criticism, however prejudiced or exaggerated such opinion or criticism might be. The penal jurisdiction of the House should be exercised as sparingly as possible and only when it is essential to protect the House from improper obstruction. In future, when a member has a remedy in courts, he should not be permitted to invoke the penal jurisdiction of the House in lieu of, or in addition to, that remedy. We may also draw on our own experience during the last 32 years and define the limits of privileges of Parliament. When, for example, a person who has been committed to prison for contempt approaches a court under article 32 or 226 of the Constitution, it should be clearly laid down that no contempt proceedings would lie against the lawyer representing him or the judges hearing the case.

At present, the penalties which may be imposed for contempt include suspension of a member and imprisonment of the contemner for duration of the session. Admonition and reprimand are milder forms of punishment. Our Parliament, in common with the House of Commons, does not possess the power to impose a fine. This power should be conferred on Parliament, particularly when it is the only penalty which may be imposed on a company or corporation. Parliament may also be empowered to impose a fixed term of imprisonment and to remit, suspend or vary any penalty it imposes. An interesting question arises in regard to expulsion of a member. There have been seven cases of expulsion so far in India. Two concerned Parliament and five State legislatures. The Punjab and Haryana High Court has held that legislatures in India have no power to expel a member. Another High Court has taken a different view. There is yet no authoritative decision of the Supreme Court on the point. But we feel that as expulsion involves vacation of a seat, this should not be a recognised mode of punishment.

In dealing with the substantive question of privileges, it is also necessary to lay down by law the procedure to be followed by Parliament. There is considerable resentment among newspapermen with regard to the procedure now followed by

Parliament for dealing with cases of alleged contempt. Rule 314 of the Rules of Procedure and conduct of business in the Lok Sabha which is the relevant rule on the subject does not prescribe the procedure at all. Rule 228 empowers the Speaker to issue such directions as may be necessary. The position is unsatisfactory. The proceedings before the Privileges Committee are quasi-judicial and the procedure followed by courts should be adopted by the Committee. In these proceedings article 21 would apply and Bhagwati, J. in *Maneka Gandhi's* case[35] observed that the procedure has to be 'right, just and fair' and in accordance with the principles of natural justice. Mathew Commission has, therefore, recommended that the alleged contemners should be given reasonable opportunity to defend themselves and to be represented by lawyers. The rules framed should not violate fundamental rights. A limitation of one year should be prescribed for taking cognizance of publication of offending material in the newspapers on the ground of breach of privilege. The right of the Press to be present in the Committee of Privileges, as in courts, should be recognised.

The legislative proposals outlined above are by no means complete or exhaustive. The problem of contempt of Parliament raises delicate questions affecting Parliament, Press and Judiciary which are indispensable organs of democratic life. It is suggested that a high powered commission consisting of eminent jurists, judges, legislators, journalists and public men should be appointed to recommend legislative measures defining parliamentary privileges and the respective jurisdiction of the various organs of our democratic society so that they may function in a spirit of understanding within their respective spheres and help the peaceful development of the democratic life in this country. Codification of privileges may not remove all conflicts between the Press and Parliament but it will certainly ensure better understanding between the two.

35. *Maneka Gandhi* v. *Union of India*, A.I.R. 1978 S.C. 597.

CHAPTER VII

The Press and Right to Privacy

Right to privacy is generally recognised as a cherished right in our modern complex society. But there is no specific provision in our Constitution conferring this right on the citizens. It is not also protected by any law of the country. The Mathew Commission was, therefore, required by item 3 of the terms of reference to "examine and make recommendations on the constitutional and legal safeguards to protect the citizen's right to privacy."

The question whether the right to privacy flows from the right to personal liberty under article 21 or from the freedoms guaranteed under article 19 was considered by the Supreme Court in several cases. In *Kharak Singh's* case,[1] Subba Rao, J. (as he then was) made the following observations in the context of personal liberty under article 21 :

"It is true our Constitution does not expressly declare a right to privacy as a fundamental right, but the said right is an essential ingredient of personal liberty.... In the last resort, a person's house where he lives with his family is his 'castle'; it is a rampart against encroachment on his personal liberty.... If physical restraints on a person's movements affect his personal liberty, physical encroachments on his private life affect it in a larger degree. Indeed nothing is more deleterious to a man's physical happiness and health than a calculated interference with his privacy."

1. *Kharak Singh* v. *the State of U.P.*, (1964) 1 S.C.R. 332

In *Govind* v. *M.P. State*,[2] the petitioner alleged that on the basis that he was a habitual offender, the police were making domiciliary visits both by day and night at frequent intervals and that they were secretly picketing his house. He contended that these actions of the police were violative of the fundamental rights guaranteed to him under articles 19(1)(d) and 21 of the Constitution. In this case, the Supreme Court observed :

"Rights and freedoms of citizens are set forth in the Constitution in order to guarantee that the individual, his personality and those things stamped with his personality shall be free from official interference except where a reasonable basis for intrusion exists.

"The right to privacy in any event will necessarily have to go through a process of case-by-case development. Therefore, even assuming that the right to personal liberty, the right to move throughout the territory of India and the freedom of speech create an independent right of privacy as an emanation from them, which one can characterise as a fundamental right, we do not think that the right is absolute."

From the two cases referred to above, it cannot be said that the Supreme Court has categorically recognised a general right of privacy as a fundamental right even as an emanation from other fundamental rights guaranteed to the citizens. The right of privacy, as such, does not also find a place in any law of the country, though the laws relating to trespass, defamation, criminal breach of trust, copy right etc., protect certain aspects of privacy indirectly.

The right to privacy may be violated not only by the Press but also by government and other persons. The modern State has grown into a powerful administrative body controlling every aspect of the life of its citizens. It has vast powers and the technological revolution has thrown up devices like wiretapping, eavesdropping and bugging which enable the government to probe into the deepest and farthest corners of a man's

2. *Govind* v. *M.P. State* (1975) 3 S.C.R. 946.
12—TPI

house even without his knowledge. Man's house is no longer sacrosanct and inviolate. There is a widespread belief that government interferes with the privacy of its citizens in many ways but this is beyond the scope of our study. We are, in this chapter, concerned only with intrusion of privacy of citizens by the Press.

The Concept of the right to privacy

The word 'privacy' as generally understood, means seclusion, the state of being withdrawn from society, being away from others, alone and undisturbed. It also means secrecy and avoidance of publicity. The right to privacy has as its basis the inherent uniqueness of every human being and his or her right to private life free from unwanted intrusion and disclosure. While discussing privacy, we have to keep clearly in mind the distinction between the notion of the interest in privacy on the one hand and such interests as those in 'secrecy,' 'confidentiality' and 'reputation' on the other. While these notions overlap and the legal protection for secrecy, confidentiality and reputation has indirect consequences on the protection of privacy, it is vital not to confuse the notions. It is also important to distinguish the 'interest' in privacy from the concept of a 'right' to privacy. For the purpose of the law, it is only appropriate to speak of a right to privacy where the legal system affords an enforceable remedy for interference with the interest in privacy.

Legislation in relation to privacy

Position in other countries

The right to privacy was most forcefully articulated for the first time in U.S.A., by Warren and Brandeis in their famous article[3] published in 1890. The Supreme Court of U.S.A. has now held that privacy is a fundamental personal right emanating from the totality of the constitutional scheme. The broadest definition of privacy was given by Justice Brandeis :

"The makers of our Constitution conferred, as against the Government, the right to be let alone, the most comprehensive

3. *The Right of Privacy*, 4 Harvard Law Rev. 193.

of rights and the right most valued by civilised man."[4]

It is obvious that a legal right to privacy as broadly framed as this would be enormous in scope. Today, violation of privacy has been recognised as a tort in U.S.A. and there is a series of decisions of the courts at various levels. This right has been recognised in France and also in the Federal Republic of Germany. U.S.A. was the first country to enact specific legislation on various aspects of privacy covering its invasion by modern technological devices. Canada, Scandanavia and some European countries have also legislation on similar lines. In several Australian States, legislation has been enacted to give protection to certain aspects of privacy, such as surveillance devices, data banks, credit reporting etc.

It is significant that no generalised right of privacy has been recognised in the common law of U.K. although there have been several attempts at legislation on the subject of privacy. The Younger Committee in U.K. submitted a comprehensive report on privacy in 1972. It rejected the need for a general right to privacy on the ground that it would introduce uncertainties into the law, the repercussions of which upon free circulation of information were difficult to foresee in detail. The Committee argued that it was appropriate to narrow the definition of privacy and the best way to ensure regard for privacy was to provide specific and effective sanction against clearly defined activities which unreasonably frustrate the individual in his search for privacy. The Committee, accordingly, suggested several areas where legislation may be undertaken. The Royal Commission on the Press presided over by Prof. McGregor, which submitted its report in July, 1977, agreed with the views of the Younger Committee.

International recognition of the right

The right to privacy received international recognition in 1948. Article 12 of the Universal Declaration of Human Rights states :

"No one shall be subjected to arbitrary interference with his privacy, family, home or correspondence, nor to attacks

4. *Olmstead* v. *U.S.* (1928) 277 U.S. 438

upon his honour and reputation. Every one has the right to the protection of the law against such interference or attacks."

The General Assembly of the United Nations in article 17 of the International Covenant of Civil and Political Rights reiterated the right to privacy enunciated in article 12 of the Universal Declaration of Human Rights. This right has also been recognised by the European Convention on Human Rights. Article 8 of the said Convention adopted in 1953 states :

"1.   Everyone has the right to respect for his private and family life, his home and his correspondence; and

"2.   There shall be no interference by a public authority with the exercise of this right except such as is in accordance with the law and is necessary in a democratic society in the interests of national security, public safety or the economic well-being of the country, for the prevention of disorder or crime, for the protection of health or morals or for the protection of the rights and freedoms of others."

Position in India

The Law Commission of India had occasion to examine this question in 1971. In chapter 23 of its 42nd Report on the Indian Penal Code, it observed that the law on the subject of privacy was still rudimentary even in advanced countries, and it was not advisable to have a comprehensive legislation to deal with all aspects of invasion of privacy. The Law Commission rightly thought it better to make a beginning with those invasions which would amount to eavesdropping and unauthorised publication of photographs and leave the rest to be considered later in the light of the experience gained and legislation introduced in other countries.

Pursuant to the above recommendation of the Law Commission, a Bill was introduced in the Rajya Sabha to amend the Indian Penal Code by substituting a new Chapter entitled 'Offence against Privacy' in place of the existing Chapter XIX. It was a short Bill with a limited purpose. By this Bill, use of artificial listening or recording apparatus was made an offence. If any person, knowing that any artificial listening or recording apparatus has been introduced into or in the vicinity of any premises without the knowledge or consent of the person in possession of the premises, listens to any conversation with the aid of such apparatus or uses such apparatus for the purposes of recording any conversation, he shall be liable to imprisonment which may extend to six months or with fine or with both. If any person publishes any such conversation or a record thereof, he would be liable to imprisonment for one year. Unauthorised photography was also made an offence. If any person publishes any such unauthorised photograph, he would be liable to one year's imprisonment. Exception has, however, been made in favour of a public servant who uses artificial listening or recording apparatus or takes unauthorised photographs, if he acts in good faith in the course of his duties connected with the security of the State, the prevention, detection or investigation of offences, the administration of justice, or the maintenance of public order.

This Bill was passed by Rajya Sabha on 23rd November 1978 but the Bill lapsed with the dissolution of the Lok Sabha. At present, there is no general law of privacy in our country.

Violation of privacy by the Press
Experience of other countries

We shall now turn to the specific problem of violation of privacy by the Press. Experience shows that in U.S.A., three kinds of mass media action have generally led to privacy suits. Firstly, the most common form of invasion of privacy by the Press is the publication about private affairs of an individual. To be actionable, the publication must be something that would be offensive or embarrassing to a man of ordinary sensibilities. Typical of such cases are those involving publicity concerning a private debt, publication of distressing matters out of the past and disclosure of intimate details about the body, sexual practices and the like. But if the publication is truthful and "newsworthy," it is protected. The expression "newsworthy" has no generally accepted meaning. According to American courts, the concept of "newsworthiness" has three basic parts : (a) public interest, (b) public figure, and (c) public record. Material taken from the 'public record' is normally immune from privacy suit. A public figure is a person who places himself voluntarily in the public eye by becoming a politician, an actor or a controversial personality. A person may also involuntarily become participant in an occurrence of public or general interest. The expression 'public interest' is also vague and an almost endless variety of topics have public interest. It is pointed out that from a privacy point of view, the more newsworthy the publication is, the greater will be the invasion of privacy and it is argued that the test of newsworthiness should be discarded and some other suitable test should be adopted. Secondly, the Press sometimes uses an individual's name or photograph in an advertisement without his consent. In such cases, there is generally some kind of profit-making or commercial endeavour involved. If a man has a publicity value in his name or photograph, he should enjoy the exclusive privilege of capitalising on it and the Press cannot be allowed to deprive him of that privilege. But if the name or photograph which is published in an advertisement is incidental to other legitimate publication, it is not considered objectionable. Thirdly, the Press may publish matters which are false and, while not defamatory, place the individual in a false light in the public eye. For example, the use of a photograph in a misleading way or an inaccurate or fictitious account of a person's life and character. It has been held[5] that in such cases, actual malice should be proved to sustain the suit.

In U.K., the Younger Committee considered the question of invasion of privacy by the Press. It noted that objectionable means are sometimes adopted by the Press to obtain information, e.g., gaining entry into private premises and conducting interviews by deception, pestering and harassing people in private places for obtaining news, etc. The Press also gives

5. *Time* v. *Hill*, 395 U.S. 374 (1967).

wide publicity to private information, totally regardless of the means adopted for obtaining such information, e.g., publication of news and comment, mainly to satisfy idle curiosity about private misfortunes, calamities or other incidents. It also publishes, with critical innuendo, stories about unusual but lawful private activities and behaviour. Whenever such unwanted publicity is given to personal matter, there may be a conflict of interests between the need for the public to be informed and the need to respect the individual's privacy. The Committee recommended that the balancing of interests in each such case should be left to the judgment of the Press Council.

Pursuant to the recommendation of the Younger Committee, the Law Commission of U.K. produced a working paper on the Law of Confidence. The matter was also considered by the Royal Press Commission. This matter, however, came into prominence during legal proceedings relating to the publication in the *Sunday Times* of the diaries of the late Mr. Richard Crossman. The way in which certain newspapers had dealt with the private lives of well known people was heavily criticised and the Press Council of U.K. had to issue in 1976 a declaration of principles on privacy setting out certain rules for the guidance of editors in deciding when to publish stories about people's private lives :

(i) The publication of information about the private lives of individuals without their consent is permissible only if there is a legitimate public interest overriding the right of privacy.

(ii) Inquiries into matters affecting the private life of an individual can be undertaken only where the editor is clearly of opinion that public interest in such matters may arise.

(iii) The public interest which is relied on as justification for publication or inquiry referred to above must be a legitimate and proper public interest and not merely a prurient or morbid curiosity. A distinction has also to be made between "of interest to the public" and "in the public interest." Whatever is of interest to the public is not 'in the public interest.' It should also be recognised that entry into public life does disqualify an individual from his right to privacy. But the information about the private life of an individual occupying a public position may be published only when circumstances relating to his private life are likely to affect the performance of his duties or public confidence in him or his office.

(iv) Invasion of privacy by deception, eavesdropping or technological methods which are not in themselves unlawful can, however, be justified only when it is in pursuit of information which ought to be published in the public interest and there is no other reasonably practicable method of obtaining or confirming it.

(v) The Council expects that the obtaining of news or pictures shall be carried out with sympathy and discretion. Reporters and photographers should do nothing to cause pain or humiliation to the bereaved or distressed people, unless it is clear that the publication of the news or pictures will serve a legitimate public interest and there is no other reasonably practicable means of obtaining the material.

(vi) Editors are responsible for the actions of those employed by their newspapers and have a duty to ensure that all concerned are aware of the importance of respecting all legitimate claims to personal privacy.

Position in India and recommendations of the Mathew Commission

In India, there is no general law of privacy. Complaints relating to privacy to the Press Council have also been few. It is reported that the Press Council received only five such complaints. One of these was not maintainable. Another had to be dropped as the newspaper in question had ceased publication and the remaining three were in various stages of inquiry. No guidlines have also been issued for the Press to follow in deciding what matters may be published about people's private lives. But the question has now assumed considerable importance and some way has to be found for the protection of personal information.

Privacy concerns the individual, but individuals interact when they live in a community and this leads to communication of personal information. Knowledge of what other people are doing is essential to members of a society who are interdependent. Such knowledge is the raw material out of which public opinion is formed and by which standards of public and private customs and morals are evolved. Much of the knowledge referred to above is of a purely public character relating to issues of international, national or local policy. But it often extends into the personal activities of individuals or groups where the borderline between the private and public domains is less distinct. Some matters, although highly personal, raise issues of public concern. All members of the community have an interest to receive information on topics of public significance. Thus the claim to privacy tends to conflict with the claim to public information. The dilemma is to strike a proper balance between these two interests. It becomes more complex when the private activities of a public figure are in question.

Today, privacy has grown into an unwieldy and nebulous concept and a general law relating to privacy may not be advisable. This has been the experience of other countries also. In England, several attempts have been made to legislate on this subject, namely, the Lyon Bill, the Walden Bill, the N.C.C.L. draft and the Justice draft, but none of them were found satisfactory, because all of them required the court to determine whether the infringement of privacy was unreasonable. There was, however, no yardstick to determine what was unreasonable and uncertainty would be introduced into the law. Moreover, litigation in our country is proverbially expensive and dilatory. It would affect both the Press and the complainant. If invasion of privacy becomes a ground of legal action, the Press may become exceptionally vulnerable to malicious action. The potential cost of possible actions of invasion of privacy might inhibit a newspaper from proceeding with a story. As for the complainant, apart from expenses, resort to court will involve washing of dirty linen in public and the very purpose of ensuring his privacy would be frustrated.

The examination of the legislation enacted or contemplated shows that privacy is an extremely nebulous concept and the criteria which may constitute its violation cannot be easily drawn up. The Mathew Commission is, therefore, of the view that it would not be advisable to undertake either an amendment of the Constitution or the enactment of a general law on the subject. The Law Commission has recommended legislation intended to make a beginning with those invasions which amount to eavesdropping and unauthorised publication of photographs. The Mathew Commission endorses the recommendation that the Indian Penal Code be amended to include a Chapter on 'Offence against privacy.' To give effect to the recommendation of the Law Commission, a Bill was actually introduced into, and passed by, Rajya Sabha but it lapsed with the dissolution of the Lok Sabha. The Mathew Commission recommends that the Bill should be reintroduced in Parliament as early as possible.

The proposed legislation has a very limited objective. In all other cases, the Press Council could appropriately be entrusted with the task of taking cognizance of complaints of unfair publication relating to matters concerning privacy. The Mathew Commission, therefore, suggests that Section 13(2)(c) of the Press Council Act, 1978, which deals with the functions of the Press Council, may be suitably amended by inserting therein the phrase "including respect for privacy."

The Mathew Commission further suggests that in disposing of complaints relating to privacy, the Press Council should keep certain principles in view. Every person is entitled to the refuge of his home and family free from unwarranted intrusion and the threat of unwanted publicity. Personal and sexual relations, for example, are normally entirely private matters as are family quarrels, illness, an individual's mode of life in his home and personal letters. Such intimate matters should not be published. Sensitive private facts relating to the health, private behaviour, home life or personal or family relationships should not be published, except when it is in public interest to do so. Similarly, appropriation of the name, identity, reputation or likeness of an individual for commercial or political purposes or for advancement of one's career should be treated as objectionable.

Much news is published to satisfy curiosity or a desire to be entertained. Such news may be 'of public interest' but not 'in public interest.' Even a determined and substantial invasion of privacy may be justified, if it can be shown that the object is to give news 'in public interest.' The real test is whether the news is in public interest. But public interest is a vague term and is not capable of precise definition. The Mathew Commission, therefore, suggests that the facets of 'public interest' dealt with in the exceptions to Section 499 I.P.C. (defamation) should be utilised in deciding whether the publication is in public interest or not.

The Commission further suggests that a matter may be said to relate to public interest, if it belongs to one of the following categories :

(a) Conduct of a public servant in the discharge of his public functions, or his character in so far as his character appears in that conduct, and no further;

(b) Conduct of any person touching any public question, or his character in so far as his character appears in that conduct, and no further;

(c) Any performance which its author has submitted to the judgment of the public, or the character of the author in so far as his character appears in such performance, and no further;

(d) Matters arising out of any authority conferred by law or contract on one person to pass, in good faith, any censure on the conduct of another person, in matters to which such lawful authority relates;

(e) Matters concerning any accusation made against any person to a person who has lawful authority over that person, with respect to the subject-matter of the accusation.

It may also be noted that certain publications are privileged. The following are some of the examples :

    (i) fair and accurate report of judicial proceedings not
        held in *camera*;

    (ii) fair and accurate report of proceedings in Parlia-
         ment or State Legislatures not held in *camera*; and

    (iii) fair and accurate report of proceedings befor a pub-
          lic body or public servant not held in private.

The public interest relied on as the justification for any
publication must be a legitimate and proper interest and not
only a prurient or morbid curiosity. Apart from the plea of
public interest, the following may be deemed as valid defence
against a complaint of invasion of privacy :

    (i) consent to publication;

    (ii) availability of published matter from public record
        open to public inspection;

    (iii) innocent publication, i.e., publication where the pub-
         lisher did not know or had no reason to believe that
         it would cause distress, annoyance or embarrassment
         to particular individuals;

    (iv) matters published under legal authority to which a
         claim of privilege, as understood in the law of defa-
         mation, applies; and

    (v) publication which is for the protection of the pub-
        lisher himself.

There has been a tendency in a section of the Press to
write fictional stories with reference to an existing person. In
U.S.A. writings of this kind have been taken adverse notice
by the courts. In some cases, the offence may attract the defamation law, and the aggrieved person would have legal remedy.
Where this is not possible, the aggrieved person should have
recourse to the Press Council.

'Investigative' or 'exposure' journalism involves prolonged enquiries based on suspicion. Sometimes it is in public
interest and sometimes it ends up in character assassination.
However, the Press views it as an important public service

and claims immunity in this area. But the Mathew Commission thinks that the processes of inquiry involved in investigative journalism should not be treated by the law in any way different from other journalistic activities. The Commission is of the view that it should be carried on within the same rules as are applicable to ordinary citizens.

The Press should not be unduly inhibited in performing its important function of giving news in the public interest as distinct from news that may pander to prurient or morbid curiosity. But a correct balance has to be struck between the citizen's claim to privacy and the public's right to information. The Press Council should be entrusted with the responsibility of looking into complaints of invasion of privacy and of monitoring the performance of the Press in this regard.

CHAPTER VIII

The Press Council

Freedom of the Press always entails certain obligations and responsibilities. As Pandit Nehru observed : "If there is no responsibility and no obligation attached to it, freedom gradually withers away. This is true of a nation's freedom and it applies as much to the Press as to any other group, organisation or individual." In its survey of the functioning of the Press in India, the first Press Commission found that a large section of the Press is behaving irresponsibly and came across a great deal of "scurrilous writing," of 'indecency and vulgarity' and 'personal attacks on individuals.' Though the well-established newspapers had, on the whole, maintained a high standard of journalism, yellow journalism was on the increase in the country and was not confined to any particular area or language. In the war for increased circulation, many newspapers abdicated their responsibility and pandered to the baser instincts of their readers and the image of the Press as an institution had greatly suffered. The Commission remarked that "whatever the law relating to the Press may be, there would still be a large quantum of objectionable journalism which, though not falling within the purview of the law, would still require to be checked." It was of the view that the best way of maintaining professional standards would be to bring into existence a body of people principally connected with the industry whose responsibility it would be to arbitrate on doubtful points and to censure any one guilty of infraction of the code of journalistic ethics. The Commission recommended the setting up of a Press Council 'to safeguard the freedom of the Press' and 'to encourage the growth of the sense of responsibility and public service among all those engaged in the profession of journalism.'

Establishment of Press Council in India

Pursuant to the recommendation of the First Press Commission, a Press Council Bill was introduced into, and passed by, Rajya Sabha but the Bill lapsed on account of the dissolution of the Lok Sabha in April, 1957. Eight years later, on the recommendation of the National Integration Council, the Press Council Act was passed by Parliament in 1965 and the Press Council of India was set up on 4th July, 1966. The Council was reconstituted and its terms extended from time to time. During Internal Emergency, the Press Council Act, 1965 was repealed with effect from 1st January, 1976 by an Ordinance which was replaced by an Act. The objects and reasons appended to the Press Council (Repeal) Act, 1976 stated that the Council was being abolished because "it was not able to carry on its functions to achieve the objects for which the Council was established." The Annual Report of the Ministry of Information and Broadcasting for 1975-76 said : "The Press Council during the nine years of its existence, had failed to curb the tendentious, provocative and unrestrained writings in the Press. It was unable to frame a code of conduct for editors and complaints of minor character mostly engaged its attention. Accordingly, the Press Council of India was abolished with effect from 1st January, 1976." Subsequently, a fresh legislation providing for the establishment of a Press Council was enacted by the Press Council Act, 1978 (hereinafter referred to as "the Act"). The Act came into force on 1st March, 1979 and is continuing in operation.

Press Councils in other countries

The institution of Press Council emerged for the first time in Sweden in 1916. Italy, Holland, Denmark, West Germany Australia and other countries followed the example of Sweden and Press Councils have now been established in more than 40 countries. The British Press Council came into being in 1953. It has served as a model for many countries, including India. The first Press Council was an all-Press body which elected its own Chairman. The idea of a lay Chairman and some lay members was introduced in 1962. The Third Royal Press Commission of U.K. felt that a Council dominated by journalists and others from the Press could not keep an effective watch on the standards of the Press and could not deal satisfactorily with complaints made by citizens. It suggested that the Council should be independent of the Press and that parity should be maintained between lay and journalist members. In U.S.A., the proposal for the establishment of a Press Council was made by Hutchins Commission on Freedom of the Press as far back as 1947. But the editors and journalists of U.S.A. at that time scoffed at the idea and said that they were aware of their limitations and that no external authority was needed to do a kind of "back-seat driving." They ultimately veered round to the view of having a self-regulating body in that country too and the National News Council was established in 1973.

The functions assigned to Press Councils differ from country to country. The Italian and Netherlands Press Councils have nothing to do with publishers and confine their activities to the maintenance of professional standards of journalists. In Denmark and West Germany, the Councils address themselves only to publishers. The functions assigned to the British Press Council are more comprehensive. Its main objects are to preserve Press freedom, maintain the character of the British Press in accordance with the highest professional and commercial standards, and to deal with complaints about the conduct of the Press or the conduct of person and organisations towards the Press. Since the Council is a voluntary body, the only sanction it has is the moral obligation of newspapers and periodicals to publish adjudications upholding complaints against them.

In all the countries, except Italy and Holland, Press Councils have been set up voluntarily. In India, the Press Council has been incorporated as a statutory body and it has the same powers as are vested in a civil court while trying a suit under the Civil Procedure Code in respect of certain matters specified in Section 15 of the Act.

Composition of the Press Council

Under Section 5 of the Act, the Council consists of a Chairman and 28 other members. The Chairman is nominated by a Committee consisting of the Chairman of Rajya Sabha, the Speaker of the Lok Sabha and a person elected by the members of the Council. As the council exercises certain quasi-judicial functions, it is desirable that the Chairman should be a person with judicial background. So far, all the Chairmen have been judges of the Supreme Court.

Of the 28 members :

(a) 13 are working journalists of whom six are editors of newspapers and the remaining seven are working journalists other than editors;

(b) 6 are nominated from among persons who own or carry on the business of management of newspapers; of them, there shall be two representatives from each of the categories of big newspapers, medium newspapers and small newspapers;

(c) one is nominated from among persons who manage news agencies;

(d) three are persons having special knowledge or practical experience in respect of education and science, law, literature and culture of whom one shall be nominated by the University Grants Commission, one by the Bar Council of India, and one by the Sahitya Academy; and

(e) five are members of Parliament of whom 3 are nominated by the Speaker of the Lok Sabha and two are nominated by the Chairman of the Rajya Sabha.

An analysis of the composition of the Council would show that out of its 28 members, twenty are journalists, three are lay members and five are members of Parliament. The inclusion of lay members was intended to ensure that the voice of

13 – TPI

the public would be heard in the deliberations of the Council. But the journalist members dominate the Council and the lay members are too few in number to have an effective voice. The Third Royal Commission on Press in U.K. suggested that in order that the public may have confidence in the Press Council, parity should be maintained between its lay and journalist members. If that is not feasible, it is suggested that the number of lay members should be increased and the number of journalist members should be correspondingly reduced.

Justice Mudholkar, the first Chairman of the Press Council, in his Tagore Law Lectures expressed the view that members of Parliament need not be represented in the Council. He observed : "what useful purpose the members of Parliament can fulfil as members of the Council is difficult to see. The danger is that their presence may develop political overtones in the decisions of the Council. Used as a politician is to political thinking, such person cannot live away from politicking wherever he is placed. It would, perhaps, be better to exclude the members of Parliament from the Council and increase the strength of journalists of standing."[1] This suggestion of the Chairman of the Press Council is not acceptable. Parliament should have representation in the Council but their number may be reduced from 5 to 3 as in the 1965 Act.

Shri Yadunath Thatte, a member of the Press Council suggested retirement of members by rotation. This is a useful suggestion as it will ensure continuity in the work of the Council and the Mathew Commission has recommended that this suggestion should be given effect to. To achieve this object, the number of members of the Council has either to be increased to 30 or reduced to 27. Further, the Council should not be subject to dissolution, but as nearly as possible, one-third of the members from each category should retire on the expiration of every second year and new members should be nominated from the same category as in the case of Rajya Sabha or the Legislative Councils. The Act of 1978 may be suitably amended to achieve this object.

1. Mudholkar, J. *Press Law*, (Tagore Law Lectures) p. 103

Powers and Functions of the Council

The main objects of the Council are to preserve the freedom of the Press and to maintain and improve the standards of newspapers and news agencies in India. The various functions which the Council may perform in furtherance of its objects have been specified in Section 13. One of the important tasks of the Council is to build up a code of conduct for newspapers, news agencies and journalists in accordance with high professional standards. Among other functions which the Council has to perform are to help newspapers and news agencies to maintain their independence, to ensure on the part of newspapers, news agencies and journalists the maintenance of high standards of public taste and foster a due sense of both the rights and responsibilities of citizenship, to encourage the growth of a sense of responsibility and public service among all those engaged in the profession of journalism and also to promote a proper functional relationship among all classes of persons engaged in the production or publication of newspapers or in news agencies. The Council has also been entrusted with the task of studying the Press structure in India and to concern itself with developments such as concentration or other aspects of ownership of newspapers and news agencies which may affect the independence of the Press. The Council has also to keep under review cases of assistance received by any newspaper or news agency in India from any foreign source. These are some of the important functions assigned to the Press Council which we propose to discuss.

Inquiry into Complaints

One of the main functions of the Council is to inquire into complaints received by it. Under Section 14, where, on receipt of a complaint made to it or otherwise, the Council has reason to believe that a newspaper or news agency has offended against the standards of journalistic ethics or public taste or that an editor or a working journalist has committed any professional misconduct, the Council may hold an inquiry into the matter. The grounds on which a complaint may be filed are many and varied. A complaint may be filed if the newspaper has written something which is in extreme bad taste or if it has intruded into the privacy of an individual. A complaint may also be filed on the ground that a journalist has committed professional misconduct or on grounds such as misrepresentation of facts in a news report or because the headlines therein are misleading or on the ground that an article in a newspaper has stated as fact what was a mere conjecture and so on. Complaint may be filed by any person and it is not necessary that the complainant should have a personal interest in the matter complained against. The Council may also take notice of any misconduct of its own accord and it need not necessarily wait for someone to lodge a complaint.

Every complaint filed need not, however, be inquired into. The Council may not take cognizance of a complaint if, in the opinion of the Chairman, there is no sufficient ground for holding an inquiry. Further under Section 14(3), the Council is debarred from holding an inquiry into any matter in respect of which any proceeding is pending in a court of law.

Where it is decided that an inquiry should be held, the complaint is considered by a Committee of the Council called the Inquiry Committee. Inquiry is held after giving the newspaper or news agency or the person concerned an opportunity of being heard in accordance with the regulations made under the Act and the principles of natural justice are strictly followed. Both parties can adduce evidence before the Inquiry Committee, either oral or documentary, in support of their respective contentions. The findings of the Inquiry Committee are placed before the Council. The parties are entitled to appear before the Committee as well as the Council either in person or through a legal practitioner.

For the purpose of holding an inquiry under the Act, the Council can exercise the same powers as are vested in a Civil Court while trying a suit under the Civil Procedure Code in respect of the following matters, namely :

(a) summoning and enforcing the attendance of persons and examining them on oath;

(b) requiring the discovery and inspection of documents;

(c) receiving evidence on affidavits;

(d) requisitioning any public record or copies thereof from any court or office;

(e) issuing commissions for the examination of witnesses or documents; and

(f) any other matter which may be prescribed.

But it has been clearly laid down in Section 15(2) that the Council cannot compel any newspaper, news agency, editor or journalist to disclose the source of any news or information published by that newspaper or received or reported by that news agency, editor or journalist. It has been further provided under Section 15(3) that every inquiry held by the Council shall be a judicial proceeding within the meaning of Sections 193 and 223 of the Indian Penal Code.

After holding an inquiry, the Council may, if it is satisfied that it is necessary so to do, impose a penalty on the erring newspaper or journalist for reasons to be recorded in writing. It has power to warn, admonish or censure the newspaper, the news agency, the editor or the journalist, as the case may be. Under Section 14(2), the Council may also require any newspaper to publish therein in such manner as the Council thinks fit any particulars relating to the inquiry. The decision of the Council is final and shall not be questioned in any court of law. The public rebuke that the Council administers and the moral obligation of the offending newspaper to publish its decisions operate both as a penalty and deterrent. The reason is that it is a serious matter for a newspaper to inform its readers on whose respect it depends that it has been convicted of a breach of journalistic standards.

Since its inception in 1966 up to the end of 1981, the Council considered about 800 complaints. This does not include the figures for 1975 which are not available. Of these, 214 were complaints involving freedom of the Press, mostly against Central and State governments and local bodies, alleging discrimination in distribution of advertisements, denial of facilities and harassment. 566 complaints were made against newspapers by organisations and individuals and Central and State Governments. The Council has warned, admonished or censured 42 newspapers during the period ending in 1981. The complaints involved writings calculated to incite communal hatred, indecency and obscenity, journalistic improprieties including character assassination, unethical practices like insertion of dummy advertisements, scandalous reporting and suppression of news. Some of the newspapers have been warned, admonished or censured more than once.

The Council is not a court of law. Its verdicts are not judicial pronouncements. It cannot impose any punishment on the offending newspaper or journalist nor can it award damages to the aggrieved party. The penalty that the Council imposes has no salutary effect unless it is given due publicity and the offending newspaper publishes the decision of the Council. But the Council does not have any power to compel a newspaper to publish its decision or to punish a defaulting newspaper. The reaction of the British Press to the publication of the decisions of the British Press Council in its early years was not favourable. When a reader threatened to go to the Press Council against a newspaper, the editor replied : "As for your threat, you can report me to the Press Council, Madame Tussauds, the Society for the protection of sputniks, NATO or UNESCO as you wish. May you enjoy yourself." But the position has now changed. From "incredulous indignation" to "wary hostility" to "grumbling recognition" and ultimately to "acceptance" are the gradual stages through which the British Council passed. The experience of the British Press Council has shown that the power to require a newspaper to publish its decision properly used and constantly exercised can become extremely effective. In India also, there have been cases where the newspapers have defied the directives of the Press Council. An English daily of Bhopal was warned in 1980 on a complaint from two individuals. The paper was asked to publish the decision of the Council. The decision as published was at variance with the full text of the decision and it was "likely to create misunderstanding in the minds of the readers as to the identity of the newspaper indic· ted." The editor had also appended a small note of defiance. The Council in the course of its adjudication said : In the same issue, the paper carried an extremely objectionable editorial under the caption 'Abolish the Council,' imputing political motives to the decision of the Council.... The Editor's conduct, in the opinion of the Council, was deplorable inasmuch as he had not only flouted the directions of the Council but also published a highly objectionable editorial derogatory to an independent body like the Press Council... The Council accordingly, censured the editor of this newspaper and directed him to publish the decision of the Council in his newspaper."

It is evident that when a newspaper chooses to be recalcitrant, the Council is helpless. The Press Council has, therefore, suggested that the 1978 Act should be amended to empower it to recommend to the Central or State governments or other public bodies etc. stoppage of issue of advertisements, curtailment in the matter of allocation of newsprint or suspension of concessional rates of postage, for a specified period, in the case of newspapers which are censured thrice. In the case of jounalists and editors, who are held by the Council thrice to have violated the accepted principles of journalistic ethics, the Council desires to have the power to deny facilities of accredition for a specified period. The Council has urged that its recommendations should be binding on the concerned authorities. The majority of the Mathew Commission recommend that the Press Council should be given the powers sought by it with the modification that a newspaper would invite sanction if it comes to the adverse notice of the Council thrice, whether by way of disapproval, warning, admonition or censure. Sarvashri Girilal Jain, S. K. Mukherjea and H. K. Paranjape do not agree with the majority view that the Council should be given penal powers. We agree with the dissenting members of the Mathew Commission that the Council should not be given any penal powers. The Third Royal Commission on the Press in U.K. considered such a proposal and rejected

it on the ground that it would present a potentially dange-
rous weapon of control over the Press if given statutory back-
ing. The Press Council is not a court of law and should not
be converted into one. It is a court of honour and should
exert its moral authority. Our Press Council is struggling for
recognition and we can, as Philip Levy put it, ''Take encouragement from the United Kingdom Council which survived
the days of its rejection to become a national institution and
the accepted custodian of the freedom and the morals of the
English Press.''

In regard to complaints alleging violation of freedom of
the Press by Central or State Governments, the Council is
empowered only to inquire into and express an opinion but
not censure the government. The Press Council in the annual
report for 1980 has suggested that it should also have the
power to warn, admonish or censure the government and its
observations in this behalf should be placed before Parliament or State legislature concerned. The Mathew Commission
does not consider it necessary to vest such powers in the
Council. It is of the view that Section 15(4) which empowers
the Press Council to ''make such observations, as it thinks fit
in any of its decisions or reports, respecting the conduct of
any authority, including Government'' is adequate. The Commission, however, recommends that such observations should,
as early as possible, be placed before Parliament or the State
Legislature, as the case may be. We feel that the recommendation of the Mathew Commission should he accepted.

Code of Journalistic Conduct

Another very important function entrusted to the Council under Section 13(2)(b) is ''to build up a code of conduct
for newspapers, news agencies and journalists in accordance
with high professional standards.'' Much controversy center-
ed round the point whether a code of ethics should be framed
by the Council or whether it should be left to be evolved on
the basis of case law which the Council would build up in
course of time. Before the formation of the Press Council and
even during its early years, there was a clamour from the

journalists that the first and foremost task of the Council should be to frame a code of conduct for journalists so that they could be guided by such a code. The Council examined this question in its very first meeting in December, 1966 and decided that it would build up such a code in course of time, through precedents established in the process of dealing with specific complaints. Later in 1967, the Council pointed out that the provisions of the Act required the Council to 'build up' a code and not 'frame' one. It was of the view that the mere enunciation of certain basic principles in general terms would not prove helpful when they have to be applied to individual cases. Moreover, if these principles were to be reduced to a kind of code of conduct, they would have a tendency to attain a degree of rigidity which might give rise to difficulties. No code of conduct for journalists has so far been framed.

Among the professional bodies of journalists, only the All-India Newspaper Editors' Conference has a Code of Ethics and an Editors' Charter, both incorporated in its Constitution. The Constitution makes it obligatory for the members to abide by them. Several other attempts have also been made to frame a code of ethics but without much effect. A code of ethics for journalists and editors was drafted by a Committee of 17 editors and presented to Rajya Sabha on 8th January, 1976. The National Union of Journalists adopted, in February, 1981, a declaration pertaining to rights and duties of journalists. The All-India Small and Medium Newspapers Association had drawn up a code of ethics in 1975 but it was not approved by its general body. The Editors' Guild of India is categorically against the drawing up of any code of ethics for the guidance of journalists on the ground that "responsible people cannot be governed by codes."

In the United States, the American Society of Newspapers Editors adopted in October, 1975 a code of conduct for the editors and the code received the approval of the constituent bodies. They, however, did not contemplate a rigorous enforcement of the code. The British Press Council has always opposed the idea of the preparation of a code but the Third

Royal Commission on the Press recommended that the Council should draw up a Code of Behaviour on which it could base its adjudications.

After examining this question, the Mathew Commission has taken the view that "it would not be desirable to draw up a code of ethics for newspapers. As the Press Council has maintained, such a code could be built up case by case over a period of time."[2] We are unable to accept this view. The concept of journalistic ethics at present is vague and nebulous. Clear law is the prime need of justice. But we agree with Shri Chalapati Rau that "no code, however carefully drawn up, can possess the precision of law."[3] It would not, however, be difficult to draw up a code which would serve not only as a rough and ready guide for journalists but also as an objective standard on which the Council could base its adjudications. During the last 15 years and more, the Council has adjudicated upon a number of complaints. Taking into account the case laws and precedents so far built up and also the various codes drawn up in our country and abroad and the practices obtaining in England, the Council may draw up a code of journalistic conduct which would be helpful both to journalists and the Council. The fine distinction between 'building up' a code and 'framing' one which the Council sought to draw should not deter it from undertaking this necessary task.

Study of Press Structure

Under Section 13(2)(i) of the 1978 Act, the Council is required "to concern itself with developments such as concentration or other aspects of ownership of newspapers and news agencies which may affect the independence of the Press." Under the corresponding provisions of the 1965 Act (where the language was slightly different), the Council drew up a questionnaire on the subject and circulated it to ascertain public opinion. Very few replies were received and most of

2. *The Second Press Commission*, Ch. VII, para 32, p. 82.
3. M. Chalapati Rau, *The Press in India*, pp. 47—48.

them were 'vague, incomplete and unsatisfactory.' Subsequently, the Council set up a Monopoly Committee which held its first meeting in June, 1971. In the meantime, Government contemplated undertaking legislation on the subject and informed the Council that any suggestions that the Council might have to make in this regard would be welcome and would be given the highest consideration. The Monopoly Committee of the Council met for several days and made certain suggestions in respect of the problems of monopoly and concentration of ownership of newspapers. The Press Council's Annual Report for 1973 says : "The Council, which commenced consideration of these reports, could not complete its work as it felt that the problem required a comprehensive study of several aspects which the Council at its few sittings was unable to carry out adequately." There is no reference to this subject in the annual report for 1974. No report was published for 1975. The annual reports of the revived Press Council for the years 1979 and 1980 do not refer to any study with regard to concentration or other aspects of ownership of newspapers. It appears that no proper study of the subject was undertaken by the Press Council.

Foreign Money in Indian Press

Under Section 13(2)(f) of the Act, the Press Council is required "to keep under review cases of assistance received by any newspaper or news agency in India from any foreign source." The Council undertook a study of journals produced or circulated by foreign missions in India. A Committee was appointed for the purpose in 1971 but there is no mention of its findings in any subsequent annual report. In 1973, the Council gave a ruling in respect of advertisements published in Indian newspapers by foreign embassies. It held that advertisements must be clearly distinguishable from editorial matter carried in the papers. It further held that while publishing such advertisements, the newspapers should specify in the advertisement itself the amount received by them. The rationale behind this was that such advertisements should be charged at normal rates, since payment of more than the normal rates would amount to a subsidy to the paper.

Shri Virendra, editor of the *Daily Pratap,* invited the attention of the Council to an article published in *India Today* in its December issue, 1979 under the title ''The Invisible Forces'' in which it was alleged that some Indian journalists listed therein were in the pay of the CIA and that some newspapers including three from Jullundhur were being subsidised by communist countries. The Council decided to call for full particulars from the magazine 'India Today,' but eventually the case was treated as closed ''since the three Jullundhur dailies mentioned in the impugned article had not sent any contradiction to 'India Today.' The allegations made were serious and the manner in which the Press Council disposed of the case was, to say the least, inappropriate. The question of foreign money in the Indian Press has assumed considerable importance but the Council has not devoted much attention to it.

In order to curb the influence of foreign money on the Press, the Mathew Commission has recommended the following five steps, and the enactment of necessary changes in laws for the purpose :[4]

  (i) There should be a specific legal provision under which no newspaper undertaking should have any foreign ownership either in the form of shares or in the form of loans.

 (ii) Advertisements as well as printing contracts from foreign sources should be on normal rates which are applicable to similar work done for others.

(iii) Advertisement rates should be published each year.

 (iv) Once a year every newspaper should publish its profit and loss account, with separate information about foreign and Indian sources.

  (v) Every newspaper undertaking must submit with its

4. *The Second Press Commission Report,* Vol. I, Ch. VII, para 39, p. 83.

annual account the following information to the Press Council :

(a) Details of revenue obtained from advertisements and printing contracts in respect of foreign sources countrywise; and

(b) names of the top 100 shareholders with their nationality and address and the number and proportion of shares held.

Journalistic training

Under the 1965 Act, the Council was expected "to provide facilities for the proper education and training of persons in the profession of journalism." In pursuance of this objective, the Council set up a Committee in 1966 but no substantial work was done. This function which was assigned to the Council has now been omitted under the 1978 Act on the ground that "the Council should not be burdended with those operational functions." The Mathew Commission, however, feels that the 1978 Act should be amended to entrust the Press Council with the function of keeping under continuous review the adequacy and quality of journalism training facilities in the country. It recommends that both universities and professional institutions should share the tasks of training and research, and that there should be a National Council for Journalism Training and Communication Research with which the Press Council should be associated.

Monitoring of Press Performance

A systematic study of the performance of the Press in India is of utmost importance and the First Press Commission suggested that this task should be undertaken. But no organisation has so far undertaken this task. On the recommendation of the Commission, the Press Institute of India was formed in 1963 and the Indian Institute of Mass Communication in 1965. Neither of these institutions has taken up a comprehensive and continual review of the performance of the Indian Press. The survey that the Press Information Bureau does is oriented to the publicity needs of various Central Ministries and is not concerned with the maintenance and improvement of professional standards. The Mathew Commission, therefore, recommends that the Press Council should arrange to monitor the performance of the Press in general, and in particular, with regard to violation of privacy. Given the size that the Indian Press has attained, and its great diversity both in subject matter and in languages of publication, it would not be feasible to entrust the task of a continuous monitoring of Press performance to any single institution like the Press Council. The Commission, therefore, suggests that the Council should enter into arrangements with selected University departments of journalism, Press Institute of India, Indian Institute of Mass Communication and any other suitable organisation to take up the work of monitoring the performance of newspapers in respect of important issues. It should be ensured that the work of monitoring is done systematically and the findings communicated to the Press Council promptly. These findings should be available for study, at the offices of the monitoring agency and of the Press Council, by research scholars and others interested in the performance of the Indian Press. The arrangements may be funded by the Press Council to the extent necessary and adequate funds should be made available to the Press Council for the purpose.

Funding of the Council

Under Section 16 of the Act, the Council is empowered to levy fees from registered newspapers and news agencies. In pursuance of this power, the Council has levied fees from registered newspapers at rates varying from Rs. 100 per annum to Rs. 1,500 per annum depending on their circulation. It also levies Rs. 1,500 per annum from Class I or Class II news agencies and Rs. 1,000 per annum from all other news agencies. During the financial year 1979-80, the Press Council raised a revenue of Rs. 2,54,700 from fees levied and it received during the year grant-in-aid amounting to Rs. 9,16,000 from the Central Government. It will thus be seen that the Council is funded mainly by grants from the Government.

It is recognised that financial viability is essential to the maintenance of autonomy and independence of the Council. The Council, therefore, recommended to the government a revised scale of fees both for newspapers and news agencies. In respect of newspapers, the rates of fees vary from Rs. 200 per annum to Rs. 5,000 per annum and in respect of news agency, the rates vary from Rs. 2,500 to Rs. 5,000. There would be a stiff rise in the scale of fees but the Government has accepted the proposal and it is hoped that the Press Council will now have financial viability.

The Mathew Commission suggests the levy of a cess on newsprint consumption and a tax on newspaper advertisement and further suggests that in order to augment further the Council's resources, a portion of the yield from both should be earmarked for the Press Council. This is a controversial suggestion and has to be examined from various aspects. But even without these additional resources, the Press Council is expected to have financial viability for all practical purposes.

Working of the Press Council

The Press Council was established with certain objects and various functions were entrusted to it to achieve those objects. The Council has now been functioning for about 16 years and it may be useful to examine how far those objects have been achieved. The Council acts as a buffer between the Press and the public. It is its role as a quasi-judicial body sitting as a court to inquire into complaints against breaches of journalistic ethics. In its capacity as an adjudicating body, it has heard more than 800 complaints, most of them being against the conduct of the Press while some of them were against the conduct of governments towards the Press. But the general climate of opinion was not in its favour for quite some years. It was called a "paper tiger with rubber teeth" and "a vague and powerless body." Its reproof was characterised as "a mere slap on calloused wrists." But over the years, the Council has grown in stature and its rebukes against newspapers and journalists have had a salutary effect.

Inquiry into complaints, important as it is, is but one of the many functions entrusted to the Council. Its contribution in other spheres of its activities has not been as significant as expected. It has yet to frame a code of conduct for editors and journalists. It has not yet undertaken a proper study of the Press structure with particular reference to the concentration of ownership of newspapers nor of the influence of foreign money on the Indian Press. It has not taken up the task of providing facilities for the proper education and training of persons in the profession of journalism nor has it made proper arrangements for monitoring the performance of the Press in India. Explaining the reasons why the Council has not made much progress so far, Justice Mudholkar, the first Chairman of the Press Council, in his Tagore Law Lectures observes : "The unreasonable attitude adopted by a journalistic association, which is more a trade union than a professional body, and the equally unreasonable attitude of some politicians with a view to placating trade associations, is the chief reason why the Press Council has not made much progress."[5] The Press Council is, however, a very useful institution and it can play a significant role in maintaining and improving the freedom of the Press and ensuring propriety on the part of the Press. To achieve this object, the composition of the Council should be strengthened by inducting in it more eminent lay members. The Council should essentially be a body of elder journalists and eminent lay members by whose moral authority alone it should command the respect of the profession as well as of the people and it should adopt a more dynamic approach to its various activities and it should not be supposed that it is just a forum for ventilating personal grievances.

5. Mudholkar, J. *Press Law* (Tagore Law Lectures), p. 106.

CHAPTER IX

The Press as a Business and a Public Utility

The Press has a dual role. Primarily it is a medium of expression and communication of information and ideas; it is also an industry carrying on business with profit motive. It has, however, to be distinguished from other business establishments as it is also a public utility service. We have already dealt with the first aspect; in the present chapter we are concerned with the second.

The right to carry on any business has been conferred on citizens under article 19(1)(g) but reasonable restrictions on this right can be placed under clause (6) in the interests of the general public. But in regulating the economic and business aspects of a newspaper, the State cannot impose restrictions which would affect freedom of expression guaranteed under article 19(1)(a) by curtailing its circulation or freedom of discussion. Since grounds mentioned in clauses (2) and (6) of article 19 are different, the exercise of power by the State under both the clauses may lead to anomaly or conflict and the Supreme Court has tried to remove this anomaly by evolving the doctrine of "direct impact" in a series of cases, *Sakal Papers'* case,[1] *Express Newspapers* case[2] and *Bennet Coleman*

1. *Sakal Papers* v. *Union of India,* (1962) 3 S.C.R. 842.
2. *Express Newspapers* v. *Union of India,* (1959) S.C.R. 12.

14—TPI

case.[3] We have already discussed this theory in Chapter 3. If any law imposes restrictions on the commercial activities of the Press under clause (6) and such law, not being protected under clause (2), directly and substantially curtails freedom of expression and circulation, the law would be unconstitutional. But if the effect of such law or restriction on the freedom of expression is indirect and remote, the law would not be vitiated and would not be violative of article 19(1)(a).

Monopoly in the Indian Press

The growing dimension of the Press as a business institution calls for regulation or control by the State in the interests of the general public. The foremost danger arises from monopolistic control of the Press. This problem has arisen in other countries also. In U.S.A., though freedom of the Press has been specifically guaranteed under the Constitution, the constitutional authority for imposing restrictions upon the Press as a business is drawn from the doctrine of 'Police power.' But the restrictions must be reasonable under the 'due process' clause. In U.S.A., the business aspect of the Press has been subjected to anti-trust or anti-monopoly legislation and also to various other laws. In India also, there are various laws under clauses (2) and (6) of article 19 to regulate the Press and we have already discussed the impact of those laws on the freedom of expression. These laws, though numerous, are not such as have impeded the exercise of that freedom.

There are, however, widespread allegations that the Indian Press is in the hands of monopolists whose dictates the journalists have to obey and this affects freedom of the Press in an invidious manner. The Government made two valiant attempts in the past to control what they conceived to be monopolistic tendencies in the Press, first by enacting the Newspaper (Price and Page) Act, 1956 and then by issuing the Newsprint policy under Newsprint Control Order, 1962. They were struck down by the Supreme Court in *Sakal Papers* case[4] and

3. *Bennet Coleman* v· *Union of India*, A.I.R. 1973, S.C. 106.
4. *Sakal Papers* v. *Union of India*, (1962) 3 S.C.R. 842.

Bennet Coleman case[5] on the ground that the government could not do indirectly what it could not do directly. At present there is no law to control monopoly in our Press.

It is now asserted that there has been further concentration of ownership in the newspaper industry and what is worse, the bulk of the industry is a subsidiary to, and a handmaid of, other powerful financial empires of the industrialists. It is pointed out that to compare them with Beaverbrooks, Rothermeres, Northcliffs and Thomsons of England is misleading. The newspaper magnates in England and other Western countries are the products of the newspaper industry alone and are responsible to the public. To the Indian counterparts of Beaverbrooks and Rothermeres, the newspaper industry "is an accessory of big business and a means of exercising extraneous influence and power" with the result that in India the newspapers have lost their status and dignity and that "factory managers are managing directors of newspapers and they think that newspapers are products no different from gunny bags."[6]

It cannot be disputed that a democratic society lives and grows by free market of ideas and open public discussion. There can be no single voice of the Press in a free society. It is essential that there should be variety of ownership and opinion and different newspapers and magazines should put before the public varied and different points of view. Monopoly in the Press and a free democratic society cannot co-exist. But the questions which arise for consideration are whether a monopoly really exists and whether newspapers which have links with industrial houses present news and views in a manner detrimental to the public good.

Inadequacy of data

The difficulty that one encounters at the threshold in answering these questions is that there has been so far no proper investigation into these questions and that there is inadequacy

5. *Bennet Coleman* v. *Union of India*, A.I.R. 1973 S.C. 106.
6. See *Bennet Coleman* v. *Union of India*, A.I.R. 1973 S.C. 106.

of data on these subjects. The first Press Commission devoted
an entire chapter to ownership and control of the Press. There
was, however, no authentic published material on the subject
before it and it had to rely very heavily on certain views expressed by some of the witnesses but it had no means to test
the correctness of their statements by a close examination of
the newspapers. When the first Press Commission was appointed in 1952, there was not a single daily in the country with
a circulation of one lakh. *The Times of India* printed 94,748
copies, the *Statesman* 65,032, the *Hindu* 69,748 and the
Hindustan Times a meagre 48,141. The position of Indian
language dailies was even worse. *Swadesmitran* printed 39,000
copies while other so-called successful papers printed around
25,000 copies daily. They, however, felt that there was in the
Indian newspaper industry a considerable degree of concentration. There was no question of monopoly in the Indian
Press at that time. The Commission also did not talk of the ills
which beset the Indian Press then but of the ills which might
beset it decades later. They, therefore, recommended certain
measures to control the monopolistic tendency which might
develop in future.

The Mathew Commission has also dealt with the subject
at great length. In view of the inadequacy of data on ownership pattern, it commissioned a study on the ownership and
control structure of the Indian Press by the Indian Institute
of Public Administration, New Delhi. The result of the I.I.P.A.
study shows that out of 54 dailies, 27 newspapers which have
links with other business or industry control 40.87 per cent
of the total circulation while 20 newspapers with primary
interest in newspaper business control 18.80 per cent of the
total circulation. These figures do not show that there is monopoly in the Indian Press nor does the Commission say so. But
from these figures, the Commission has taken the view that "a
very significant part of the Press in the country in general,
and a major portion of all the important daily press in particular, is controlled by persons having strong links with other
businesses or industries."[7] Before dealing with the alleged

7. *Second Press Commission Report*, Vol. I, p. 141.

link of newspapers with other business interests, we shall briefly discuss whether there is any monopoly or monopolistic tendency in the newspaper industry.

The number of newspapers, national and regional, published in our country is very large and would, on the face of it, give a diversity of choice to the newspaper reader. In Delhi, there are six or seven English national dailies besides a number of language papers. If one does not like the *Times of India* or the *Indian Express*, one may shift to the *Patriot* or the *Statesman*. The term monopoly in its normally accepted connotation means that it is an exercise of exclusive control over the production and sale of some commodity or service. Where there is monopoly, there is no room for any kind of competition. Judged by this test, it cannot be said that there is any danger of monopoly in the Indian Press.

For want of a better definition of monopoly, we may consider the definition given in the Monopolies and Restrictive Trade Practices Act, 1969. ''Purveying of news or other information'' falls within the definition of 'service' in Section 2 of the Act. A 'dominant undertaking' with reference to a service is defined as an undertaking which either by itself or along with inter-connected undertakings controls not less than one-third of the services that are rendered in India or any substantial part thereof. Similarly, a 'monopolistic undertaking' with reference to a service has been defined as a dominant undertaking or an undertaking which together with not more than two other undertakings provides or otherwise controls not less than one-half of the services that are rendered in India or substantial part thereof. The current interpretation is that 'dominance' or 'monopoly' of a newspaper is to be ascertained in relation to circulation of newspapers in all languages in India or substantial part thereof. Applying this test, there is no monopolistic or dominant undertaking in the newspaper industry.

The Mathew Commission, however, feels that taking into account the existing state of affairs in the Indian Press, the question of monopoly should be examined from the points of view of area domination or language domination. The study undertaken by the Commission in this regard shows that the top two dailies account for more than 50 per cent of the circulation of newspapers published in a State only in the case of Kerala and Madhya Pradesh. No conclusion can be drawn from this study. The Commission has tried to examine the situation with regard to competition in another way, namely, language-wise. It says that a condition approximating to monopoly may be said to exist in respect of Bengali, Kannada, Malayalam, Tamil and Telegu. To take an example, *Ananda Bazar Patrika* has a large circulation in Bengali but there are other papers to choose from, namely, *Jugantar, Aaj Kal* or *Basumati.* The larger circulation of *Ananda Bazar Patrika* has not adversely affected other papers.

The Commission also undertook a study of the effect of new editions of chain newspapers on the circulation and growth of local dailies. A big newspaper, irrespective of the pattern of its ownership, generally expands its circulation by opening new editions from new centres. The Commission has found that the Chandigarh edition of the *Indian Express* has not affected the growth of the *Tribune* which is the only local English newspaper of standing. The new edition of *Indian Express* at Hyderabad has not affected the growth of *Deccan Chronicle.* Similar is the case with the Calcutta edition of *Economic Times* vis-a-vis *Business Standard,* the Ernakulam edition of *Malayala Manorama* vis-a-vis *Mathrubhoomi;* and the Bangalore edition of *Hindu* vis-a-vis *Deccan Herald.*

The foregoing brief survey would show that the tests laid down for monopolies in general or even for a dominant undertaking are not applicable to the newspaper industry. Some would, therefore, prefer to call it an oligopoly, which means a group of papers or owners joining together to control the news media to the exclusion of other small papers. It is said that an oligopoly either absorbs or totally eliminates the weaker competitors one by one. In this context, it would be necessary to examine in detail whether there is such an oligopoly and, if so, whether there is an implied or open understanding among them to shut out certain news from the purview of the reader solely for the purpose of promoting their personal or business interests. Commenting on this question, Mudholkar J. in his Tagore Law Lectures observes : "when there is more than one newspaper in a given area either in an Indian language or in English each competing with the other, it is difficult to say that the competing newspapers join together to indulge in any kind of sharp practices, unless it is said that they have an understanding even to share profits or in other words they are a combine or cartel. But there is no such allegation."[8] There is as yet no danger of monopoly or oligopoly in our country. The expansion in the circulation of our so-called big newspapers should not cause public concern. Our big newspapers are but pitiful pygmies by international standards. In 1979, the Japanese *Yomiuri Shimbun* sold over 13 million copies per day in a nation just over 110 million. In Britain, with a population of 55 million, the *Sun* sells 4 million copies per day. The level of circulation of newspapers in other western countries is also equally high. In India in 1982, with a population of 68 crores and 28 crores at least nominally literate, there is not a single paper which has crossed the seven figure barrier. The *Indian Express* with ten editions prints 6,47,709 copies while *Times of India* with three editions prints only 4,67,812 copies. In the case of Indian languages, there is no daily selling 5 lakh copies, although *Ananda Bazar Patrika* (4,03,047) and *Malayala Manorama* (4,70,779) may soon make it. There is only one Tamil periodical, *Kumudam,* which has crossed half-million mark. Hindi dailies are much worse off. India is thus nowhere near the point at which Japan and Western countries stood even at the beginning of this century. Their problems are, therefore, not our problems. Our problem is not to control monopolies but to encourage expansion of circulation at all levels—big, medium and small newspapers.

De-Linking and Diffusion of Ownership and Control

It is a peculiar characteristic of the pattern of ownership of the Press in India that many of the largely circulated newspapers are owned or controlled by industrial or business mag-

8. Mudholkar, J. *Press Law* (Tagore Law Lectures) p. 112.

nates. In a study of the concentration of economic power, the Mahalanobis Committee observes that "one must take into account the link between industry and newspapers which exists in our country to a much larger extent than it is found in any of the democratic countries of the world." The majority of the Mathew Commission thinks that industrial houses use these powerful media to promote their own narrow personal and business interests at the cost of public interest and this poses a danger to the freedom of expression.

Freedom of the Press is not merely a professional right that inheres in journalists. It is essentially the readers' right to know. As William Ernest Hecking put it in *Freedom of the Press* : "The phrase 'freedom of the Press" must now cover two sets of rights and not one only. With the rights of editors and publishers to express themselves, there must be associated a right of the public to be served with substantial and honest basis of fact for its judgment of public affairs. Of these two, it is the latter which today tends to take precedence." Freedom of the Press "has changed its point of focus from the editor to the citizen." The Press is a public utility discharging the basic social function of informing, educating and entertaining the public. For the public interest in this vital area to be properly served, the presentation of news and views in the Press should be fair, accurate, objective, balanced and truthful. Similar views have been expressed by the first Press Commission which says : "A man's opinions are his own, but if he claims to purvey news, the buyer is entitled to insist that it shall be untainted, unadulterated and undiluted. It is from this aspect that we are most concerned with the effect of ownership and the control it exercises on the quality of the service provided to the public."

The majority of the Mathew Commission has advanced various arguments to show that the big industrial and business houses which control the Press treat it as a kept press to serve their personal and business interests and has recommended that the newspaper industry should be delinked from other business interests. The dissenting members of the Commission S/Shri Girilal Jain, Rajendra Mathur, H. K. Paranjape and

S. K. Mukherjea do not subscribe either to the views expressed by the majority or to the recommendations made by it.

The main argument advanced by the majority in favour of its proposal is that where newspapers are controlled by other big business, they become vehicles of expression of the ideology of their owners and the selection, presentation and display of news in such newspapers would be dictated by that ideology. The newspaper industry in their hands becomes involuntarily the cultural arm of other businesses and industries. They become naturally antagonistic to the implementation of certain key directive principles contained in Part IV of the Constitution. It can hardly be disputed that the ownership structure of the newspaper establishment determines the character and style of news report and news display. What gets self-censored and blacked out might be as significant as what gets reported. The Press cannot be truly free in such a situation.

Secondly, it has been urged that the power associated with the control of means of production in the past has now been, to a great extent, transferred to those who control the mass media. Those who control the means of production try to control the media not only for profit but much more so for perpetuation of power associated with the possession of means of production.

It has been further urged that businessmen who control the newspaper do not generally have an intellectual or educational background; they are not steeped in the ethos of journalism and would not fight for its causes. They cannot brook an independent-minded editor and expect the editor to be a mere scribe. For them, newspaper is only one among many businesses they control. On the other hand, if a person has sole interest in newspaper business, he will have greater understanding and competence and is more likely to fight for the principles for which he developed the newspaper.

It has also been argued that newspapers controlled by business houses are oriented towards the urban elite and the rural masses and the poorer sections of the society are neither covered properly nor do they have as adequate choice of newspapers as the city dwellers have.

Finally, it has been pointed out that the main economic advantage accruing from de-linking would be that newspaper profits would not be capable of being easily used for purposes other than publication of newspapers.

In considering the proposal for de-linking, it is necessary to examine the extent to which newspapers are controlled by big business houses and secondly, whether the presentation of news and views by such newspapers is detrimental to public interest.

Control of newspapers by big Business Houses

Among the top dailies, *Hindustan Times* is controlled by the Birla Group and *Times of India* by Bennet Coleman Co. The Minority Report has analysed the ownership structure of other important dailies and it has been found that no other paper is substantially controlled by big Business Houses.[9] The *Indian Express* group of companies is controlled by Shri Goenka. It is true that he acquired some interest in steel and jute industries but his association with those industries has ceased. He has some interest in real estate business but the buildings belong to the Company. He is not a director of any company outside the *Indian Express* group and he has clearly stated in his evidence that "every penny earned by the Company has been ploughed back to the Company itself." The same is the case with the *Statesman*. Except for two corporate shareholders holding 12.56 per cent and 7.48 per cent of the share capital, there are no other companies among the top 10 shareholders. Andrew Yule & Co. Ltd. holding 12.56 per cent is now a government enterprise. Thus Guest Keen Willian Ltd., with 7.48 per cent shares is the only private company which is a top shareholder. It cannot be argued that the *Statesman* is controlled by any big business and to call it a 'jute press' is highly unfair. *The Amrita Bazar Patrika*, the *Ananda*

9. See *Second Press Commission Report*, Vol. I, *Minute of Dissent*, pp. 228, 229, 230, 231.

Bazar Patrika and the *Hindu* are all family papers whose primary interest is in newspaper industry.

The above analysis would show that there are but few papers which are controlled by big business Houses. That is presumably why the majority report has evolved and used a different categorisation, namely, "newspapers owned or controlled by companies or undertakings or businessmen with interests in other businesses or industries." In order to include a newspaper within this category, one of the criteria adopted is that if a newspaper in which more than 50 per cent of the directors hold directorships of other companies unconnected with newspaper publishing, such a newspaper would come within this category. It is well known that a large number of individuals are appointed on the board of directors of companies mainly for the purpose of obtaining the benefit of their knowledge and experience. They may not have any shares in those companies and they may not exercise any effective control in the management of those companies. To say on the basis of such directorships that a substantial control over the newspaper company is exercised by persons with interests outside the newspaper business is unrealistic. Linked units is a nebulous concept and the majority report has based its findings on the basis of very slender data.

Functioning of controlled newspapers

The mere fact that some newspapers have links with other industries should not be a cause for much concern. The really important point for consideration is whether such newspapers present distorted and biased news and whether their presentation of news and views is detrimental to public interest. No systematic study of the contents of newspapers has so far been undertaken. The first Press Commission within the limited time at its disposal conducted a brief survey of the contents of newspapers. The study revealed both favourable and certain unfavourable tendencies. The Commission realised that in a matter of such importance, a survey of the nature undertaken by it could not indicate whether the Press was giving a correct picture of the current events which was essential.

But the Commission said that by and large in the matter of presentation of news and the presentation of views, the general performance of newspapers has been one of satisfaction.

The majority of the Mathew Commission are also "conscious that the newspapers which will come within the proposed legislation (of de-linking) are quality newspapers rendering good service to the community."[10] Yet, they have recommended de-linking. In support of their recommendation, they have said that these papers have a 'vested interest' in protecting big business and they have opposed policies and legislation that went against the interests of private big business such as the Companies Act, the M.R.T.P. Act and all proposals for nationalisation. Now, every newspaper has a policy of its own and it should have the right to propagate its policy and views. To deny that right to a newspaper is to deny the right of freedom of expression. We have a mixed economy and the capitalist Press has a right to put forward its point of view to the public. It cannot be denied that dissemination of news should be from as many different sources and with as many different facets and colours as is possible. For this purpose, dissemination of information from diverse and antagonistic sources is essential to the welfare of the people. In considering this aspect of the question, the first Press Commission thought that it was natural for a newspaper owned by a businessman or an industrialist to adopt editorial policies which would advance directly or indirectly the interests of the business community as a whole or the particular business interests or commitments of the owner. It did not see any cause for complaint if espousal of such policies was restricted to the editorial columns. But the Commission was anxious to ensure that it did not affect the fairness, objectivity, accuracy and comprehensiveness of the news reported in the newspapers. There is, however, no evidence to show that the news coverage in the so-called linked papers in regard to the aforesaid proposals was not fair or adequate and that those newspapers which are not linked with other businesses, (e.g. the *Hindu*, the *Amrita Bazar Patrika,* the *Ananda Bazar Patrika* or *Sakal*) reported the news more comprehensively and objectively. There does not appear sufficient justification for de-linking a newspaper from other business interests merely because it advocates a policy which does not find favour with the government.

A pertinent question arises as to how far a newspaper has the power to shape public opinion or influence the government. The majority of the Mathew Commission seems to have great faith in the power of the Press in moulding public opinion and they seem to think that the present structure of big private enterprises would suffer a grievous collapse without the active support of a monopoly-dominated Press. There are others who think that the power of the Press in shaping public opinion is at the most marginal. Mudholkar, J. in his Tagore Law Lectures says that he belongs to the latter class.[11] We also share his views. Today, the people are sufficiently enlightened—at any rate the urban population—to distinguish between what is propaganda and what is plain truth. People are not unduly swayed by propaganda carried on in newspapers. On the other hand, no government worth its name would ever be cowed down by an assiduous propaganda carried on by a newspaper against its policies and performances. No government would look to newspaper opinion for shaping its foreign policy or its domestic or economic policy. We should not, therefore, be unduly concerned even if certain newspapers espouse the cause of big private enterprise.

This leads us to another question. A newspaper to be independent must be economically viable. A newspaper struggling for its existence and depending upon outside agencies to dole out funds cannot afford the luxury of freedom. On account of technological revolution, equipment for the Press has become so expensive and the cost of running a newspaper so high that it is hardly possible for an individual or a company to run a newspaper, unless it is linked with other business interests or a political party. A newspaper linked with a big busi-

11.   Mudholkar, J., *Press Law* (Tagore Law Lectures), p. 117.

ness House with ample resources at its disposal can render better service to the public.[12] It can benefit from the services of its own correspondents in different parts of the country and abroad and be in a position to offer more original news than its competitors. It can afford the services of high calibre cartoonists and also pay better for contributed articles. It can also afford to engage well-qualified trained journalists. A good printing press with various up-to-date technical facilities can be intensively used if a number of publications are sharing its use. A well-organised newspaper group, financially sound and commercially successful, would be in a better position to try its hand at new and pioneering attempts. There is no reason why a newspaper should be decried merely because it is linked with other business interests, unless it can be shown that the quality of news it serves is tainted and adulterated. Where a newspaper is linked with a big business house, there are certain inherent drawbacks but they have to balance against the advantages flowing from such links. While advocating the cause of big newspapers, the minority members do not say that small newspapers should not be encouraged. They may be helped through Newspaper Development Commission and other institutions but it is not necessary to destroy big newspapers to help the growth of small newspapers.

One of the inherent drawbacks of a newspaper undertaking controlled by a big business house is the editor's loss of autonomy in his own set up. This is a complex problem which we have briefly discussed in Chapter I, and which we propose to discuss more fully in the next chapter. This complex problem has been engaging the attention of professional bodies in the field all over the world for years with no worthwhile results that can act as guidance.

It has been argued by the majority of the Mathew Commission that "commercial newspapers are largely produced for the urban elite. Their style and content and the news they carry, are not particularly relevant to rural masses or to the

---

12. See *Second Press Commission Report*, Vol. I, Minute of Dissent, p. 238.

poor."[13] At the same time, the Commission has taken note of the fact that in spite of their urban middle class backgrounds, our journalists have an adequate sense of guilt, and they go out of their way to highlight the problems of the oft-forgotten poor. In the nature of things, a paper with multi-State circulation cannot be expected to cover adequately the problems of the rural masses. For them, a different type of paper is needed. The district Press in India has not yet come of age and efforts should be made to develop this Press.

Another argument advanced by the majority is that in order to maximise profits, commercial papers sometimes resort to sensationalism and extravagance. But the Commission has paid tribute to the soberness, responsibility and sense of social commitment of the Indian Press. Our leading dailies are generally "quality" papers or are at any rate trying to emulate the virtues of quality newspapers. There is a 'popular' Press in India as also yellow journalism which thrives on stories of sex, crime and character assassination but these blemishes cannot generally be attributed to the leading dailies.

Newspapers in India are neither all virtuous nor vicious. They are a mixed lot and call for certain remedial measures. But their plurality should not be done away with through massive State interference, because the remedy would be worse than the disease. This does not mean that we should be smugly content with things as they are. If there is any general law to curb monopoly and if it is applied to newspaper industry, no exception can be taken. This has also been the view of the Supreme Court in *Bennet Coleman's* Case[14] But any policy which affects the newspaper industry only may cause more harm than good. Moreover, there is no virtue in de-linking for its own sake. De-linking, if it is to be fruitful, must promote the growth of newspapers on right lines, and not result in their emasculation and eventual closure. It is significant that no credible answer to the question how a newspaper could be properly run after it is delinked could be provided either by

13. *Second Press Commission Report*, Vol. I, p. 146.
14. *Bennet Coleman v. Union of India*, A.I.R. 1973 S.C. 106.

the Mathew Commission or any one who appeared before the Commission. Unless a workable substitute is suggested, it would be highly undesirable to adopt a doctrinaire attitude in regard to de-linking. It might starve a quality paper and spell its ruin. Delinking should not be undertaken merely as an article of faith. Experience suggests and all the evidence shows that big newspapers have become big, successful, credible and influential because they have been serving public interest, their pattern of ownership notwithstanding.

The dissenting members of the Mathew Commission observe : "it would be tragic beyond words if, in trying to turn the Press into a public utility, its viability as an industry were to be destroyed. Press as commerce and Press as a mission may seem to be too contradictory to reconcile on a purely abstract plane, but in real life such contradictions are resolved in a working synthesis."[15] We agree.

Recommendations of Mathew Commission

With a view to prevent concentration of ownership in the Press, to delink the Press from other business interests, to eliminate unfair competition among big and small newspapers and to help the growth of the latter, the Mathew Commission has made several recommendations. In the first place, it is proposed that M.R.T.P. Act should be made applicable to newspaper industry; secondly, legislation should be undertaken to de-link newspaper industry from other business interests; thirdly, legislation should also be undertaken to provide for price-page schedule and news-to-advertisement ratio; and finally, a Newspaper Development Commission should be set up to keep the growth of newspaper industry on proper lines. We shall briefly consider all these proposals.

M.R.T.P. Act and the Press

The Mathew Commission has recommended that the Monopolies and Restrictive Trade Practices Act, 1969 should be made applicable to the newspaper industry. Earlier in 1977-78, the

15 *Second Press Commission Report*, Vol, I. *Mintue of Dissent*, p. 228.

Sachar Committee also held that there was no justification for exempting newspaper industry from the provisions of the Act, This Act is a general law to control monopolies and the Press will have little to complain if this law is made applicable to it.

The M.R.T.P. Act as it is in force and as it is interpreted is not, however, applicable to newspaper industry. "Purveying of news or other information" falls within the definition of service in Section 2 of the Act and newspaper industry is, therefore, within the scope of the Act. Difficulties, however, arise because of the definitions of monopolistic undertaking and dominant undertaking. We have already referred to these definitions. A 'dominant undertaking' with reference to a service is defined as an undertaking which, either by itself or with inter-connected undertakings, controls not less than one-third of the services that are rendered in India or substantial part thereof.   Similarly, 'a monopolistic undertaking' with reference to a service has been defined as a dominant undertaking or an undertaking which together with not more than two other independent undertakings provides or otherwise controls not less than one-half of the services that are rendered in India or substantial part thereof. We have also seen that the current interpretation of dominance or monopoly of a newspaper is to be ascertained in relation to the circulation of newspapers in all the languages of India. If this criterion is to be applied, the Act becomes a dead letter in respect of newspapers.

In order to make the Act applicable to the Press, the Mathew Commission suggests certain modifications to the criterion to be applied. It suggests that the proper way of determining 'dominance' or 'monopoly' with reference to a newspaper undertaking is to take into account the circulation of the newspaper in the area within which a substantial part of the newspaper is circulated. Further, when considering the total market for a given newspaper, the language in which the newspaper is published would be directly relevant. A newspaper cannot compete with another in a different language or in an area which it cannot reach in reasonable time. The Com-

15—TPI

mission, therefore, recommends that for determining dominance or monopoly, the effective market should be considered; it may be the whole of India in the case of some newspapers or a State or a region in the case of others. Agreeing with the Sachar Committee, it further recommends that for the purpose of determining dominance, the existing criterion of one-third should be reduced to one-fourth share of the market. It further suggests that no case relating to newspaper should be decided under the M.R.T.P. Act without a public inquiry by the M.R.T.P. Commission. This would ensure that different aspects of the question of a situation of monopoly and concentration receive fair attention by an independent quasi-judicial body. The Commission further recommends that the M.R.T.P. Commission should have the authority to act *suo moto* if allegations of monopolistic practices by a newspaper undertaking come to its notice. We agree with the recommendations of the Commission that the M.R.T.P. Act should be made applicable to the Press. But it would not be desirable to single out the Press for special treatment under the Act. It would be preferable to amend the Act suitably in general terms in the light of the recommendations of the Commission to make it automatically applicable to the Press. But if this is not found feasible, we would suggest that, in view of the peculiar position of the newspaper industry, special provisions may be made to make the Act applicable to the Press.

No study has, however, been undertaken to ascertain how many newspapers will come within the purview of the M.R.T.P. Act, even if the modified criteria recommended by the Commission are applied. Nonetheless, some newspaper undertakings have already registered themselves under the Act. Bennet Coleman & Co. Ltd., which controls the *Times of India* group of newspapers and the *Indian Express* group are already registered under Section 20 of the M.R.T.P. Act, so also the *Eastern Economist* of the Birla group and Associated Publishers of the Amalgamation group. One distinct advantage of such registration is that a company registered under the Act cannot take up new activities without the permission of the government. The inter-connections between the newspaper undertaking and other undertakings can also be scrutinised and an enquiry ordered under Section 27 of the M.R.T.P. Act, if this is found necessary. If the powers under the Act are properly exercised, it might be possible to keep a check on the monopolistic practices of a newspaper undertaking and the Commission's recommendation for de-linking the Press from other business interests would lose much of its force.

Delinking the Press from other Business interests

The majority of the Mathew Commission thinks that in the interest of the public, it is necessary to insulate the Press from the dominating influence of other business interests and recommends the enactment of a law making it mandatory for persons carrying on the business of publishing a newspaper to sever their connections with other businesses to the extent indicated by them. We have already discussed the question of de-linking and we feel that in the situation prevailing in the newspaper industry, no legislation for delinking is called for and that such legislation will do more harm than good. We shall, however, briefly examine the scheme of the proposed legislation.

There are two aspects of the proposed legislation. Firstly, the person carrying on the business of publishing a newspaper should not have, *directly or indirectly,* an interest in excess of the prescribed interest, in any other business. Secondly, the person carrying on the business of publishing a newspaper should not be in a position, of being controlled, *directly or indirectly,* by any other person having interest, in excess of the prescribed interest, in any other business. The prescribed interest is defined as interest which should not exceed ten per cent of the total interest involved in the publication of the newspaper. For example, in the case of a company publishing a newspaper, its aggregate interest in other business should not exceed ten per cent of its subscribed share capital. On the other hand, persons having interest in any other business or businesses should not, taken together, be allotted to have more than ten per cent interest in the business of publishing a newspaper. Thus, in the case of a company publishing a newspaper, not more than ten per cent of its subscribed share capital should be allowed to be held by persons having interest in other business. The proposed legislation will have to work out carefully the concept of 'control' by persons having interest in business other than that of the newspaper. It is proposed that this law, to start with, should apply to all newspapers which have circulation exceeding one lakh copies per day.

The proposed law should also provide for filing a declaration by a newspaper, once in six months, that the newspaper is not being published in contravention of the provisions of the proposed legislation. If the declaration is found to be false, the Magistrate acting under PRB Act should have the power under Section 8B thereof to cancel the declaration of the newspaper filed under Section 5 of the Act. This penalty would be in addition to the penalty attracted by a false declaration under Section 176 I.P.C.

This is the broad outline of the proposed legislation. About 32 dailies will come within the ambit of the proposed legislation and they are all quality newspapers rendering good service to the community. The proposed law will be very complex and extremely difficult to work.

Firstly, it has been proposed that in the case of a Company publishing a newspaper, its aggregate interest in other business has to be limited to ten per cent of its subscribed capital. If this limitation is to apply only to the newspaper undertaking itself, it may be possible to work out the scheme. But if we have to take into account the interest of directors and shareholders also, it will be very difficult to work the scheme.

Secondly, the scheme speaks of limiting the control over the newspaper company by other businesses. Control may be exercised in various ways such as proprietory control, control by legal means, inter-member control arrangements, management control, voting trusts, irrevocable proxy, cross-holdings etc. The majority report says : "the concept of control which we contemplate is one which includes control as a result of or by means of agreements, *benami* transactions, trusts, arrangements, understandings and practices whether or not having legal or equitable force and whether or not based on legal or equitable rights.'' It goes further on to say that ''it is of utmost importance to ensure that the shareholders as well as the directors of the newspaper company are not controlled directly or indirectly by other business interests.'' It is very difficult, if not impracticable, to work out such a scheme of control. Moreover, in order to give effect to the scheme of control, it would be necessary to sell the shares of newspaper company to eligible persons from the open market. But the shares of newspaper companies are not attractive because often there are no profits or very small ones. They will be still less attractive when the newspaper is delinked from other business interests. The majority of the Commission recognises this difficulty and suggests that such shares should be acquired and held by an autonomous body or agency to be specified by the legislation till they are purchased by eligible persons. The effect of this proposal would be that control will pass from business houses to the government which would strike at the root of freedom of the Press. On this ground alone, the idea of the proposed legislation should be dropped.

The proposed law further stipulates that every newspaper has to file a declaration once in six months that it is not being published in contravention of the law and if the declaration is found to be false, the declaration made by the newspaper under Section 5 of the P.R.B. Act may be cancelled. Putting forward impracticable conditions to be fulfilled by newspaper undertakings and then threatening them with closure would be, to say the least, unfair.

A pertinent question arises as to whether as a result of delinking, the performance of the de-linked newspapers would be better. There is no reason to suppose that the owners of delinked papers would change their attitude to news and views and they would turn the industry into a vocation or a mission. There are about 17,000 non-linked newspapers in our country which are poorly run and whose professional norms and ethical standards are by no means higher than those of the linked ones. On the other hand, as the de-linked papers would not have ample resources at their disposal, the quality of the papers would suffer and their concern with profitability is likely to be more absolute and obsessive and there may be a tendency among them to sensationalise and pander to the baser instincts of the readers for the sake of circulation and advertisement.

As we have said before there is no virtue in delinking for its own sake and it should not be undertaken merely as an article of faith. The proposed legislation might spell ruin to quality papers without any appreciable improvement in non-linked newspapers.

The dissenting members of the Commission have made certain alternative suggestions. They suggest that in a newspaper undertaking owned by a joint stock company, one-third of its directors should be persons of eminence with experience in journalism, literature, administration, economics, law, science or such other professional fields. These special directors should be selected by way of co-option by the Board of Directors and they should have a fixed tenure. In the case of other newspaper undertakings, (not owned by Joint Stock Companies), there should be an advisory board consisting of three members who should have the same background as that of special directors. They may be appointed by the owners of the newspaper undertaking for a fixed tenure. The minority report further recommends that in all cases of appointments, promotions, dismissals or other disciplinary action relating to editorial and journalistic staff, the views of the Special directors or of the advisory board, as the case may be, have to be ascertained by the managements of the newspaper undertakings and, in case there is a persistent difference between them, the matter should go to arbitration. These are simple recommendations, easy to implement, without affecting the ownership pattern of newspaper undertakings. Yet, they may act as a salutary check on any arbitrary action of the management. They may be accepted.

Price-page Schedule and News-to-advertisement ratio

Apart from the proposals for the application of the

M.R.T.P.' Act to the Press and its de-linking from other business interests, the Mathew Commission makes another important but controversial recommendation for prescribing a price-page schedule with a statutory news-to-advertisement ratio. The question of a price-page schedule has been the subject of debate for the last three decades and we may briefly note the vicissitudes through which this proposal has passed.

History of the Proposal

The First Press Commission suggested the prescription of a price-page schedule and was firmly of the view that the quantum of advertisements should not exceed 40 per cent of the total area. In pursuance of this recommendation Parliament enacted the Newspapers (Price and Page) Act, 1956 to regulate the prices of newspapers in relation to their pages and sizes and to regulate the allocation of space for advertising matter. The Daily Newspapers (Price and Page) Order, 1960 made under the said Act fixed the number of pages that could be published by a newspaper according to the prices charged. However, both the Act and the Order were struck down by the Supreme Court in *Sakal Papers* case.[16]

The need for a price-page schedule was again examined by the Enquiry Committee on small newspapers. The Committee was divided in its opinion and by a five to four majority, it recommended a price-page schedule and also that not more than 40 per cent of the space in a newspaper should be occupied by advertisements. Later, an excise duty of two paise per copy was imposed by the Government on newspapers having daily circulation of more than 15,000 with effect from 15th November, 1971. Under the pretext of covering the levy of this duty, many newspapers disproportionately raised their selling price. Government, therefore, enacted the Newspapers (Price Control) Act, 1972 which empowered the Government to determine the maximum price which could be charged by a newspaper. The provisions of the Act were, however, never invoked and being a temporary measure, the Act lapsed after

16. *Sakal Papers* v. *Union of India*, (1962) 3 S.C.R. 842.

two years. This question was again examined by the Fact Finding Committee on Newspaper Economics under the Chairmanship of Dr. Bhabotosh Datta which submitted its report in
1975. It was definitely opposed to the price-page schedule but
advocated a news-to-advertisement ratio of 50 : 50 so long as
newsprint was in short supply. In the Second Press Commission also, there has been a sharp difference of opinion and the
dissenting members have opposed the proposal of a price-page
schedule and news-to-advertisement ratio.

Arguments in favour of the proposal

In support of the proposal, the majority of the Mathew
Commission argues that freedom of the Press rests on the
assumption that widest possible dissemination of information
from diverse and antagonistic sources is essential to the welfare of the people. It is, therefore, necessary to reduce the
differences due to economic or other causes. It is necessary to
ensure that newcomers should be enabled to start publication
with a fair chance of achieving success and that there should
not be unfair competition between big and small newspapers.
But established newspapers with a large circulation enjoy certain special advantages. It has a lower cost of production per
copy and because of its large capital resources, it is free from
certain handicaps which affect a paper with limited resources.
A paper of long standing and with a large circulation is able
to build up a large and stable volume of advertisement
revenue and is in an advantageous position compared to small
newspapers or others who have just entered the field.

It is true that such economic advantages and handicaps
exist in a number of industries but the newspaper industry
stands on a different footing. As the Enquiry Committee on
Small Newspapers observed, whereas the selling price of an
industrial product is always above the cost of production, a
daily newspaper may sell at a price which is much below its
cost of production. In other industries, in spite of the existence of a few big units, a new entrepreneur can enter the field
because the big units cannot reduce the sale price of the product below its cost of production. But in newspaper industry,

big units can afford to sell their newspapers at a price lower than their cost of production, because of the disproportionately large advertisement revenue at their disposal. Further, the re-sale value of old newspapers in our country is very high and in view of this, a newspaper giving more pages for the same price commands a larger circulation which enables it to get more advertisements which in turn puts it in a position to be able to further reduce its selling price. There is another handicap for a new entrant in the field, because a stale issue cannot be sold as a newspaper.

The Mathew Commission feels that for the freedom of the Press to be effective, the present degree of dependence of newspapers on advertisements has to be lessened and that the prescription of a price-page schedule with a news-to-advertisement ratio is absolutely essential for promoting fair competition among the existing units and for providing a chance of success to newcomers in the interest of dissemination of information from diverse sources. The Commission does not, however, lay down any scheme for price-page schedule but suggests that an Expert Committee should be set up to work out a price-page schedule after taking into account the present-day economics of publishing a newspaper. It, however, makes a firm recommendation that the news-to-advertisement ratio should be fixed at 60 : 40 for big, 50 : 50 for medium and 40 : 60 for small newspapers.

Examination of the proposals

Arguments advanced by the Mathew Commission in favour of its proposals are persuasive and there can be no dispute over the question that we should not allow the development of a monopoly Press where larger newspapers will have maximum freedom to destroy all the existing or potential competition. But the question which needs to be examined is whether the proposed measures will eliminate unfair competition without destroying our quality papers and whether they would be legally defensible.

One initial difficulty in examining this question arises from the fact that the price-page schedule is yet to be worked out. The Commission was uncertain about the impact of the proposed measure on the economics of the newspaper industry and, therefore, suggested the setting up of an Expert Committee to work out a price-page schedule after examining the relevant facts. Without a clear picture of the proposed schedule, a discussion on its impact on different classes of newspapers can take place only on certain presumptions and would be somewhat academic and unrealistic. Even for such a restricted discussion, it would be useful to take note of the existing price-page level of some selected newspapers and the space occupied by advertisements in them.

Price-page level of certain selected dailies[17]   November, 1981

Name of the Daily	Selling price (in paise)		Average number of pages in a single issue
	Weekdays	Sundays	
1. Hindu, Madras	70	75	21.6
2. Hindustan Times, New Delhi	60	60	22.0
3. Indian Express, New Delhi	60	70	13.85
4. Times of India New Delhi.	60	70	18.27
5. Statesman, New Delhi	50	50	12.8
6. Deccan Herald, Bangalore	60	70	16.13

Advertisement Space[18]

Name of Newspaper	Percentage of space devoted to advertisements in the year 1981
1. Statesman, Calcutta	67.0
2. Hindustan Times, New Delhi	63.0
3. Times of India, Bombay	60.0
4. Indian Express, Madras	55.0
5. Ananda Bazar Patrika, (Bengali) Calcutta.	58.6
6. Assam Tribune (English) Gauhati.	58.1

From the above tables, it will be seen that the advertisement ratio varies from 67 per cent to 55 per cent and the aver-

17.   See *Second Press Commission Report*, Vol. I, p. 12.
18.   *Second Press Commission Report*, Vol. I, p. 155.

age number of pages in a single issue varies from 22 to 12.8.
The average number of pages of our dailies is not at all high
by international standards and should not be a cause of much
public concern. The introduction of a price-page schedule
would presumably affect all important dailies and would certainly reduce their advertisement revenue. If a newspaper
retains its existing page level, it may have to raise its selling
price which will be beyond the reach of common readers and
this will lead to a decrease in the volume of its circulation
which in turn will further reduce its advertisement revenue.
If, on the other hand, a newspaper reduces its page level, its
advertisement revenue will substantially fall and the paper
may cease to be economically viable. The quality of a newspaper depends to a large extent on its financial resources and
advertisement is the main source of income for a newspaper.
The Mathew Commission recognises that our important dailies
are utilising advertisement revenue to a certain extent for
improving their quality and subsidising the selling price for
the benefit of the readers. With a substantial fall in the
advertisement revenue, the quality of our newspapers will
suffer. It is generally accepted that the quality of the Indian
newspapers leaves much to be desired. Even the best known
of our newspapers like the *Times of India,* the *Hindu,* the
Indian Express, the *Statesman* or the *Hindustan Times* cannot be considered anywhere near the top class newspapers in
developed countries either in the quality of news that they
provide or the quality of information, feature articles and
cartoons etc. that they contain. If they have to improve, they
will require more pages rather than less.

The introduction of a price-page schedule may adversely
affect the quality of important dailies and may also raise their
selling price. The question which arises is whether it will help
small papers and new entrants in the field. It cannot be
assumed that if advertisements are not permitted to be published in the large newspapers, they would automatically shift
to others. The dissenting members of the Mathew Commission
do not, therefore, favour a strait jacket solution to the problem because "this will merely create difficulties for the exist-

ing good quality newspapers, only because they have large circulations, and at the same time may not necessarily help the sustenance or coming into existence of similarly good quality but smaller circulation papers.''[19] In the absence of clear provisions of a price-page schedule, we tentatively agree with the Bhabotosh Datta Committee, the only Committee so far on newspaper economics, that in the present state of newspaper industry, it is not necessary to introduce this schedule.

Tax on advertisement

This is not to say that there is no case for some limit on the use of advertisement by newspapers. Our problem is to encourage small newspapers without unduly hurting quality papers. To achieve this object, it may be necessary to put some curb on excessive advertisements. We suggest a news-to-advertisement ratio of 50 : 50 to be applicable to all classes of newspapers, big or small. This suggestion is in keeping with the recommendations of the Bhabotosh Datta Committee as also of the minority report of the Mathew Commission. If, however, any newspaper makes use of excessive advertisement beyond 50 per cent of the total newspaper space, it should be subject to a progressive tax on advertisement. We think that such a flexible approach would be better than a fixed general prohibition. In order to help small newspapers as also for administrative convenience, small newspapers with circulation below 25,000 may be exempt from the tax on advertisement.

Constitutional Position

We shall now consider the legal aspect of prescribing a price-page schedule with a news-to-advertisement ratio. It may be recalled that in pursuance of the recommendation of the First Press Commission, the Newspapers (Price and Page) Act, 1956 was enacted to regulate the prices of newspapers in relation to their pages and sizes and to regulate the allocation of space for advertising matter. The Daily Newspapers (Price

---

19. *Second Press Commission Report*, Vol. I, *Minute of Dissent*, p. 239.

and Page) Order, 1960 made under the said Act fixed the number of pages that could be published by a newspaper according to the prices charged. But both the Act and the Order were struck down by the Supreme Court in *Sakal Papers* Case.[20] The Mathew Commission has now made exactly the same recommendation and to give effect to it, the Newspapers (Price and Page) Act has to be re-enacted. But such a law would obviously be invalid in view of *Sakal Papers* case. But the Mathew Commission thinks that the *Sakal Papers* case was incorrectly decided and it should be reviewed. We shall briefly examine this aspect of the question.

The Press is not only a medium of expression but it is also an industry carrying on business with profit motive. Restrictions may be placed on freedom of expression only on the grounds mentioned in clause (2) of that article. Reasonable restrictions may also be imposed in the interests of the general public to regulate the business or commercial activities of the Press. But in regulating the economic and business aspects of a newspaper, the State cannot impose restrictions which would affect freedom of expression guaranteed to the Press under article 19(i)(a) by curtailing its circulation or freedom of discussion unless such restrictions are also protected under clause (2) of the article. Since grounds mentioned in clause (2) and clause (6) are different, the exercise of power by the State under both the clauses may lead to anomaly or conflict and the Supreme Court has tried to remove this anomaly by evolving the doctrine of "direct impact." If a law regulating the business aspect of the Press imposes restrictions which *directly* affect its volume of circulation or its freedom of discussion or otherwise affect freedom of expression, such a law would be unconstitutional. On the other hand, if a law is directly aimed at regulating the business aspect of the Press but as a result of operation of such law, freedom of expression of a newspaper is *indirectly* or *remotely* affected depending on contingencies which may or may not happen, the law cannot be declared invalid as violative of articles 19(i) (a). This doctrine of 'direct impact' has been evolved by the

20. *Sakal Papers* v. *Union of India*, (1962) 3 S.C.R. 842.

Supreme Court in the leading cases of *Express Newspapers* case, *Sakal Papers* case and *Bennet Coleman* case.[21]

The doctrine of direct impact applies also to general laws not specifically directed against the Press. Thus laws of taxation, factory laws etc. may have some effect on freedom of the Press when applied to newspaper industry. If any law or restriction not protected by clause (2) of article 19 directly and substantially curtails freedom of expression, the law or restriction would be unconstitutional. But if the effect of such law or restriction on freedom of expression is indirect and remote, the law would not be vitiated and would not be violative of article 19(1)(a).

The doctrine of 'direct impact' evolved by the Supreme Court embodies a sound proposition of law and no exception can be taken to it. The Mathew Commission, however, seeks to rely on the doctrine of pith and substance. It recognises that while imposing restrictions on the Press under clause (6) of article 19, "such restrictions might apparently conflict with the right conferred under article 19(1)(a)." In such a case, the Commission suggests that the solution is to decide what exactly is the pith and substance of the legislation. In other words, the appropriate mode of resolving the conflict is to look at the true nature and character of the legislation and decide whether it is really a restriction upon the freedom to carry on business or an indirect attempt to suppress freedom of expression. The test is the pith and substance of the matter and not the indirect effect of the legislation."[22] The doctrine of pith and substance is a well recognised doctrine and to my mind, it makes no difference whether we apply the doctrine of direct impact or the doctrine of pith and substance. The question which ultimately arises for consideration is a question of fact, whether the impugned law relating to a price-page schedule will have a direct bearing on freedom of expression or whether it will have only indirect or remote effect.

21. *Express Newspapers* v. *Union of India,* (1959) S.C.R. 12. *Sakal Papers* v. *Union of India,* (1962) 3 S.C.R. 842. *Bennet Coleman* v. *Union of India,* A.I.R. 1973 S.C. 106.
22. *Second Press Commission Report,* Vol. I, p. 157.

In *Sakal papers* case, the Supreme Court held as a fact that the Newspapers (Price and Page) Act, 1960 directly affected freedom of expression guaranteed under article 19(1)(a). It says : "The impugned law far from being one which merely interferes with the right of freedom of speech incidentally, does so directly though it seeks to achieve the end by purporting to regulate the business aspect of a newspaper. Such a course is not permissible." While no exception can be taken either to the doctrine of direct impact or to the doctrine of pith and substance, there may be honest difference of opinion as to whether the Supreme Court has correctly applied the law to the facts of the case. But we feel that it would be too risky and also inappropriate to confront the Supreme Court by re-enacting the Newspapers (Price and Page) Act.

Though the Mathew Commission is clearly of the opinion that the decision of the Supreme Court in *Sakal papers* case merits a review, it realises the difficulties involved in getting it done. It, therefore, suggests that, if necessary, the Constitution should be suitably amended to give effect to its proposals. A law prescribing a price-page schedule and news-to-advertisement ratio may be protected by suitably amending clause (2) of article 19. But we have discussed earlier that such a law may not achieve the desired objective and may do more harm than good. An amendment of the Constitution should not be lightly undertaken and we feel that it should not be undertaken to give effect to a law of doubtful utility.

Legislation prescribing a price-page schedule and news-to-advertisement ratio cannot be justified on merits and there are legal obstacles to such legislation. We have, therefore, suggested a tax on excessive advertisement. Such a measure would be easy to operate. As a taxation law, its impact on freedom of expression would not be direct and would, if at all, be indirect and remote and the law would not be vitiated and would not be violative of article 19(1)(a).

Newspaper Development Commission

The number of newspapers in our country is fairly

large, exceeding 17,000 and it is steadily on the increase. But most of them are poorly run. Established newspapers with large circulation enjoy certain special advantages and the smaller units cannot compete with them. It is necessary to encourage the growth of small newspapers and to eliminate unfair competition to the extent possible.

One of the handicaps from which smaller newspapers suffer is the lack of easy credit facilities. Big newspaper undertakings have been able to secure credit on a significant scale from the apex credit institutions. But small newspapers are experiencing difficulties in securing such credit on easy terms. A proposal was, therefore, made to set up a Newspaper Finance Corporation to give soft loans to small newspapers. Mudholkar, J. in his Tagore Law Lectures opposed this proposal on the ground that subsidising newspaper industry would strike at the root of the freedom of the Press. The Mathew Commission is not also in favour of any such separate finance corporation. It suggests that priority status may be allotted to small and medium newspaper undertakings for credit from the nationalised banks, State Finance Corporations and institutions for promotion of small-scale industries. We agree.

The quality of our newspapers, particularly of small and medium newspapers, leaves much to be desired. In order that smaller newspapers may compete with big newspapers, it is necessary that all possible assistance should be rendered for the growth of small newspapers and for improvement of their quality. For this purpose, the Mathew Commission recommends the setting up of a Newspaper Development Commission.

Functions of the Commission

This Commission will seek to promote the development of the Press as a whole. But it will make special effort in facilitating the growth of Indian language newspapers, newspapers of local interest such as district newspapers and all small and medium newspapers. It will not give financial subsidy directly to any individual newspaper but it will offer technical and all other assistance on a generalised, non-discriminating and non-discretionary basis.

The objects envisaged for the Development Commission are briefly as follows :

(i) to promote R & D in the newspaper industry, particularly research in and development of teleprinters in Indian languages and of composing and printing technologies suitable for small and medium newspapers;

(ii) to promote the development of Indian language news agencies;

(iii) to provide development assistance to the Press, especially to small and medium newspapers, through such means as the provision of subsidised teleprinter services on a non-discriminatory basis;

(iv) to arrange supply of newsprint to newspapers, other than those belonging to newspaper chains, in interior or remote areas at prices comparable to those prevailing at port-towns;

(v) to assist the emergence and growth of daily newspapers in remote and interior areas by subsidising the news agencies' teleprinter links;

(vi) to assist in obtaining for newspapers and news agencies reasonable tariffs for internal and external communication;

(vii) to appraise proposals for the publication of daily newspapers by the Government in areas without a daily Press;

(viii) to liaise with various Government departments concerned with the needs of the newspaper industry;

(ix) to promote and coordinate training in journalism, in case the Press Council does not assume this function;

(x) to provide financial assistance through grants to institutions engaged in R & D in newspaper publishing;

(xi) to commission studies relevant to the promotion of above objects; and

(xii) to undertake such other functions as the Commission considers to be appropriate in pursuance of the above objectives :

Composition

The composition of the Commission may be broadly as follows :

(1) One full-time Chairman who should be a person with experience in finance, industry, development administration or newspaper management and generally well-versed in public life but not connected with any newspaper undertaking at the time of appointment.

(2) Two whole-time members.

(3) Three representatives from newspaper organisations, like IENS, ILNA and AISMNA.

(4) Three representatives of working journalists.

(5) The Chairman of the Press Council or his nominee.

(6) The Chairman of the Indian Institute of Mass Communication or his nominee.

(7) One representative each from the Ministries of Information & Broadcasting, Finance and Industry.

This is only a broad outline of the scheme of composition of the Commission.

Funding

Financing of the Commission poses certain difficulties. In order that the Commission may maintain its autonomy, it should not be a fully subsidised body. The Mathew Commission, therefore, suggests that the Commission should be funded through a small cess on all newsprint consumption by newspapers and a tax on the advertisement revenue of newspapers. Advertisement revenue is major source of revenue for a newspaper and a general tax on advertisement revenue may create complications. We have, therefore, suggested a tax only on excessive advertisements, that is to say, a tax on advertisement when the space occupied by it exceeds 50 per cent of the total space of the newspaper. The cess and tax so collected should be earmarked for the Development Commission. But there is constitutional difficulty in earmarking advertisement tax to the Commission. Under article 269, advertisement tax is levied and collected by the Union but it is assigned to the States. This provision has to be suitably amended to ensure that the advertisement tax may be given to the Commission. But by such amendment, the States will not lose anything, because this taxation power has not so far been exercised by the Government of India.

To sum up : The newspapers in India are still in the embryo as compared to those in the developed countries. They have a far smaller reach as yet compared to what is necessary in a democracy. Yet it is necessary to control the monopolistic tendencies and prevent concentration of ownership in the Indian Press. It is also necessary to help the growth of small and medium newspapers and to improve their quality. But nothing should be done which would cripple big newspapers which are quality papers by our standard. It is also to be recognised that newspapr industry is a sensitive industry and external control and interference with the industry should be as little as possible. Keeping these considerations in mind, we have suggested that the M.R.T.P. Act should be made applicable to the newspaper industry. If this Act is effectively used, it would be possible to use the provisions regarding monopolistic and restrictive trade practices as well as the new category of unfair trade practices, to safeguard the interests of readers and of smaller papers. We do not favour the proposal for delinking the Press from other business interests nor do we consider it necessary to undertake legislation prescribing a price-page schedule and news-to-advertisement ratio. We would not like to restrict a major source of revenue like advertising but we have advocated a tax on excessive advertisement. We have also lent our full support to the proposal for a Newspaper Development Commission to promote the development of the Press as a whole and in particular of Indian language papers, and small and medium newspapers. We have suggested external control over the newspaper industry, only when it is a must.

CHAPTER X

Rights and Liabilities of the Editor and Others

In this Chapter, we shall discuss the rights and liabilities of the editor and certain other persons associated with the publishing of a newspaper.

Editor

The 'editor' of a newspaper, as defined in Sec. 1(1) of the Press and Registration of Books Act, 1867, means the person who controls the *selection* of the matter that is published in a newspaper. The editor is thus individually liable for any illegal matter published in his newspaper, independently of the liability of the printer, publisher or proprietor, e.g. obscene matter, a prejudical report under D.I. Rules, a seditious letter from a correspondent, a defamatory article or even a news item[1] or a signed petition by third parties or any matter constituting contempt of court or contempt of the legislature. Absence of intention or knowledge of the contents of the offending matter published will be no defence for an editor. But such plea may be taken into consideration as a mitigating circumstance, while awarding punishment. Thus, where an inaccurate report of a judicial proceeding, likely to be prejudicial to the accused, was sent by a reporter and published and the editor

---

1. *Joshi* v. *State of U.P.* A.I.R. 1961 S.C. 387.

had no reason to suppose that it was inaccurate, the Court awarded a substantial fine against the newspaper but no separate sentence against the editor.[2]

The editor is an employee of the proprietor and the relationship of master and servant subsists between them. Since the term 'editor' has been defined by a statute, a person is an editor, only if the contract of his employment under the proprietor gives him control over the selection of the matter that is to be published in the newspaper. It follows that if the proprietor unduly interferes with the right of the editor to select or reject a matter, it would constitute a breach of contract.

Editorial autonomy and independence

The editor is responsible for the production of the newspaper and since he is also personally liable for everything published therein, he should have full freedom to choose what to publish and what not to publish. But a newspaper is a private enterprise operating for private profit. In terms of investments in men and machinery and its operations, a modern newspaper unit is like any other commercial or industrial enterprise. The interest of the owner of the newspaper generally lies in its economic success. But commercial considerations, though relevant, ought not to override editorial considerations.

Some of the largely circulated newspapers in our country are owned by commercial houses or industrialists who run the newspapers as a subsidiary to their business interests or for exerting political pressure. Such proprietors naturally do not want anything to be published which is against their business interests or the interests of their fellow businessmen. They also cannot afford to take the risk of offending the government or other authorities which regulate industry in a planned economy. A newspaper owner has the basic right to have his point of view expressed through his newspaper. But the freedom of the owner is only a part of the freedom of the Press. Journa-

---

2. Re *Odham's Press* (1956) 1 All E.R. 494.

listic freedom is the heart of freedom of the Press. The effective exercise of journalistic freedom depends largely on the editor. The freedom and independence of the editor is the crux of the matter. The editing of big newspapers cannot be done or supervised by one person. Proper distribution of responsibility is inescapable. The adequacy of the editor can be sustained only by proper delegation of authority, viable distribution of work and by the habit of the widest possible consultation. It is only the co-operative endeavour of the entire editorial staff that can make for standards in a newspaper. However, the ultimate responsibility in the production of a newspaper should vest in the editor.

Conflicts may arise between editorial independence and the interests of the proprietor. Theoretically, such conflicts may be resolved by demarcating the functions of the proprietor and the editor. The proprietor of a newspaper has certainly the right to lay down the policy of the paper. He who pays the piper has also the right to order the tune. But the right of the owner should not extend beyond laying down the policy and the appointment of an editor of his choice. When an editor accepts his appointment in a newspaper, he accepts also the broad principles of the policy of the paper. He is expected to operate within the four corners of that policy but there should not be any interference in his day-to-day work. In practice, the proprietor very often leaves the control of the newspaper to an executive or manager who hardly knows the contours of freedom of the Press. Yet, the manager dictates to the editor what to say and what not to say and the editor becomes no more than a mere scribe of the proprietor. This involves not only a breach of contract but severely undermines freedom of the Press. Independence of the editor is vital to freedom of the Press. If the editor has to play second fiddle to the general manager, the paper is bound to be dull and unenterprising. The status and prestige of the editor in his own set up must be enhanced commensurate with his pivotal role in a newspaper.

We find that, by and large, the policy of a newspaper is not reduced to writing and the editor's sphere of autonomy is not clearly defined. Taking advantage of the situation, the proprietors attempt to put fetters on their editors to facilitate creation of public opinion which will enable them not only to pursue but to expand their commercial activities and make larger and larger profits openly and covertly. This is one of the day-to-day problems which editors have to face. Despite loud protests to the contrary, the fact remains that most editors try to gauge or anticipate the wishes of the proprietors of their papers and by toeing their line, circumvent the possibility of being handed over explicit instructions to them on policies to be followed in matters of public interest which vitally affect the proprietors. But even so, there are some editors who have 'run the gauntlet' of such constraints and have stuck bravely to the pursuit of an independent editorial policy, though occasionally they had to quit or change their newspapers. The Mathew Commission has cited two examples of conflicts between the management and the editor. They relate to important dailies, namely, the *Hindustan Times* and the *Statesman*. In both the cases, the editors had to quit and seek employment elsewhere.

The independence of the editor is threatened not only by internal pressure from the proprietors but also by external pressure. Government has been responsible, in a way, for denigrating the position and status of the editor, as it prefers to discuss the problems of the Press with working journalists, trade unions or the proprietors' organisations. The recognition which is due to editors is not sometimes given. Mudholkar, J. in his Tagore Law Lectures further points out that "government pressures are the greatest menace to editorial independence. Particularly, at the State level, these pressures range from the withdrawal of advertisements for an offending newspaper to physical violence to its editor and reporter, destruction of property by arson and similar activities of goondas let loose with the connivance of the police. In the face of such pressures, several papers have been snuffed out of existence."[3] The statement might be somewhat exaggerated but there is an element of truth in it.

3. Mudholkar, J. *Press Law* (Tagore Law Lectures), p. 46.

Newspapers serve a vital public purpose in making available news and views to the community. Editorial independence is of utmost importance, if newspapers are to discharge this function satisfactorily. All interferences in this area have to be guarded against, whether through external or internal pressure. Steps have to be taken to put a check on external pressure. In order to provide an effective safeguard against proprietorial or managerial interference in editorial independence, it will be necessary to take several measures.

In the first place, it is necessary to provide security of employment for the editor. The editor will be appointed by the owner of the newspaper but the person chosen ought to be a man of known ability and integrity and should have sufficient authority to conduct the newspaper in public interest, while following the policy laid down by the owner. The First Press Commission noted a decline in the status of the editor. It suggested that the appointment of an editor should be attended with the execution of a contract of employment. The contract should provide for appointment of the editor for a term of five years or till he attains the age of superannuation whichever is earlier. It should further provide that the period of notice for the termination of the services of an editor should be not less than three months during the first three years of service and not less than six months thereafter and that he should be entitled to compensation for involuntary unemployment, the measure of such compensation being determined by an independent authority. These are welcome suggestions and may be accepted.

Secondly, the editor should have full control over journalistic staff. It appears that in many cases, editors do not have enough say in the selection of journalists and assignment of professional duties to them. This is not conducive to co-operative endeavour which is so very necessary for the success of the paper. In the matter of selection of journalists, if the editor does not have a free hand, he should, at any rate, have a big say in such selection. In all other matters, including assignment of duties to journalists, the editor should have full control.

Thirdly, the policy of every newspaper should be clearly laid down in as precise terms as possible and the editor's sphere of autonomy should be clearly defined. Such policy statement, however, is bound to be in broad, general terms and disputes are bound to arise between the editor and the management of the newspaper whether full effect is being given to the policy. An independent machinery should, therefore, be set up to settle such disputes.

The editor-management relationship is an extremely complex problem which has been the subject of debate all over the world. Various attempts have been made in other countries to define this relationship and to safeguard the autonomy of the editor with no worthwhile results that can act as guidance in our country.

In America, the views columns and news columns are two separate, almost autonomous, departments with an editor at the head of each department—the former being called editor of the editorial page and the latter news editor. Above them, sits the editor-in-chief (or whatever the designation) who constitutes the link between the two departments. Between these two departments, the news department enjoys greater importance because it is responsible for four-fifths of the paper. The news editor and his deputy are top flight men who are actually responsible for shaping the journalistic personality of the paper. It is they who decide what should go into the paper and in what form. The news editor being directly responsible to the editor-in-chief, his autonomy vis-a-vis the general manager is generally assured.

In U.K., while allowing the transfer of *Times Newspapers* to Mr. Rupert Mudroch's *News International*, Government laid down stringent conditions to ensure editorial independence. The conditions laid down provide *inter alia* :[4]

(1) that there shall be six independent national directors and in future national directors shall not be appointed without the approval of the existing independent national directors;

4. See *Second Press Commission Report*, Vol. I, p. 161.

(2) that editors shall not be appointed or dismissed without the approval of the majority of the independent national directors;

(3) that the editor shall retain control over any political comment published in his newspaper and in particular, shall not be subject to any restraint in expressing opinion or in reporting news that might directly or indirectly conflict with the opinions or interests of any of the newspaper proprietors;

(4) that the editor shall retain control over the appointment and dismissal of journalists and of assigning duties to them and also of the content of the newspaper; and

(5) that disputes between the editors and the management are to be settled by independent national directors.

Similar arrangements were worked out in July, 1981 in the case of the *Observer*.

In India, the situation is far worse compared to other countries, because very often the general managers of our country are ill-equipped for performing their duties and they are appointed for reasons other than professional and technical qualifications for the post. They do not understand even the language of the editors and the importance in a newspaper of headlines, spot news, objectivity, scoops and cost of news. It is, therefore, all the more necessary in our country to set up a machinery to settle disputes between the editor and the management of a newspaper. In order to provide an effective safeguard against proprietorial or managerial interference in editorial independence, the Mathew Commission recommends legislation for the imposition of a board of trustees between the management of a large daily newspaper and its editor. The legislation should be applicable in the first instance only to daily newspapers with a circulation of over one lakh copies. The function of the board of trustees would be to ensure that full effect is given to the policy of the newspaper and to act as umpire in disputes between the editor and the management of the newspaper. The trustees should be public men of unquestionable integrity and of eminence in the field of journalism, law, science, education or such other learned professions.

They should be appointed by the management of the news-papers themselves in consultation with, and with the approval of, the Chairman of the Press Council and the Chief Justice of the High Court or the Chief Justice of India, as the case may be, depending upon the area of the circulation of the newspaper concerned. Every board of trustees should consist of three members and in the event of a difference of opinion between the Chairman of the Press Council and the Chief Jus-tice on the choice of the members of the board of trustees, the view of the Chief Justice should prevail.

S/Shri Girilal Jain, Rajendra Mathur, R. K. Paranjape and S. K. Mukherjea are, however, not in favour of the above recommendation of the majority. They regard it highly invi-dious that the proposed scheme of board of trustees should apply only to newspapers which by all accounts are reasonably well managed and conducted, and that small and medium news-papers should be left alone, even though many of them may be far from being professionally well conducted and the treat-ment of editors and journalists may be far from satisfactory. They think that it is only appropriate that all categories of newspapers should be obliged to have a system to ensure that a degree of protection is provided to editors and journalists from capricious interference and treatment by the manage-ments. They, however, exclude from this scheme newspapers whose circulation does not exceed 25,000 on practical grounds. They recommend that in all other cases, if a newspaper is owned by a joint stock company, one-third of its directors should be persons of eminence with experience in journalism, litera-ture, administration, economics, law, science or such other pro-fessional fields. These special directors should be selected by way of co-option by the Board of Directors and they should have a fixed tenure. In the case of other newspaper under-takings (not owned by joint stock companies), there should be an advisory board consisting of three members who should have the same background as that of special directors. They may be appointed by the owners of the newspaper undertak-ings for a fixed tenure. They further recommend that in all cases of appointments, promotions, dismissals or other disciplinary action relating to editorial and journalistic staff, the view of the special directors or of the advisory board, as the case may be, has to be ascertained by the managements of the newspaper undertakings and, in case there is persistent difference between them, the matter should go to arbitration. They further suggest that it would be the function of the special directors or of the advisory board, as the case may be, to act as umpire in disputes between the editor and the management of the newspaper.

It may be recalled that we discussed this very scheme in Chapter 9 as an alternative to de-linking the Press from other business interests. This scheme is also very similar to the scheme of independent national directors which was made applicable by the government in U.K. to *Times Newspapers* while allowing its transfer to Mr. Rupert Mudroch. This is a simple scheme applicable to all categories of newspapers without affecting their ownership pattern and it may help in securing editorial independence.

Proprietor

The proprietor is not responsible for anything published in the newspaper. In the case of the editor, there is a presumption under Section 7 of the Press & Registration of Books Act, 1867, that he is responsible for the publication of any offending article or matter published in the newspaper, but there is no such presumption in the case of the proprietor.[5] Hence, the owner or proprietor cannot be made liable for any matter published in his newspaper, e.g. on the ground that it is defamatory or obscene, unless there is positive proof that he was responsible for publishing that matter[5] or for its selection for publication.[6]

In contempt of court proceedings, however, the proprietor would be vicariously liable for the publication of any matter in his newspaper which constitutes contempt of court. Absence of knowledge or of intention would be no defence in

5. *Bhagat* v. *Lachman* (1967) 73 C.W.N. 1(3).
6. *State of Maharashtra* v. *Chowdhuri,* (1967) 73 C.W.N. 549.

such proceedings, though it may mitigate damages. On the other hand, the damages would be aggravated where it is shown that a sensational matter was published with the sole object of increasing circulation or profit.[7] This liability of the proprietor for contempt committed by the employees of the Press is vicarious.

We have already discussed the relationship between the editor and proprietor of a newspaper. The editor is an employee of the proprietor and the relationship of master and servant subsists between them. The function of the proprietor extends to the laying down the policy of the paper and the appointment of an editor of his choice. The editor is responsible for the selection of the matter to be published in the newspaper.

As owner of the Press, the proprietor has, however, certain liabilities. Thus, when a notice is served by the Statistics Authority upon the proprietor under Section 5 of the Industrial Statistics Act, 1942, the proprietor must, under pain of penalty, furnish such returns or information as may be called for in the notice. He must also allow access to his records and documents to any person authorised by the Authority. This Act applies to all factories and information may be required as to matters relating to the factory and labour conditions therein. Similarly, the proprietor will have the duty to maintain records under Section 18 of the Minimum Wages Act, 1948, if the Act has been extended to the Press. The proprietor of a newspaper will have all the liabilities which are applicable to the owner of a factory.

Printer and Publisher

Under Section 3 of the Press and Registration of Books Act, 1867, the names of the printer and publisher have to be printed on the newspaper. If this obligation is violated, they are liable to be punished under Section 12 of the Act. Under Section 7 to the Act, there is a presumption that a printer or publisher, as the case may be, is the printer or publisher of every

7. Re *Odham's Press* (1956) 1 ALL E.R. 494.

portion of the newspaper. They are, therefore, liable for every item of objectionable matter published in the newspaper.

The printer and publisher are individually as also jointly liable for anything illegally published in the newspaper, e.g., defamation, obscenity, contempt of court, contempt of legislature etc. Even for an advertisement published in newspaper at the instance of an advertiser, the publisher may be liable if the advertisement is defamatory of a third person.

We have discussed in Chapter 4 in detail the individual liability of the printer and the publisher as also their joint liability along with the editor in cases of defamation.

Under the existing law, the printers and publishers stand on the same footing and they are presumed to know what is being printed. But in practice, the printers print the materials given to them without trying to analyse their content. The Faulks Committee which dealt extensively with the question recommended that the defence of innocent dissemination which is available to vendors, news agents etc. should be extended to printers also. The Mathew Commission has suggested that the recommendation of the Faulks Committee with regard to the liability of the printer should be accepted and incorporated into our law. But until the law is changed, the legal liability of the printer in regard to any offending matter will remain on the same footing as that of the publisher.

Disclosure of Sources of Information

The claim of the journalists that they should not be forced to disclose their sources of information raises a question of great practical interest and has been the subject of discussion in all the free democratic countries. Much information is given to the Press under a pledge of confidentiality and the journalist has a moral as well as an ethical duty to protect the anonymity of his source of information. If this confidentiality is not preserved, some sources of information would naturally dry up and much of the information would cease to flow and the journalists would be disabled from performing their legitimate functions.

In investigative journalism in particular, information is supplied to the Press on the clear understanding that the source would not be divulged. Investigative journalism has of late assumed great importance and has generally been beneficial to the public. The Press has brought to light many public scandals and exposed wrong doings which would otherwise have remained concealed. No doubt there is a public interest in ensuring a regular supply of reliable information to the Press and, therefore, its sources of information should not be dried up.

It may be noted here that the Indian Evidence Act gives protection to a lawyer who declines to disclose information given to him by his client in certain circumstances. So also, a communication between husband and wife is placed above enquiry by courts so long as the marriage subsists. By convention, courts respect the confidence which arises between a doctor and his patient, a priest and a penitent and between a banker and his customer. Privilege can be claimed in respect of all such communications. A question arises why should a journalist who seeks to serve the public be required to disclose the source of his information, particularly when he takes the responsibility for its authenticity.

This question arose in U.K. as early as 1888, when a claim for immunity from disclosing the source of information was made on behalf of the Press before the Parnell Commission. But this claim was rejected by Sir James Hannen sitting with two other judges. This question was again considered in 1963 in the two cases arising out of Vassal Inquiry. The question was whether a journalist had any special privilege, under the law, not to disclose the source of his information relating to any matter, analogous to that which exists in the case of confidential relationship between attorney and client, husband and wife etc. and the usual argument was strongly put that if disclosure is ordered in such cases, the source of information would dry up. In both the cases, the claim of the journalists was firmly repelled. Lord Parker expressed the clear opinion in *A. G.* v. *Clough*[8] that no such immunity had been recognised or existed. The same view was taken by the Court of *A. G.* v. *Mutholland* and *A. G.* v. *Fosster*[9] and Lord Denning observed :

"The only profession that I know which is given a privilege from disclosing information to a court of law is the legal profession and then it is not the privilege of the lawyer but of his client. Take the clergyman, the banker or the medical man. None of these is entitled to refuse to answer when directed to by a Judge.... The judge will respect the confidence which each member of these honourable professions receives in the course of it, and will not direct him to answer unless not only it is relevant but also it is a proper and indeed, necessary question in the course of justice to be put and answered. A Judge is a person entrusted, on behalf of the community, to weigh these conflicting interests—to weigh on the one hand the respect due to confidence in the profession and on the other hand, the ultimate interest of the community in justice being done... If the judge determines that the journalist must answer, then no privilege will avail him to refuse."

This question was recently considered by the House of Lords in *British Steel Corporation* v. *Granada Television Ltd.*[10] and the Court held that there is no absolute immunity for journalists from disclosing their sources of information. If the judge considers that disclosure is necessary for doing justice in the case, he has a duty to insist upon the disclosure and the journalist cannot claim any immunity in such cases.

Courts in U.S.A. have been trying to strike a balance between the various public interests involved. While on the one hand, the importance of the Press not being compelled to disclose its source of information is recognised, on the other, the importance of a private individual being in a position to obtain redress for wrongs done to him is also acknowledged.

8. *A.G.* v. *Clough* (1963) 1 Q.B. 773.
9. *A.G.* v. *Mutholland* and *A.G.* v. *Fosster* (1963) 2 Q.B. 477.
10. *British Steel Corporation* v. *Granada Television Ltd.* (1980) 3 W.L.R. 774.

Neither interest overrides the other. A balance has to be struck between the two conflicting interests and each case depends on its own facts. The U.S. Supreme Court has taken the same position as the House of Lords in the *British Steel Corporation* case.

In India, all persons who are competent to be witnesses under Section 118 of the Evidence Act may also be compelled to give evidence and answer relevant questions, unless exempted by law. Such exemptions are contained in :

(i) Section 5 of the Bankers' Books of Evidence Act, 1891;

(ii) Sections 51-52 of the Divorce Act, 1869; and

(iii) Sections 121, 122, 123, 124, 125, 126, 127 and 129 of the Evidence Act.

Hence, under the law, a journalist has no special privilege as to non-disclosure of his source of information. The Press does not enjoy a higher legal status than an ordinary citizen. It enjoys the same rights and shares the same duties which any citizen of the country enjoys. At the same time, it has to be recognised that the Press undoubtedly performs a function of great public importance when it brings to light public scandals. A major function of the Press is to expose public evils. Unless the Press is afforded a privilege about the source of its information, it may well-nigh be impossible for any one to lay these facts before the journalist. Experience of the past has shown that non-disclosure of sources of information has not in any way caused serious harm to society. It is also a fact that the journalist does enjoy certain special privileges. In the legislatures, the journalist has a special enclosure, the Press gallery; he gets invitations for and is provided with a special place to sit in all important meetings; further, he gets priority allotment of a house, telephone connections and so on. These facilities are provided to him because they are essential for enabling him to perform his duties satisfactorily.

On the other hand, all journalists are not paragons of virtue. There have been instances of exposure of scandals

17—TPI

which have turned out to be no scandals at all, but only the prelude to expensive claim for defamation. There have been instances where the fair conduct of criminal trials has been impaired and there have also been instances of grave and un-warranted invasions of privacy.

The courts in adjudicating cases before them shall have to strike a balance between conflicting public interests. A relationship of confidence between a journalist and his source of information is in a different category from confidential relationship between attorney and client or between husband and wife. But this does not involve any principle that such confidence is not to be respected. In all such cases, the court will have to decide on the particular facts and circumstances whether the interest in preserving this confidence is outweighed by other interests to which the law attaches importance.

The Mathew Commission has taken the view that there is no absolute immunity for journalists from disclosing their sources of information. It has, however, taken note of Section 15(2) of the Press Council Act, 1978 which provides that no newspaper, news agency, editor or journalist shall be compelled to disclose the source of any news or information in a proceeding before the Press Council, though it is vested with the same powers as that of a civil court in the matter of receiving evidence and examination of witnesses. The public interest in the free flow of information and hence in protecting a journalist's source of information has to receive wide recognition in our country. The strength of the public interest involved will vary from case to case. The court will have to weigh in each case the public interest in doing justice in a case against the public interest involved in the free flow of information through protection of the confidential source of information. The court may compel the Press to disclose its source of information only when it is absolutely necessary in the interests of justice. This is not a matter of law but of convention and it should normally be followed.

S/Shri Girilal Jain, Rajendra Mathur, S. K. Mukherjea,

H. K. Paranjape and Ishrat Ali Siddiqui do not agree with the above view. They hold that journalists should not be compelled to disclose their sources of information and if they are compelled to do so in extreme cases, they should disclose their sources of information only to the Judge and that too in confidence and any changes in law that may be necessary for this purpose should be made. We do not think that any changes in law are called for.

CHAPTER XI

News Flow : Internal, Regional and International

Communication, which is at the heart of all social inter-courses, thrives only when there is a system of efficient, adequate and equitable arrangement for flow of news within one country and also between various countries and regions of the world. In the early stages of the development of the mass media, particularly of the Press, a good deal of the news was provided by the News Agencies which developed early in the 19th century in the developed western countries and ex-tended their operations on an international scale. The exten-sion and modernisation of these agencies have simultaneously contributed to, and followed, the emergence of the mass circu-lation press by expanding the sources as well as coverage and transmission of news. Rapid technological progress, particu-larly in the past two decades, has revolutionised further the facilities for communication. The recent decade and a half has been particulaily inventive, productive and imaginative. Inter-national satellite systems, application of space technology, use of domestic satellites, lasers, fibre optics, video-cassettes, faci-lities for facsimile transmission, a variety of micro-processors, the invention and use of the silicon chip, binary codes of trans-mission etc. represent significant inputs for more extensive and efficient means for data collection, storage, retrieval and diffu-sion. These new technologies, use of which is at present mainly

260

concentrated in a few developed, industrialised countries, provide a glimpse of the new era in communication.

Internal News Flow

The basic function of a news agency is to survey news and provide news reports of current events to the newspapers and others who subscribe to its service. More broadly, a news agency is "an undertaking of which the principal objective, whatever its legal form, is to gather news and news material with the sole purpose of expressing or presenting facts and distributing it to a group of news enterprises and in exceptional circumstances to private individuals with a view to providing them with as complete and impartial news service as far as possible against payment and under conditions compatible with business terms and usage." Consequently, its news coverage should be fast, complete and accurate, as well as fair, objective and unbiased.

India fortunately is in a much better position in this area than many other developing countries. There are at present four premier wire news agencies in India—apart from a large number of small non-wire, feature and specialised agencies which came into existence mostly in the last one or two decades. The Press Trust of India (PTI) and the United News of India (UNI) disseminate news in English (though UNI has recently started a service in Hindi also). The Hindusthan Samachar and the Samachar Bharati provide their services mainly in Hindi. PTI, which was registered in 1947, started functioning in 1949; the Hindusthan Samachar, in 1948 and was subsequently reorganised in 1957; the UNI, in 1961 and the Samachar Bharati in 1967. All these four agencies are in the private sector. The PTI is registered as a joint-stock company under the Companies Act, 1913. The UNI and the Samachar Bharati are registered under the Companies Act, 1956. The Hindusthan Samachar is registered as a co-operative society. A brief description of the history, organisation and operations of these four agencies is given next.

Press Trust of India

The Press Trust of India, sponsored by seven newspapers of India as a Joint Stock Company in August, 1947, started operations on 1.2.1949. At the time of its formation, it took over the business of the Associated Press of India (API), a subsidiary of Reuters. The Agency began as a non-profit venture. According to the Memorandum and the Articles of Association of the Company, shareholding is restricted to newspapers regularly published in India which subscribe to its services. The shareholders are not paid any dividend, the income being invested solely on the promotion of professional activities originally set out for it. Its Constitution also provides that the control shall at no time pass into the hands of any interests, group or section. It is interesting to note that with the liquidation of the United Press of India in 1958, PTI was left as the sole English News Agency in the country for about 3 years till 1961 when UNI started functioning.

The agency is administered under the supervision of a General Manager and a Board of 14 Directors. A Chairman is elected annually. The Agency's administrative headquarters are in Bombay but the news operations are carried out from Delhi. The agency, when it took over the business from Associated Press of India, inherited 30,000 km. of teleprinter lines. This network has now grown to about 60,000 km. It has, in addition, teleprinter links with Dhaka and Islamabad and satellite links with important news centres of Asia, Europe as well as Latin America, viz. Jakarta, Kuala Lumpur, Colombo, Bahrain, Moscow, Belgrade and Havana. The Agency functions round the clock and puts out on an average of 1,00,000 words every day of which 40% (approx.) is international news including reports of its own correspondents abroad.

PTI has over 1100 employees, including 193 Staff Correspondents and 90 Teleprinter bureaux all over the country. It employs 297 part-time correspondents or stringers. It has full time correspondents in 11 important world cities including New York, London, Moscow, Beijing, Kuala Lumpur, Nairobi, Islamabad, Kathmandu, Colombo, Dhaka and Bahrain. In addition, there are part-tive correspondents filing stories from

19 foreign news centres. It subscribes to three international news agencies, viz. Reuter, AFP and the UPI. In addition, it gets foreign news from a host of other national and inter-regional news agencies.

PTI offers to its clients three classes of services—'A', 'B' and 'C'. The 'A' Service is the most comprehensive consisting of about one lakh words daily. The 'B' Service is about 60 per cent of 'A' Service, and 'C', about forty per cent. In addition, PTI has a General Service for small newspapers. It also offers some Special Services to its clients. The Economic Service is intended for institutional subscribers other than newspapers. The Feature Service gives an account of important events placing them in their national and international context. The Money Service gives all important news about the international money market and is meant for banks and financial institutions. It has recently introduced a News-Scan Service and plans to start a photo service.

PTI has at present over 1,000 subscribers of which newspapers account for over 25 per cent. The subscription rate to the newspaper organisation is dependent upon the class of service offered to it by the Agency.

The basic subscription for an English Newspaper with a circulation of 10,000 for the 'A' Class Service is Rs. 8,400 per month. The subscription charged by the Agency from non-newspaper organisations is at the rate of Rs. 2,000 per month inclusive of rental for teleprinter machines.

United News of India

The First Press Commission's Report had spoken of the need to have at least two news agencies each competing with the other and also acting as a corrective on the other. The newspapers shared this feeling in the wake of the collapse of United Press of India in 1958. The UNI was sponsored by eight newspapers and started its operations in 1961. From a modest start, the UNI expanded substantially within the last two decades. It has 64 teleprinter Bureaux in the country, with 60,000 km. (approx.) of teleprinter lines. The total wordage put out on an average every day is 1,00,000 (approx.) on a round the clock basis.

The administrative headquarters of this agency are located at Delhi. It has a staff strength of about 550. The agency employs full-time and part-time correspondents for its news gathering operations. The number of full-time correspondents deployed by UNI is 164, who are posted at 43 Centres spread over the country. The total number of part-time correspondents servicing the agency is 199.

The agency offers a uniform service to its subscribers, as against the three categories of Service offered by PTI. However, UNI has more newspaper subscribers than PTI. PTI, on the other hand, has twice as many government subscribers (including semi-government and autonomous bodies) as UNI. Also UNI has more non-government, non-newspaper subscribers than PTI. UNI also offers a number of special services to its clients. The UNI Economic Service provides economic information for the use of banks, financial institutions and business houses. The UNI Agricultural Service is meant for, among others, researchers, educational institutions and Panchayats as well as newspapers. The UNI Backgrounder Service is meant for educational institutions, business houses, Government departments as well as newspapers. The UNI Energy Service is meant for mass media and institutions dealing with energy problems. The UNI Financial News Service is a teleprinter service for economic dailies, banks and financial institutions. It has also recently started a Hindi Service.

The agency has, like PTI, based its subscription rates on the circulation of a newspaper. It is pertinent to note that the subscription rates were substantially increased both by PTI and UNI in March, 1981 to meet the additional expenditure to be incurred as a result of the Palekar Award. The basic subscription for UNI in the case of an English newspaper with a circulation of up to 10,000 has recently gone up by 41 per cent from Rs. 1,845 to Rs. 2,600. The surcharge on every additional circulation of 2,500 copies over 10,000 copies has been increased from Rs. 127 to Rs. 180. The new rates include the rental of the teleprinter machine.

Hindusthan Samachar

India's first multi-lingual agency, Hindusthan Samachar, was set up by Shri S. S. Apte as a private limited company in 1948. Its avowed aim was to educate the masses and to strive for the promotion of all Indian languages. The early effort was limited to the distributing of news amongst the newspapers in Bombay, Delhi, Patna and Nagpur through Devanagri telegrams. With the advent of Devanagri teleprinters in 1957, the situation improved but the heavy transmission costs forced Shri Apte to hand over the agency to a co-operative society of employees. In 1957, it became a society called the Hindusthan Samachar Co-operative Society.

The administrative headquarters of the society are located in Delhi. Hindusthan Samachar has 54 teleprinter bureaux and 5 other units. The total length of teleprinter lines is about 25,000 kms. The agency functions for 14 hours a day and turns out about 48,000 words daily. The agency has about 250 employees, 134 of whom are journalists. It employs full-time as well as part-time correspondents for its news gathering operations throughout the country. The total number of full-time correspondents deployed by the agency at the beginning of 1981 was 134. These correspondents are posted at 37 centres throughout the country. The total number of stringers appointed by Hindusthan Samachar is stated to be about 400.

Hindusthan Samachar provides teleprinter service in Hindi, Marathi, Nepali, Gujarati, Oriya and Kannada. Gujarati and Oriya subscribers take the service in the Devanagri script. The Kannada service in the Roman script is taken by the Karnataka Government. Some Malayalam, Telugu, Urdu, Bengali, Punjabi, Oriya and Kannada papers subscribe to non-teleprinter services in type-written or hand-written sheets. There are no fixed subscription rates. The rates are fixed through negotiations. However, since March, 1981, Hindusthan Samachar rates have been increased by 20 per cent for newspaper subscribers and 30 per cent for non-newspaper subscribers.

It may be pertinent to mention that the Managing Committee of Hindusthan Samachar was superseded and an Administrator appointed as per Section 32 of the Delhi Co-operative Societies Act, 1972, by the Registrar of Co-operative Societies, Delhi in May, 1982.

Samachar Bharati

The second language news agency, Samachar Bharati, was registered in 1966 under the Companies Act, 1956 and commenced operations in 1967. In 1970, four State Governments namely, the Governments of Bihar, Gujarat, Rajasthan and Karnataka purchased more than 50 per cent of its shares.

The administrative headquarters of the agency are located in Delhi. It has 35 teleprinter bureaux and 10 other Units. It utilises some 25,000 kms. of teleprinter lines. The agency operates for 18 hours a day and turns out about 48,000 words daily on an average. It has about 240 employees on its rolls, 109 of whom are journalists. It has also employed full-time and part-time correspondents to help it for its news gathering operations. 94 full-time correspondents are posted at 28 centres throughout the country. The number of stringers appointed by the agency is reported to be 400.

Samachar Bharati's main services are in Hindi. It also provides services in Gujarati, Marathi, Punjabi, Urdu, Telugu Kannada, Malayalam and Tamil using Hindi as the link language. The agency charges a uniform rate of Rs. 1250 per month from newspapers and non-newspaper organisations alike.

It is apparent from the brief overview above that the Indian news agencies have come a long way since their modest beginning and have widened and improved their coverage and transmission of news. However, a number of deficiencies— organisational, functional and financial—still remain as impediments to their providing an even better service. The Second Press Commission in its recent report has drawn pointed attention to this aspect. However, before we examine these issues in the context of the Press Commission's suggestions, we might briefly recall an interesting episode in the structure and working of our news agencies.

The four news agencies mentioned above were merged

together on February 1, 1976 into one news agency, called "Samachar." This agency was expected to collect and disseminate news both within the country and abroad. Subsequently, in March, 1977, Government appointed an expert committee under the Chairmanship of Shri Kuldip Nayar, an eminent journalist, to examine the functioning of Samachar taking into consideration various aspects like freedom of the Press, independence of news agencies, and the possibility of a competitive service being freely available to all users.

This Committee recommended that Samachar should be dissolved and re-structured by the creation of two news agencies—'Varta' and 'Sandesh'. These in their turn should jointly set up an organisation for international news services which may be called 'News India.' News India would buy foreign agency services and make them available to subscribers of Varta and Sandesh.

While Varta was suggested as a news agency to organise and develop news services in Indian languages, along with an English service, Sandesh was visualized as an exclusively English news agency. News India was not to be a separate news agency as such but would be financed and managed in partnership by the two agencies jointly. News India was to have a monopoly in foreign news. The Committee also recommended that an interim body be set up by the Government to bring about the reorganisation within a period of three months.

The acceptance of the Kuldip Nayar Committee report, it was argued by the critics, would have created three monopoly news agencies—one each in the field of English language, Indian languages, and international news service.

In fact, the critics argued that each would be a monopoly in its field—News India in foreign news, Sandesh in English news at home and Varta in news in Indian languages. There could hardly be any competition between Sandesh and Varta, because Sandesh would be only in English and, therefore, would necessarily have to resort to time-consuming translation at each major centre. The set-up would not have the merit of competition. Also, if the Government had to make up the budget deficit of Rs. 1.7 crores every year in respect of the proposed three agencies, the agencies would hardly enjoy any independence.

The Government of India decided in November, 1977 not to accept the recommendations of the Kuldip Nayar Committee. It decided to undo the merger and restore *status quo ante* prior to the merger. The Government, however, agreed to protect the higher emoluments drawn by the employees during the Samachar period by providing grant-in-aid on a tapering basis for six years. The previous names were restored and the agencies started functioning separately from 15th August, 1978. Presumably, the considerations which weighed with Government were the need to restore the credibility of the news agencies and to reintroduce an element of competitiveness in their operations. One may recall in this context the perceptive remarks of the First Press Commission in 1954 : "However objective a news agency strives to be, there are certain drawbacks which arise from monopoly and which could be obviated only by competitive service available freely to all users." Taking into account the performance of 'Samachar' during its short existence and the essential requirement of ensuring credibility of news agencies, the decision of the Government seems to be on sound lines.

The Second Press Commission has in its recent report reviewed the organisational adequacy and functional efficiency of Indian news agencies. It has recognised the need for encouragement and expansion of the useful role the small non-wire, feature and specialised agencies are playing. At the same time, it has brought out the continuing deficiencies of the premier wire agencies, particularly with regard to the content and quality of coverage, urban bias in reporting, small capital base, restricted shareholding, managerial and financial weaknesses as well as lack of modern technology. Further, in their view, "the development of a first rate news service in Indian language brooks no further delay."[1] They have suggested in this context that if none of the existing agencies comes forward with a viable scheme, "we would like to see the Indian

1. *Second Press Commission Report*, Vol. I, Chap. XI, para 50.

language newspapers in different parts of the country taking the initiative to form a news agency which will offer an efficient service in Indian languages."[2] If this does not materialise, the majority view of the Press Commission is for setting up a statutory corporation for the purpose.

The Second Press Commission is on strong ground in highlighting the functional weaknesses and operational inadequacies of the four premier wire news agencies. As regards coverage, none of the four agencies has a full-time correspondent in 350 out of the 405 district headquarters in the country. Four Union Territories also fall in the same category. Reliance on part-time correspondent (stringers) for coverage from these areas is very often unsatisfactory as they lack professional skill, expertise and facilities. As a consequence, quality reporting from rural areas of development news or social changes is virtually non-existent. The financial weakness of the news agencies prevents them from acquiring more teleprinter links or telecommunication facilities. These hindrances as well as the concentration of correspondents in selected metropolitan and urban areas leads inevitably to an "urban bias" in news coverage.

The Commission's stress on removing the financial constraints and making the news agencies economically viable primarily through their own efforts is welcome. There is force in the criticism that subscription rates charged from big newspapers are on the low side and the Commission has commented "that the big newspapers are in a position to pay much more."[3] There is also some room for more liberal payments from AIR and Doordarshan for utilisation of their services. Further, in all the four news agencies, the subscribed capital is far below the authorised capital, which itself is not very large. Expansion of their capital base through a larger spread of shareholding particularly among small and medium papers (for which a vigorous effort as well as will on the part of the newspaper industry to help are prerequisites) would certainly help

2. *Second Press Commission Report*, Vol. I, Chap. XI, para 50.
3. *Second Press Commission Report*, Vol. I, Ch. XI, para 29.

the agencies to secure more long-term credit from the banks and financial institutions for technological innovations and the much needed modernisation. However, in this context, the suggestion, *inter alia*, of the Commission that to ensure 'public accountability,' the board of directors of each wire agency should have "a director jointly nominated by the Speaker, Lok Sabha and the Chairman, Rajya Sabha (who need not necessarily be a Member of Parliament)"[4] appears to be rather impractical as well as undesirable. Such a step would certainly impair the credibility of the news agencies and detract from their professional efficiency. The ultimate accountability of news agencies is (and should continue to be) to their end users, *i.e.*, the newspapers and the general reading public and they should continue to be tested on the touchstones of impartiality, objectivity, fairness and credibility.

The Commission's view regarding the pattern of future development of English and the language news agencies deserves careful examination. Given the present stage of development of PTI and the UNI, their fund of professional skill and expertise and organisation as well as potential for their expansion, we may accept the Commission's recommendation that for providing news services in English, "the present position in which PTI and UNI offer competing services"[5] be left undisturbed. This would also be appropriate for preserving their professional independence and credibility in a country like ours.

However, the Commission seems to be on weaker ground when they recommend in their majority view (as stated earlier), the formation of a new news agency to offer an efficient service in Indian languages. The basic premise is that "as regards the provision of news services in Indian languages, opinion tendered before the Commission has been unanimous that the services now provided by the two Indian language agencies are quite inadequate, both quantitatively and qualitatively."[6] It is true that both the existing language

4. *Second Press Commission Report*, Vol. I, Ch. XI, para 59.
5. *Second Press Commission Report*, Vol. I, Ch. XI, para 47.
6. *Second Press Commission Report*, Vol. I, Ch. XI, para 49.

agencies (Hindusthan Samachar and Samachar Bharati) are much smaller in size, quality and coverage compared to the two news agencies in English (PTI and UNI). Their financial position is also much weaker. None of them seems to be in a position to attract large-scale infusion of fresh capital which is so vital not only for their expansion but even for their continuation as efficient viable units. However, in our view, the remedy does not necessarily lie in forming a fresh language agency either through cooperation from the language papers or even on a statutory basis. In all likelihood, any such news agency would founder on the same rock of financial weakness, paucity of professional skills and the absence of modern technology and necessary facilities. A statutory cooperation would have the added disadvantage of starting its activities in the face of legitimate reservations about its "credibility."

A more pragmatic alternative might be to encourage both PTI and the UNI to convert themselves gradually to multilingual agencies. UNI has already taken a step recently in this direction by introducing a Hindi service (UNIVARTA). PTI is reported to be thinking of introducing language services also. Taking into account their existing infrastructure both in terms of hardware, professional skills and managerial expertise, introduction of multilingual service would be easier as well as financially more viable for these two agencies. To start with, the cost of collection as well as overheads would be lower through utilisation of the existing network for gathering and dissemination of news. It would also be easier for them to secure the necessary capital infusion and long-term credits for acquisition of hardware as well as trained manpower. In the long run, this would add to their viability and potential for further expansion on a planned and sustained basis.

Regional and International news flow

The brief survey about the national scene has revealed the existence of distinct gaps in news flow in qualitative as well as quantitative terms even within the country—between rural and urban areas, between political, spot news and developmental stories etc. Such imbalances are even more pronounced

in the flow of information and news between the developing
countries of the Third World and the industrialised developed countries on the one hand and between the developing
countries themselves on the other. Such disparities persist even
today though the past decade has witnessed the setting up as
well as the expansion of news agencies in a number of developing countries. It would be relevant to recall here that the
late sixties and seventies had witnessed a raging controversy
about the inadequate, imbalanced and unfair flow of news between the developed and the developing countries. The demand
for a New World Information and Communication Order
emerged out of this prolonged, stormy and often acrimonious
debate and was ultimately accepted by the world community.

A few examples illustrate the point. According to the
information cited in the Report by the Internnational Commission for the study of Communication Problems (UNESCO
1980) popularly known as the MacBride Commission after its
Chairman, "..... A.P. (Associated Press of USA) sends out
its general world wire service to Asia from New York an average of 90,000 words daily. In return, Asia files 19,000 words
to New York for worldwide distribution. UPI's (United Press
International, USA) general news wire service from New York
to Asia totals some 100,000 words and the file from all points
in Asia to New York varies between 40,000 to 45,000 daily...
AFP's (Associated France Press, France) service from Paris
to Asia is 30,000 strong. In addition, some 8,000 words are
collected in Asia and distributed within the region to Asian
clients. The same 8,000 words file is sent back to Paris for
incorporation into other world services of AFP. The flow of
news is uneven in that a lot more is sent from London or New
York to Asia than the other way round. Although the feed
from the West is supposed to contain news of the rest of the
world, it is heavily weighted in favour of news from North
America and West Europe.[7] The same is true of developing

7. *Many Voices, One World*—Report by the International Commission
    for the study of Communication Problems (UNESCO, 1980)
    p. 146(f.n.)

countries in Latin America and other parts of the Third World.

It is against this sombre background that we have to appreciate the continuing efforts by the developing countries to correct the imbalances in the so-called 'one way flow' of news and information through various international forums including the United Nations, the UNESCO and the Non-Aligned Movement. Some of the important developments in this context are, in chronological order :

(i) Adoption of the Declaration on Fundamental Principles concerning the contribution of the Mass Media to the strengthening of Peace and International Understanding, the promotion of Human Rights and to countering Racialism, Apartheid and Incitement to War at the twentieth Session of the General Conference of UNESCO in Paris in 1978. This was followed up in the 21st General Conference at Belgrade in 1980 with a resolution calling upon the Director-General to present *inter alia* a detailed implementation report before the next (1983) General Conference.

(ii) The submission of the final report of the MacBride Commission to Director-General, UNESCO in early 1980 and the detailed discussion on its recommendations in the twentyfirst Session of the General Conference of UNESCO in Belgrade, in 1980 leading to the adoption of a consensus resolution on the relevant issues. This Resolution, *inter alia*, lays down the basic factors on which the New World Information & Communication Order might be based.

(iii) The setting up of the International Programme for the Development of Communication (IPDC) under the aegis of UNESCO in the 21st General Conference in October, 1980. An Inter-governmental Council consisting of 35 elected member states of which India is one has also been created to supervise its activities. The IPDC would draw up projects

and programmes for the communication systems in
Member-States, giving particular attention to the
special needs of each developing country. To start
with, the IPDC had a budget of US $ 1.75 million
appropriated by UNESCO.

It is accepted today that the most important result of the
whole debate is "the wider recognition of the implicit flaws
in the "free flow" concept as well as of the fact that in the present day world, preconditions have to be created for the implementation of a real free flow of information, if a generous principle is not to continue as an advantage for the few and a
detriment for many on both national and international levels."[8]
As a result, some encouraging concrete initiatives have
already been taken or are being taken : (a) arrangements between News Agencies and Broadcasting organisations in developing or non-aligned countries for wider dissemination of
news from and about them viz. Non-Aligned News Agencies
Pool; (b) increased interest by some major newspapers and
news agencies in industrialised countries to collect and publish
news and reports on socio-economic issues from developing
countries; (c) suggestions for the creation of resource centres
(for exchange of news, television programmes, films etc.) in
Africa and Asia; (d) the growing regional co-operation among
News Agencies and broadcasters and programmes for establishing regional exchange arrangements, viz. Asia Pacific
News Network, Pan African News Agency etc.; (e) the agreement between sixteen important newspapers in different parts
of the developed and developing world, to produce a common
quarterly newspaper supplement featuring views regarding
the New International Economic Order; (f) increasing efforts
by international and professional organisations and media of
industrialised nations to augment technical and educational
cooperation for communication development; (g) the setting
up of the International Programme for Development of Communication (IPDC) under the aegis of UNESCO (referred
to earlier) to draw up plans and formulate projects in the

8. *Many Voices, One World* (UNESCO, 1980) p. 143.

communication sector for developing countries; and (h) inter-professional meetings and seminars on such topics as implementation of and links between the New Economic and Communication Orders.

Among these hopeful developments, the setting up of the Non-Aligned News Agencies Pool in 1976, and the emerging regional organisations of news agencies, viz. Asia Pacific News Network (ANN) and the Pan African News Agency (PANA) deserve slightly more detailed examination to show, if nothing else, how difficult it is to transform the present order and implement in practice the free flow of information.

From a modest beginning in 1976, the Non-Aligned News Agencies Pool has steadily expanded its operations. There are at present about 80 participating news agencies from developing countries of four continents with an average daily output of 50,000 words. The Pool does not aim at supplanting the existing multinational news agencies of developed countries but seeks simply to supplement their service. From its point of view, exchange of developmental news and feature articles and visuals depicting the experience of each Pool partner is of utmost importance so that the non-aligned developinng countries might be better informed about themselves and learn from the experience of one another. The Pool members have also been persistent in their efforts to remove two major hindrances, namely, building up professional skills and improving telecommunication facilities for ensuring larger acceptance of its despatches by the Press in the developed countries. Five Institutes of Journalism/communication at New Delhi, Belgrade, Cairo, Tunis and Havana have introduced special courses in "News Agency Journalism." In fact, the Indian Institute of Mass Communication (IIMC), New Delhi, has already trained in this course 105 foreign students from 91 countries over five years. A Style Book has also been finalised by the Press Trust of India (the Pool participant from India) in collaboration with the IIMC, New Delhi, to help the Pool Desk news editors to give a distinct character to the Pool news. However, the emphasis is not on "Spot news" but on "developmental news." Regular exchange of impact reports among the participating agencies is also being attempted. For ensuring faster transmission and dissemination of news, reduction of the existing tariff structure and establishment of more and more satellite links are urgent necessities. Only a few countries like Sri Lanka and India have so far introduced the concessional Press Bulletin Service and have taken advantage, albeit in a very modest way, of satellite transmission.

The UNESCO has in recent years encouraged the growth of regional organisation of news agencies like OANA (Organisation of Asian News Agencies), ANN (Asia Pacific News Network), PANA (Pan African News Agency), FANA (Federation of Arab News Agencies) and the CANA (Caribbean News Agencies) as complementary to the establishment of the New World Information and Communication Order. The Non-Aligned News Agencies Pool (which is an international news exchange arrangement) has also endorsed this move and resolved to support regional and sub-regional news exchange arrangements and decided to coordinate news exchange with these organisations in the interest of avoiding duplication and overlapping of efforts.

One example of such regional news exchange is the Asia Pacific News Network (ANN) which was launched on January 1, 1982. 24 news agencies of the region are members of the network. All countries of Asia are represented (except Papua, New Guinea, Singapore and Maldive Islands which have no news agencies). The network is based, like the Non-Aligned News Agencies Pool, on the principle of self-reliance and pooling of expertise and reports for mutual benefit. Each participating news agency is to contribute daily up to a maximum of ten minutes' transmission or two or three items of major news value. Redistribution Centres (of which New Delhi is one) are expected to pass on this traffic without editing to the agencies connected with them. During the first year of its existence, ANN has registered considerable progress and overcome a number of initial problems. The effort is now on to activate the relatively weaker member agencies through infrastructural support and training assistance.

A very brief glance at PTI's experience as a participating news agency in the Non-Aligned News Agency Pool (and also in ANN) illustrates vividly the importance of both professional expertise and faster transmission in securing greater acceptability in the developed countries. Till the end of 1980, when PTI satellite links came into operation, Pool transmission used to be done entirely by wireless through the overseas communication service. The reception as well as transmission were largely dependent on uncertain weather conditions. The daily average volume of outflow of news pool was a meagre 300 to 500 words. However, with the commissioning of 7 satellite links between November, 1980 and July, 1981, the volume of outflow of Pool news increased significantly to about 8,500 words in November, 1982 transmitted simultaneously to all the Pool participants. The receipt from other Pool members also almost doubled—from 15,000 words per day to about 28,000 words per day. Switching over to satellite links has also reduced the time for news to travel to the editorial desks in the receiving agencies. This enhanced considerably the prospect of Pool news being accepted by the media in the receiving countries. Available reports show that Indian Pool news is getting published in increasing volume in the newspapers of the receiving countries. In fact, the Pool service during the recent Asian Games had a most encouraging response. This has also been the outcome of diligent efforts over a period of time to improve the professional input.

It has also been noticed that while the incoming Pool stories continue to be predominantly political in nature, PTI is endeavouring to change the character of Pool news outflow by emphasising the transmission of economic and developmental news. However, both in volume and nature of service, there is considerable scope for improvement. Although time for news transmission has been reduced because of introduction of satellite links and better telecommunication facilities, its actual utilisation is still limited. Utilisaton of the service by the foreign media is to some extent linked with the difficulties of translation into another language. The answer to this problem will lie in the direction of transmission of Pool news in the languages predominantly used in the Pool member countries, e.g., French, Spanish and Arabic. Such changes will of course require considerable efforts as well as investment over a period of time.

The conclusion which emerges from the brief overview above is that quantitatively as well as qualitatively, imbalances in news flow persist at different levels and in different forms. This may be between developed and the developing countries so far as the news flow is governed by the existence or non-existence of appropriate infrastructure. It also exists between the developing countries themselves and also between various regions within the same country. There is no single universal criterion by which to measure these imbalances and disparities since news values differ from one country to another and sometimes even from one region to another within same country. It is also apparent that the concrete steps so far initiated in this direction, have not been able to make much of a dent in the existing situation. However, these efforts must continue and be reinforced by providing better professional inputs as well as up-dated technological facilities as the present situation cannot continue without detriment both to international understanding and to cooperation between nations.

CHAPTER XII

Review of the Working of the Press in India

Ever since the publication of the first newspaper in India in 1780, the Indian Press has passed through many political vicissitudes during the last two centuries and it has been steadily growing. In 1981, there were 1,264 daily newspapers as against 1,173 in the previous year. The circulation of dailies improved by 5 per cent in 1981 as compared to the circulation in 1980 and touched the figure of 15.25 million copies. There were 17,782 periodicals in 1981, including monthlies, weeklies, fortnightlies, quarterlies, annuals, bi-monthlies, half-yearlies etc. The total circulation of the periodicals in 1981 was 35.7 million copies. The circulation of the Indian Press, including dailies and periodicals, advanced to 51.1 million copies in 1981 from 50.9 million copies in 1980, showing a modest increase of 0.4 per cent.

The newspapers in India are still in the embryo as compared to those in the developed countries. They have a far smaller reach as yet compared to what is necessary in a democracy and the quality of our newspapers also leaves much to be desired. In 1979, the Japanese *Yomiuri Shimbun* sold over 13 million copies per day in a nation just over 110 million. In Britain, with a population of 55 million, the *Sun* sells 4 million copies per day. Many such instances may be cited; but these should suffice. The level of circulation of newspapers in other western countries is also equally high. In India, with a population of 68 crores, there is not a single newspaper which can expect to reach the target of even one million copies per day. There are only three multi-edition dailies which have a circulation of about 5 lakhs copies per day. They are the *Times of India* published from Bombay, Delhi and Ahmedabad, *Malayala Manorama* published from Calicut, Cochin and Kottayam and the *Indian Express* from 10 different centres. We have been complaining of a population explosion in our country and since Independence there has been an accelerated advance in education and eradication of illiteracy. This should naturally tend towards what one might call a readership explosion but that is significantly absent. There has no doubt been slight improvement in the level of circulation, but the total circulation of all the newspapers put together is pitifully low, not merely compared to that in other countries but also compared to what one might expect in the circumstances prevailing in our country.

Readership Research

If the Indian Press has to play its expected role of informing, educating and entertaining the public and of moulding public opinion, it is imperative that there should be expansion of circulation at all levels—big, medium and small newspapers and the quality of the newspapers should also be improved. It is necessary, therefore, to analyse and diagnose the causes for the inadequate growth of the Indian Press. Is it that the Press as a whole or in greater part is lacking in readership appeal ? Is it a case that the public are indifferent to what is happening in the country ? Is it a case where the price of a newspaper is too high for the readers for whom it is designed to cater ? This involves an informed readership research which we believe would be worthwhile for the Press Council to undertake.

Mathew Commission

The Indian Press suffers from many ailments. The Second Press Commission in its voluminous report which was placed before Parliament on 5th November, 1982, has made as many as 278 recommendations. Though the report is voluminous, the Commission has not adequately dealt with certain important problems affecting the Press. The Commission has not also spoken in one voice. The Commission consisted of a Chairman and 10 other members. Out of them, 4 members have append-ed a long joint minute of dissent. The area of difference is large and the dissenting members do not subscribe to the views expounded and to most of the major recommendations of the Commission. Two other members have also submitted a minute of dissent on certain particular issues. The recommendations of the Commission were not very well received by the Press either. While placing the report before Parliament, Govern-ment did not clearly indicate its reactions to the various re-commendations. A Committee of Ministers has been set up to consider the recommendations of the Commission and its report is (at the time of writing) still awaited. We have, however, discussed all the major recommendations of the Commission in the preceding Chapters.

Freedom of the Press

At the outset a pertinent question arises whether the Press in India is free and independent. Freedom of the Press has been guaranteed by the Constitution under article 19(1) (a). We have, however, seen earlier that the freedom which the Press enjoys in this country is not higher than what a citizen enjoys. There is at present no central repressive Press law directed against the Press. But in a civilised society, free-dom of the Press cannot be absolute or unfettered. Restrictions may be placed on freedom of the Press under clause (2) of article 19. The economic and business aspects of the Press may be regulated under clause (6) of that article. Restrictions may be imposed on the Press during an Emergency. There are various general laws which affect the Press and we have dis-cussed them in Chapter 4. Contempt of Court and privileges of Parliament put further restrictions on the Press. We have seen earlier that the laws and restrictions, though numerous, are not such as have impeded the exercise of freedom by the

Press. It is sometimes alleged that the Government exercises executive control over the Press through its advertisement policy and newsprint policy. These policies are published from time to time and by and large, they are objectively implemented.

Press (Objectionable Matter) Act, 1951

In the very nature of things, conflict between the Government and the Press may easily arise in any democracy and, within limits, there is nothing alarming in it. Mutual criticism is useful, healthy and beneficial to both the Press and the Government in the performance of their respective roles. Soon after Independence, a certain tension started emerging between the Government and the Press. This led to the enactment of the Press (Objectionable Matter) Act, 1951. This was an Act with adequate safeguards and no action could be taken against the Press except after a judicial inquiry. This Act was seldom used and never misused. In the beginning, the usual noises about its being a black Act were no doubt made, but in retrospect no one would say that the Government had any authoritarian designs; even unconscious ones. Even while piloting the Bill, Rajaji visualised the appointment of a Press Council which will look after all matters relating to the Press. He observed : ''At some future time, I know the organised Press will frame its own code of professional ethics and discipline and appoint its own Council of discipline and ask for statutory powers to execute its decisions regarding breaches of discipline, regardless of whether one is a member of the organisation or keeps out of it, as in the case of the Bar Council or the Medical Council.... I think that the Press organisation will certainly be able to get these powers and then the Bill may be torn and thrown out into the waste paper basket.'' This was a temporary Act and was allowed to lapse in February, 1956 and was formally repealed by a subsequent Repealing Act, of 1957. Later, the Press Council Act was enacted in 1965.

Newspaper (Price and Page) Act and Newsprint Policy

The Government made two valiant attempts in the past

to control what it conceived to be the monopolistic tendencies in the Press, first by enacting the Newspaper (Price and Page) Act, 1956 and then by promulgating the newsprint policy for 1972-73. They were not intended to interfere with the freedom of the Press but to prevent unfair competition among newspapers by controlling prices and pages. In both cases, the Supreme Court held that they would affect the circulation of newspapers and would be violative of article 19(1)(a) and struck them down. We have earlier discussed these cases. Later, the Government enacted Newspaper (Price Control) Act, 1972 to enable it to fix the maximum prices which may be charged by newspapers. This Act was never implemented, and in course of time lapsed.

Effect of Emergency on the Press

Emergency provisions have far reaching effects on the Press. Under article 358 as originally enacted, there was automatic suspension of fundamental rights guaranteed by article 19, whenever a Proclamation of Emergency was issued. It has now been provided by the 44th Amendment that such automatic suspension will take place only when the Proclamation is issued either on the ground of war or external aggression. This means that when a Proclamation is issued on the ground of armed rebellion, article 358 will not be automatically attracted but it would be possible to suspend article 19 by issuing a Presidential order under article 359. Three such Proclamations have so far been issued. The first Proclamation was issued in the wake of the Chinese aggression on 26 October, 1962 and it was revoked by a subsequent proclamation on January 10, 1968. The second Proclamation was issued on December 3, 1971 when Pakistan launched an undeclared war against India. While the second Proclamation was still in force, a third Proclamation of Emergency on the ground of 'internal disturbance' was issued on June 25, 1975. The second and third Proclamations were revoked on March 21, 1977. During an Emergency, the Government has vast powers to control the Press and impose censorship. But during the first two Emergencies when the Government was engaged in an armed conflict with China and Pakistan, the Government did not take any steps to interfere with the freedom of the Press. The entire nation and the Press were behind the Government and the Press also, on its part, exhibited a unity of purpose and exercised commendable restraint in presenting news and views. There was no necessity to control the Press. It is true that after the Chinese aggression, the Indian Press for the first time became critical of the Himalayan policy of the Government but Nehru, liberal to the core, never resented the Press criticisms, because he himself had suffered a great disappointment. It was only during the internal Emergency imposed in June 1975 that censorship was imposed. Government seldom undertook the task of pre-censoring any newspaper but a set of guidelines was issued whose breach was to be censured and penalised.

It cannot be denied that there have been occasions where some newspapers have conducted themselves without a proper sense of responsibility. There are instances of aberration when the Government became critical of the Press. But there is no repressive law to discipline the Press and, by and large, the Indian Press enjoys freedom to an extent which very few democratic countries have. Speaking on the subject, Mudholkar, J. the first Chairman of the Press Council in his Tagore Law Lectures observed : "It is well known that India, like Japan, is one of the few countries in which the freedom of the Press is the maximum when compared with other democratic countries of the world."[1] Lord Lane, Lord Chief Justice of England, commenting on the Press in India observed :

"They are marvellous, easy to read and critical when criticism is called for. You can't ask for more."[2] The International Press Institute, however, in its annual report for the year 1982 observes that the Press freedom deteriorated worldwide this year and almost every nation violated free speech "in one form or another." It has accused Britain and U.S.A. also for curbing Press freedom and restrictions ranged from official attempts to withhold information or mislead reporters.

1.   Mudholkar, J., *Press Law* (Tagore Law Lectures), p. 108.
2,   Lord Lane, See *Statesman*, October 25, 1982.

The review, however, praised Indian newspapers for jointly fighting an attempt by the Bihar Government to outlaw publication of anything the authorities consider objectionable. The campaign is an object lesson of what can be achieved if the Press speaks with one voice and is firm in its resolve. The Institute Director Mr. Pater Galliner, however, in an introduction to the report singled out certain countries including India as nations with already poor records which slid down further in the scale of freedom in 1982. We are unable to accept the assessment of Mr. Galliner in regard to the Indian Press. Except for a short period during Internal Emergency which is in the nature of an exception, the Indian Press has always been free of State control and could and did criticise the Government and gave prominence to opposition views. The author discussed the matter with several journalists and they are of the view that there is no interference by the Government with freedom of discussion but there have been occasions when there was interference from proprietors of newspapers. Mr. D. R. Mankekar, a veteran journalist ably sums up the position when he says that the Indian Press as a whole may be free but it is not independent.[3]

The Bihar Press Bill

It is now necessary to refer briefly to the Bihar Press Bill which has generated a great deal of heat and strong wave of opposition and protest throughout the country. The proposed legislation is not in the form of a separate Press Bill. The so-called Bihar Press Bill seeks to amend I.P.C. and Cr.P.C. by inserting a new Section 292A in both the Codes. Section 292A I.P.C. provides that the publication in a newspaper of any matter which is grossly indecent or is scurrilous or intended for blackmail would be an offence which will be punishable on first conviction with imprisonment of either description for a term which may extend to two years or with fine or with both, and in the event of a second or subsequent conviction, with imprisonment of either description for a term

---

3. See D. R. Mankekar, an article *Free Not Independent* in the book "What ails the Indian Press."

which may extend to five years and also with fine. It further provides that for a second or any subsequent conviction, the minimum sentence should be imprisonment for six months and also fine. An offence under this section is committed not only by the printer and publisher of the newspaper but also by the agent, distributor, vendor and also by every person who is even remotely connected with the publication of the offending newspaper. Even a person possessing the offending document would be liable. This is too large a sweep. The only safeguard provided is that a competent court will not take cognizance of a complaint by a public servant until the State Government accords sanction for prosecution. Section 292A Cr.P.C. makes the offence cognizable, non-bailable and triable by any magistrate, including executive magistrates. In order to consider the impact of the Bihar Press Bill on the Press, it is necessary to take note of another legislation passed by the Bihar Legislature, namely, the Code of Criminal Procedure (Bihar Amendment) Bill, 1982 which seeks to give enlarged jurisdiction to executive magistrates.

The first question which arises for consideration is whether the proposed legislation is constitutionally valid. The Press does not have a fundamental right to vilify any person or indulge in character assassination. Libellous matters can and ought to be punished because they can cause untold harm and injury to a person. The State has undoubted powers to enact legislation which penalises publication of any matter but only on the grounds specified in clause (2) of article 19. Decency or morality and defamation are the relevant grounds on which freedom of expression may be curtailed. There can be no doubt that the publication of any matter which is grossly indecent or intended for blackmail is covered by these grounds. The expression 'scurrilous' is not, however, capable of precise definition and doubts have been expressed whether scurrilous writings can be penalised on these grounds. The expression 'scurrilous' was used in the Press (Objectionable Matter) Act also which was in force for four years and no exception was taken to this expression. Scurrilous writings may be either obscene or defamatory or an infringement of the right to privacy. I am clearly of opinion that scurrilous writings can also be pena- lised on the grounds specified in clause (2) of article 19.

While restrictions may be imposed on the publication of any matter which is grossly indecent or is scurrilous or inten- ded for blackmail, it is necessary to ensure that these restric- tions are reasonable. They must not be excessive or go beyond what is necessary to achieve the object of the law under which they are sought to be imposed. In considering the reasonable- ness of the restrictions, both the substantive as well as the pro- cedural provisions have to be taken into account. The proce- dure and the manner of imposition of the restrictions must also be fair, just and reasonable.[4] The substance and practical result of the legislation should be considered rather than its pure legal aspect. The correct approach should be what in substance is the loss or injury caused to the citizen and not merely the phraseology and the method which has been adop- ted by the State in placing the restrictions.[5]

Now, under Section 292A Cr.P.C., as introduced by the Bihar Press Bill, the offence has been made cognizable, non- bailable and triable by executive magistrates also.

A Police Officer will have powers to arrest a journalist even without a warrant and harass him. It is too much to expect an average police officer to have clear conceptions of indecency, gross or otherwise, or what is scurrilous or to expect him to be familiar with the legal ingredients of 'intended for blackmail.' The offence is also non-bailable. Under the Code of Criminal Procedure, 1973, every person who is arrested on the allegation of having committed an offence has to be pro- duced before a judicial magistrate who decides whether the accused should be released on bail or remanded to judicial or police custody. Section 167 Cr. P.C. contains a valuable pro- viso which provides that no person can be kept in custody for more than 60 days before a chargesheet is filed against him. After the lapse of that period, he is entitled to be released on

---

4. *Express Newspapers* v. *Union of India*, A.I.R. 1958 S.C. 578. *State of Bihar* v. *H.N. Mishra*, A.I.R. 1971 S.C. 1667.
5. *Sakal Papers* v. *Union of India*, A.I.R. 1962 S.C. 305. *Express News- papers* case, *Ibid*.

bail, even if the investigation is not concluded. The 1982 Cr.
P.C. Bihar Amendment Bill has vested these powers in the
executive magistrates. Warrants under Section 73 including
warrants against any person who is accused of non-bailable
offence and of 'evading arrest' which could hitherto be issued
only by judicial magistrates, can after the amendment be issued by executive magistrate also. Again, by the proposed amendment, the period of detention has been extended to 180 days.
Thus an executive magistrate who is directly subordinate to
the State Government may keep an accused person in jail for
six months, even if no chargesheet is filed against him during that period. A later provision lays down that an executive
magistrate, after taking cognizance, may make over the case
for inquiry or trial to any competent magistrate. The practical effect of the combined operation of Section 292A Cr. P.C.
and the aforesaid Bihar amendments in the Criminal Procedure Code will be that it would become not only possible but
easy to arrest newsmen, publishers, printers, distributors and
even hawkers and not to allow them bail for six months on the
mere orders of an executive magistrate. The fear of being kept
in custody for six months on vague charges may seriously
affect freedom of the Press.

Another important consequence of 1982 Cr. P.C. Bihar
Amendment Bill is to nullify to a large extent the cardinal
principle of separation between the executive and judiciary.
The scope of executive interference in matters which are essentially judicial has been vastly increased. It is interesting in
this connection to compare the Bihar Press Bill with the Press
(Objectionable Matter) Act, 1951. The Act of 1951 covers the
same grounds as the Bihar Press Bill but the Act of 1951 provided adequate safeguards against unjustified harassment and
no action could be taken against a newspaper except after a
judicial inquiry by a Sessions Judge. The only safeguard provided in the Bihar Press Bill is that a competent court will
not take cognizance of a complaint by a public servant without the sanction of the State Government. This cannot be
regarded as a real safeguard.

It has been argued with great force that as a result of the

amendments to the Code of Criminal Procedure, procedural unreasonableness has been injected into the provisions of Section 292A, I.P.C. as introduced by the Bihar Press Bill which render them violative of article 19(1)(a). It is difficult to say what view the courts will take in this matter, but the operation of the proposed legislation may place severe impediments in the way of newspapers and may effectively prevent them from exercising their guaranteed right and function of free and fearless criticism of the administration. Provisions which enable the police to arrest without a warrant on mere suspicion of commission of an offence, which again is made non-bailable and the powers entrusted to executive magistrates to discharge the various important functions which were hitherto discharged by judicial magistrates may deter even honest and responsible journalists from criticising the conduct of Ministers and Government servants. I am, therefore, of the opinion that Section 292A Cr. P.C. should be omitted.

It may also be noted that in a prosecution for defamation under Section 500 I.P.C., Exception 1 to Section 499 provides a valid defence for the accused. There is no such safeguard in Section 292A I.P.C. If in a matter involving the personal liberty of an individual, the State government is given discretion to pick and choose whether to proceed under Section 500 or Section 292A I.P.C. without any definite guidelines or norms in the matter, Section 292A would be violative of article 14 and may be struck down. Moreover, as the circulation of a newspaper is not confined to a State, all matters relating to the Press should be dealt with under Central laws. It is for this reason that when the Press (Objectionable Matter) Act, 1951 was enacted, all the State laws in force in Part A and Part B states were repealed.

It now appears from Press report (Statesman, December 7, 1982) that the Union Minister for Information and Broadcasting held three rounds of talks on the Bihar Press Bill with representatives of eight journalist and newspaper organisations. The Editors' Guild of India, however, abstained from the meeting on the ground that their demand was total withdrawal of the Bill and no useful purpose would be served by

19—TPI

discussing amendments to the Bill. The attitude of the Editors' Guild, to my mind, was undemocratic. Even if the proposed measure has to be scrapped lock, stock and barrel, some discussion is called for. Be that as it may, Government has realised that the proposed measure would be harsh and has suggested certain principles on the basis of which the Bill could be amended. The organisations of journalists did not agree to the proposal of the Government as they had unequivocally asked for the withdrawal of the Bill. Government has proposed firstly that the offence under Section 292A I.P.C. should be made bailable and non-cognizable. It should also be clearly defined that the offence should be taken cognizance of by a judicial magistrate, first class and executive magistrates should have nothing to do with it. In other words, Section 292A Cr. P.C. should be omitted which I have advocated. Secondly, in regard to Section 292A I.P.C. it should be made clear that the intention is to proceed against the printer, publisher, writer and the editor only. The possibility of innocent and unsuspecting readers, vendors, transporters, advertisers etc. being prosecuted should be expressly removed. Thirdly, the word 'scurrilous' should be redefined clearly. If these amendments are carried out, the Bill would become innocuous and no serious objection can be taken to it.

A question, however, arises whether the Bill as amended would serve any useful purpose. We have already laws on obscenity and defamation under Sections 292, 293, 294 and 499 read with 500 I.P.C. It is not clear in what manner the existing provisions have been found inadequate. Even if they are inadequate, there can be no valid objection, if the existing provisions about obscenity and defamation are tightened by imposing more severe punishment and the existing procedure is streamlined and simplified without affecting the basic safeguards and requirements of a fair trial. The word 'scurrilous' does not find place in I.P.C. But a scurrilous publication may be either obscene or defamatory or an invasion of the right to privacy. There is at present no general law on the right to privacy. We have discussed this matter in Chapter 7 and suggested the enactment of a law with a limited objective. In all other cases, the Press Council could appropriately be entrusted with the task of taking cognizance of complaints relating to invasion of the right to privacy. Taking all these factors into account, it appears that the Bill would not serve much useful purpose.

There can be no difference of opinion about the objectives of the Bihar Press Bill which are aimed at curbing rag journalism. To achieve that end, existing provisions of law may be more vigorously enforced and the Press Council should take more active interest in tackling the problem. The means adopted in the Bihar Press Bill may defeat the end and the Government may, as a gesture to public demand, drop the measure. It appears from Press reports that the Chief Minister of Bihar has agreed not to proceed with the Bill. This is a welcome news.

Functions of the Press

We now propose to discuss some of the important aspects of the functioning of the Press in India and what ails it. Commenting on the ailments of the Press, Shri Mankekar, a veteran journalist, says : ''Since Independence, the Indian Press has remained stagnant and lost its idealism and, in the process, its soul...... Our Press has turned routineer and, therefore, unenterprising. The crusading spirit and zeal for public causes that distinguished the pre-Independence Press of the country are conspicuous by their absence in our present-day newspapers.''[6] In pre-Independence days, the Press had a mission to rouse mass consciousness and serve the cause of freedom movement. Newspapers were run by national leaders of eminence who had indomitable courage and spirit of self-sacrifice. Journalism was not then a profession but a service. Today, the Press is a business with a profit motive. Exceptions apart, people take up the profession of journalism not as a matter of choice but only when other avenues of employment are not open to them. No wonder that the crusading spirit and zeal are often absent in the present-day news-

6. D. R. Mankekar, *Free Not Independent, Ibid,* p. 8.

papers. But with the vastly improved service conditions of working journalists, journalism has of late been an attractive profession and given the proper type of training as recommended by the Mathew Commission, the Press may regain its past glory.

Too Much Politics

Another peculiar feature of our newspapers is that there is an abnormal accent on politics and politicians and they give too much coverage to the activities of ministers. Even on an occasion like the World Religious Conference that was held in Delhi in November, 1981, the important thing for most of the newspapers was what the Home Minister had said at the Conference; what the religious leaders had to say about the oneness of religion was of secondary importance to them. Unfortunately, in India, life revolves round politics, and politicians. In other countries, distinguished scientists and economists, successful industrialists, outstanding artists and sportsmen and their achievements are given greater coverage. The dailies may claim that in self-interest they have to cater to the tastes of readers and that so long as they are politically oriented, there is no escape. But newspapers are expected not only to mould public opinion but also to mould public choice. There should, therefore, be a gradual swing and greater prominence should be given to artistic, sporting, scientific and economic trends, both inside and outside the country.

The Press and Government

Before Independence, the nationalist Press had always played an adversary role in relation to the then Government. That was understandable. But even after Independence, some of the newspapers have always been criticising the Government and its policies, perhaps, because they think that criticism sells and appreciation does not. But in the context of the enormous task of nation-building which the Government has undertaken, the Press has to reassess its role *vis-a-vis* the Government which has ceased to be alien. It should prominently display the nation-building activities of the Government and shower praises when they are due and criticise the Government when criticism is called for. To be a mindless adversary or an unquestioning ally would be to abdicate judgment. A free Press should, in our view, be a constructive critic.

Rag Journalism

Rag journalism is a scourge that afflicts the Press. Sex, scandal, blackmail, stories of corruption, true or false, appeal to the readers and tend to increase the circulation of a newspaper. Rag journalism is a temptation with all journalists which has to be curbed. But our national dailies are generally more responsible and yellow journalism is not as rampant in our country as in the West, though it exists on a fairly large scale. One would, however, hesitate to endorse the idea of controlling the Press in the name of curbing yellow journalism. Repressive Press laws are no answer to the problem. There are existing general laws which may act as deterrent to journalists engaged in sensational scandal-mongering but primarily, it is the duty of the Press Council to frame a code of ethics and enforce it strictly. The argument of the Press Council that under the statute, it can only build up a voluntary code of ethics and not frame one is not at all convincing.

Development Journalism

Our Government has undertaken huge development projects to improve the standard of living of the common man. People must know about these projects and how they would affect their lives. Development journalism has, therefore, assumed great importance.

From the beginning of the First Plan in the early fifties, newspapers have carried articles publicising river valley schemes, fertiliser plants, the new steel townships and other such Plan projects. However, there has not been much reporting of the change that is taking place—or intended changes not taking place—in the lives of the people, specially of the majority who live in the countryside. It is only lately that the Indian Press has made a beginning with in-depth development writing (to be distinguished from publicity) which should occupy a pride of place in the Press of a developing country.

The Mathew Commission undertook a quick study to find out the extent of development writing which showed that some widely read newspapers in regional languages, besides English, have taken to reporting regularly on development topics and major socio-economic issues, such as the conditions of tea garden labour, problems of drought and irrigation, 'dowry deaths' and the general ill-treatment of women, the plight of under-trial prisoners and the living conditions of urban slum dwellers. This is a welcome trend which should be encouraged and strengthened.

Many of the development stories put out in India by the Press Information Bureau at the Centre, and by the Information Departments of the States, tend to paint a one-sided picture of the change whereas development in real life is not a painless process but entails difficulties, setbacks and determined effort. Development reporting should tell the story of what is going well as well as what is going wrong. It should investigate into the reasons for success as well as for failure, at different places under different conditions, of various development programmes affecting the lives of the common people.

Most of our newspapers merely carry official handouts. They do not enable the reader to meet the extension workers who are the agents of change, or the beneficiaries of the programmes, and to hear what they have to say about their triumphs and difficulties. The reporting of non-official initiatives in rural development, educational reforms, leprosy relief and other areas is even less extensive than that of official development programmes. Surely, the free Press in a developing country should be more socially conscious and enterprising.

Internal Stability and the Press

For development to take place, maintenance of internal stability is as important as safeguarding of national security. Since Independence, threats to internal stability have arisen from different sources : (i) communal disturbances; (ii) secessionist or insurrectionary movements in some parts of the country; and (iii) agitations on political or other issues by resort to unconstitutional methods. The Press has a useful role to play in maintaining internal stability and public order.

(i) Communal harmony

Ever since Independence, communal disturbances from time to time have disfigured our national life. The first Press Commission observed : "A great deal of the scurrilous writing that is noticeable in the Press is often directed against communities or groups. Events preceding and following the partition of the country have left so many people with a sense of grievance against one community or the other that the newspapers have found it a lucrative business to exploit these feelings." The Enquiry Committee on Small Newspapers observed in Chapter VI of its report that while a substantial section of the Press had behaved with responsibility, there were some newspapers which indulged in objectionable writings calculated to incite communal passions. Harmony between people belonging to different social groups and religious faiths is desirable in itself; it is also a necessary pre-condition for development. The senseless and suicidal violence triggered by conflicts based on religion or sects is inimical to development.

The Press Council noted that the function of the Press in this area had to be viewed from two angles. One was what could be called the positive role of the Press, namely, of bringing together the diverse elements in the nation's life, by emphasising those aspects of national life which would tend towards unifying the communities. The other angle was the negative one, namely, "what the Press should not do."

The Press Council framed certain guidlines in November, 1968 for avoidance of 'objectionable communal writing' and the Mathew Commission has endorsed those guidelines. We are of the view that, on the outbreak of communal disturbance, newspapers should refrain from sensational presentation of the news and from giving community-wise figures of those killed or injured. However, when the situation gets stabilised, there should be no hesitation in investigating the cause of the rioting and its consequences with identification of communities concerned.

Communal tensions have economic, political and social causes. There have been allegations of foreign money at work. These causes should be investigated and exposed. The Mathew Commission thinks that suppression of truth would worsen rather than improve the atmosphere. However, it is difficult to lay down hard and fast rules, and a newspaper should, so to say, play it by the ear, in accordance with the circumstances of each case and with due sense of responsibility. It is further necessary that there should be stricter enforcement of the provisions of the Indian Penal Code with regard to communal incitement.

The positive role of the Press of bringing together the diverse elements in the nation's life by emphasising those aspects which tend towards unifying the communities—is as important as the avoidance of objectionable communal writing. This calls for a sustained campaign to promote the concept of human brotherhood taught and exemplified by the founders and saints of all religions. The Press should communicate widely the humanistic teachings of great religious leaders to strengthen social harmony. The Press can play a major role in opposing obscurantists of every religion and in drawing attention to the humanist teachings of saints of every religion.

(ii) Secessionist and insurrectionary movements

It is a matter of concern that insurrectionary and secessionist activities are still evident in some parts of the country. Sovereignty and integrity of India have to be maintained at all costs and it is the duty of the Press to condemn strongly and unequivocally any secessionist activity or any movement that affects national integrity. There can be no difference of opinion on this point and all newspapers, irrespective of their policy, must speak in one voice in condemning such anti-national activity. Under article 19(2) of the Constitution, the State has been empowered to enact legislation to impose reasonable restrictions on the Press in the interests of sovereignty and integrity of India and if any newspaper is found to encourage, even indirectly, any secessionist activity, the newspaper should be penalised. If any region has legitimate grievances on account of economic neglect, exploitation or apprehension of loss of cultural identity, the Press may play a useful role by bringing those causes to public notice but at the same time, advocating adherence to lawful methods of ventilating grievances and condemning any violent methods.

(iii) Agitations and the Press

The country has been witnessing frequently incidents of violence and disruption of normal life by agitators trying to bring their grievances to public notice. Leaders of agitation take resort to various methods, such as stoppage of trains and buses, burning of public property or incitement to other forms of violence. Agitations leading to the disruption of normal life have taken place in recent years in Assam on the question of foreign nationals, in Maharashtra in support of the demand for textile workers and demand for higher prices of agricultural produce and elsewhere also on similar issues. Many newspapers find themselves in dilemma while dealing with such events. On the one hand, grievances of even large sections of the public appear to gain Government attention only when there is widespread agitation and issues are taken to the streets; on the other, newspapers realise that a developing country cannot afford ventilation of grievances in such form. Assam movement for example, has caused irreparable loss to the economy not only of the country but of Assam as well on account of some of the unreasonable and anti-national demands of movement leaders. Newspapers have, however, failed to condemn such anti-national demands and create public opinion against such agitation. There is no easy solution to such problems. While the Press should bring to light and extend support to genuine public grievances, it should take a forthright stand against unreasonable demands and unconstitutional methods of agitation.

Investigative Reporting

The concept of 'investigative reporting' has rapidly gained recognition and momentum in recent years. It is not necessarily developmental reporting, since investigation could be in such areas as the personal lives of celebrities in the film world or high society, or of persons in public life or corruption in public administration. Investigative reporting is still in its infancy in our country when compared to what it has achieved in other countries like U.S.A. where investigative reporting has led even to fall of government.

We welcome the trend towards investigative reporting in so far as it is oriented to social and economic issues, for example, bringing to light the exploitation of harijans, tribals or contract labour, the trading in human flesh, or delays and corruption in public administration. Investigative reporting should be 'of public interest,' if not 'in public interest.' An article on Kuo Oil deal and similar articles are in public interest. Some newspapers, including the *Indian Express* and the *Statesman,* have started investigative reporting. A journalist of our country was given Magsaysay Award for investigative journalism. All this is encouraging but care should be taken that investigative reporting does not degenerate into character assassination or yellow journalism.

Investigative reporting entails hard work. It is said that "comment is free, but facts are sacred." One might add that facts are difficult to gather and require the expenditure of time and energy. Investigative reporting is not for lazy journalists. The enterprising reporter who engages himself in investigative journalism should not give occasion for the criticism of lack of follow-up, which is a widespread failing in the Indian Press. It is not enough to report in depth a present problem; it is necessary to keep track of the further development of a situation that has been reported.

It may be noted here that economic journalism has made great strides during the last two decades both as a part of the contents of general newspapers and through the emergence of specialised dailies and periodicals. There is a good deal of policy discussion in the Press by experts on various economic issues. But these articles, even when they appear in ordinary dailies, are written in highly technical language which are not intelligible to an average reader. They should be written in popular language so that an average reader may also appreciate the economic problems facing the country.

We must acknowledge that there could be risk in investigative reporting, as when a reporter exposes local tyranny and corruption. The Mathew Commission has cited in this connection the tragic example of Chabirani Mohapatra of Cuttack in Orissa who was violated and done to death in October, 1980 in the wake of exposure by her journalist husband of the linkage, at the block level, between propertied interests, corrupt officials and goondas masquerading as political workers. There is no easy remedy to such happenings. But the State Government should be vigilant that investigative reporters do not come to harm and public opinion should assert itself in this matter.

Public Grievance

The Mathew Commission has complained[7] that while the newspapers have the fundamental right to freedom of expression under article 19(1)(a), that article does not confer on ordinary citizens any fundamental right to express their views through a newspaper. It suggests that article 19(1)(a) should be reviewed so as to permit an ordinary citizen to exercise his fundamental right of freedom of speech and expression through a newspaper. We discussed this question in Chapter 3 under the head "Review of article 19(1)(a)" and found that the recommendation of the Commission was not acceptable.

It is, however, necessary that there should be some forum in a newspaper through which the public may express their views. We have noted that some newspapers have started earmarking regular columns for ventilation of public grievances and publication of suggestions from readers. This is a welcome trend. While the newspapers try to secure comments of the public authorities concerned on the grievances, these authorities do not respond at all in some cases or the response

7, *Second Press Commission Report*, Ch. IV, para 33, p. 37.

is not prompt. The Mathew Commission recommends that public grievance columns should be more widely offered and that the public authorities concerned should take note of the grievances published and take prompt action.

The public can also express their views through letters to the Editor. The space provided for such letters is generally very restricted. Newspapers should try to provide more space for these letters. The demand of the public to express their views through a newspaper may, to a certain extent, be met by public grievance columns and letters to the Editor.

De-linking and Diffusion of Ownership and Control

Viewed as an industry, the Press is highly capital intensive and those who have sizeable capital resources have a special advantage over those who cannot afford or manage to procure that amount of capital. It is alleged that big industrial and business houses which have ample resources control the Press and they treat it as a kept Press to serve their personal and business interests. With a view to prevent concentration of ownership in Press, to de-link the Press from other business interests, to eliminate unfair competition among big and small newspapers and to help the growth of small and medium newspapers, the Mathew Commission has made a number of recommendations. In the first place, it is proposed that M.R.T.P. Act should be made applicable to newspaper industry; secondly, legislation should be undertaken to de-link newspaper industry from other business interests; thirdly, legislation should also be undertaken to provide for price-page schedule and news-to-advertisement ratio; and a Newspaper Development Commission should also be set up to help the growth of newspaper industry and in particular, the growth of small and medium newspapers. Proposals have also been made for the interposition of trustees between the management and the editor and also the imposition of a penal duty on daily newspapers whose average page level exceeds 12 per day. All these measures have been recommended by the majority of the Commission to insulate the newspaper industry from other business interests so that the Press does not become a spokesman of the propertied classes.

These are controversial recommendations and four members of the Commission do not subscribe to the views expounded and recommendations made and they have appended a long joint minute of dissent. We have discussed these recommendations in detail in Chapter 9 and the question of editorial autonomy has been discussed in Chapter 10.

We agree with the Mathew Commission that M.R.T.P. Act should be made applicable to newspaper industry. The Commission, has however, suggested that certain modifications should be made in that Act to make it applicable to the Press. It appears that the Government would not accept this proposal as it is not considered necessary that provisions about substantial and procedural matters regarding the M.R.T.P. Act should be different in respect of newspaper industry. There is a good deal of force in the contention of the government that it would not be desirable to single out the Press for special treatment under the Act. It would be preferable to amend the Act suitably in general terms in the light of the recommendations of the Commission to make it automatically applicable to the Press. But if this is not found feasible, we would suggest that, in view of the peculiar position of the newspaper industry, special provisions may be made to make the Act applicable to the Press.

We, however, do not favour the proposal of the Commission to undertake legislation either for de-linking the Press from other business interests or for providing price-page schedule and news-to-advertisement ratio. De-linking should not be an article of faith. In the present situation of newspaper industry, it is not called for. It will do more harm than good. De-linking along with price-page schedule and news-to-advertisement ratio will merely create difficulties for the existing good quality newspapers, only because they have large circulations, and at the same time may not necessarily help the sustenance or coming into existence of similarly good quality but smaller circulation papers. These proposals cannot be justified on merits and there are also legal obstacles to them.

This is not to say that there is no case for some limit on the use of advertisement by newspapers. We have suggested a tax on excessive advertisement. If any newspaper makes use of excessive advertisement beyond 50 per cent of the total newspaper space, it should be subject to a progressive tax on advertisement. We think that such a flexible approach would be better than a fixed general prohibition. Such a measure would be easy to operate. As a taxation law, its impact on freedom of the Press would not be direct and the law would not be violative of article 19(1)(a).

Editorial autonomy

The editor-management relationship is an extremely complex problem which has been the subject of debate all over the world. Various attempts have been made in other countries to define this relationship and to safeguard the autonomy of the editor with no worthwhile results that can act as guidance in our country. The position of the editor in our country is unenviable. In order to provide an effective safeguard against managerial interference in editorial independence, the Mathew Commission recommends that legislation should be undertaken for interposition of a board of trustees between the management and the editor of a newspaper. The function of the board of trustees would be to act as umpire in disputes between the editor and the management. We discussed this proposal in detail in Chapter 10. We do not favour this proposal which affects the ownership pattern of the newspaper company. We, however, agree to an alternative scheme suggested by dissenting members of the Commission. In the case of a newspaper owned by a Joint-stock company, there should be some independent special directors. In other cases, there should be an advisory body. These special directors and the advisory body should have a big say in the appointment and dismissal of the editor and should act as umpire in disputes between the editor and the management of the newspaper. This is a simple scheme applicable to all categories of newspapers, without affecting their ownership pattern and it may help in securing editorial independence.

Newspaper Development Commission

The Mathew Commission foresaw a crucial role for the Indian language Press in the coming years as the proportion of members of legislatures and Parliament entirely relying on it for news and analysis of events at home and abroad was steadily increasing. The small and medium newspapers serving a district or a number of districts have also a very useful role to play. But the quality of the Indian language Press as also of small and medium newspapers leaves much to be desired and they cannot also compete with big newspapers. In order to provide a free market of ideas, it is necessary that all possible assistance should be rendered for the growth of Indian language Press as also of small and medium newspapers and for the improvement of their quality. For this purpose, the Mathew Commission recommends the setting up of a Newspaper Development Commission.

The Development Commission will seek to promote the development of the Press as a whole. But it will make special effort in facilitating the growth of Indian language newspapers as also small and medium newspapers including district newspapers. It will not give financial subsidy directly to any individual newspaper but it will offer technical and all other assistance on a generalised, non-discriminating and non-discretionary basis. There are indications that the Government would not accept this proposal. It has been argued that in view of the Constitutional provision for freedom of expression and Government's policy in support of the freedom of the Press, it is considered that the development of the Press should be left to itself and no outside authority or institution should interfere or be concerned with it. As a general proposition the view of the government is unexceptionable. But having regard to the peculiar position of small and medium newspapers and the need for their growth, there should be no serious objection, if technical assistance is given to them on a non-discriminatory basis by an independent and autonomous body. No doubt the Development Commission will receive some grant from the Government but it will be mainly financed by tax on excessive advertisement which we have advocated elsewhere. The Press Council is also financed mainly by government grants but the Council has not lost its independence or autonomy. There is no reason to suppose that the Development Commission will not be an independent and autonomous body. Taking all these factors into consideration, it is suggested that the Government should reconsider its view about the Development Commission.

In dealing with the recommendations of the Mathew Commission certain considerations have to be kept in view. The newspapers in India have a far smaller reach than what is necessary in a democracy. It is essential that circulation of newspapers should be increased and their quality also improved at all levels—big, medium and small. While monopolistic tendencies in the Indian Press have to be curbed and encouragement should be given to the growth of small and medium newspapers, no measures should be undertaken which might have the effect of crippling our big and quality newspapers. It is also to be recognised that the newspaper industry is a sensitive industry and it should not be interfered with by any outside authority except for compelling reasons. The recommendations of the Mathew Commission are such that if they are to be implemented, it would be necessary to enact a large number of laws to control various aspects of the newspaper industry. All the measures, taken together, will seriously affect the functioning of big newspapers but they may not necessarily help the growth of smaller newspapers. Keeping in view that the interference with the Press should be kept at the barest minimum, we have suggested only two measures, namely that M.R.T.P. Act should be made applicable to the newspaper industry and a tax may be imposed on excessive advertisement. We have also lent our support to the proposal for a Newspaper Development Commission and have suggested that the advertisement tax may be earmarked for the Commission.

The Press Council

Newspapers in our country are not all virtuous. They have their failings; they take liberties and the freedom enjoyed by them is sometimes misused. Few would deny the existence of yellow journalism in our country or the fact that it has been on the increase in recent years. It is in everybody's and the nation's interest to contain this menace. But a 'captive Press' is unthinkable in a democracy. Repressive press law is not also an answer to the problem. The temptation to rag journalism should be overcome by the journalists themselves. The Press Council may also play a useful role in curbing this evil. It is the duty of the Council not only to maintain freedom of the Press but also to maintain high standards of journalistic ethics and good taste. It is its duty to frame a code of ethics and enforce it. It is the Council and Council alone that can be the guardian of the Press in this country. But we have seen earlier in Chapter 8 that the Press Council has not been functioning as effectively and as vigorously as it should. Out of the 28 members of the Council, twenty are journalists and there are only three lay members representing education, science, law, literature and culture. The journalist members dominate the Council. They have naturally a soft corner for fellow journalists and they behave like a trade union rather than as a professional and impartial body. It is no wonder that the Council cannot function effectively. The inclusion of lay members was intended to ensure that the voice of the public would be heard in the deliberations of the Council but they are too few in number to have an effective voice. It is necessary that the number of lay members should be considerably increased to give them an effective voice and to make the Council function more effectively and vigorously.

We are the proud inheritors of so valuable a freedom as the freedom of the Press. The area of freedom which we enjoy is quite large indeed and the restraints that have been placed on the exercise of that freedom are neither too many nor too onerous. They are perhaps the barest minimum that any civilised society should impose on the exercise of such right. An objective assessment of the enforcement of Press laws by the Governments in this country would reveal that they have been circumspect in their handling of the Press. It is now for the Press to make proper use of the freedom it enjoys and not compel the government to take to repressive measures.

20—TPI

In our political set up, the Press has a special responsibility. We have adopted a parliamentary system where the opposition parties have an important role to play. But in our country, there is the dominance of the party in power and the opposition is weak and fragmented, incapable of offering any national alternative or keeping the abuses of the government in check. A heavy responsibility has thus devolved on the Press. It has to function as an extra-parliamentary opposition to strengthen the roots of democracy and democratic institutions and to keep the government in check. It has to guard against the erosion of democratic values and create a vocal public opinion for realising the goal of social and economic justice. To enable the Press to discharge its onerous responsibilities, it must put its own house in order and try to recapture, to some extent, the missionary zeal and the crusading spirit of the great men of the past who distinguished themselves in the field of journalism in pre-Independence days.

Some Facts about the Indian Press

Statiscal data, in relation to the Indian Press, are incomplete and inadequate.

Number of newspapers

The total number of newspapers, including dailies and periodicals, was 19,144 in 1981 as against 18,140 in 1980 indicating an annual growth of 5.5 per cent. Of them, 1,264 were daily newspapers in 1981 as against 1,173 in 1980. The remaining 17,800 were periodicals of which 6,729 were monthlies, 5624 weeklies, 2,555 fortnightlies, 1859 quarterlies and 230 annuals. The remaining periodicals were bi-monthlies, half-yearlies etc.

Circulation levels

The total circulation of all newspapers taken together advanced from 50.9 million copies in 1980 to 51.1 million copies in 1981 showing a modest increase of 0.4 per cent.

The circulation of dailies touched the figure of 15.25 million copies in 1981 and showed an increase of 5 per cent compared to their circulation in 1980.

The total circulation of the periodicals was 35.7 million copies in 1981. The weeklies led in circulation with a share of 42.9 per cent followed by monthlies with 39.4 per cent.

In India in 1982, with a population of 68 crores and 28 crores at least nominally literate, there was not a single paper which had crossed the seven figure barrier. *The Indian Express* with ten editions prints 6,47,709 copies; *Times of India* with three editions prints 4,67,812 copies; *Malayala Manorama* with three editions, 4,70,779 and *Navabharat Times*, with two edi-

itons, 4,17,514 copies. *Ananda Bazar Patrika,* the largest circulated single-edition daily has a circulation of 4,03,047
copies.

No daily newspaper in Indian languages sells 5 lakh
copies. A Tamil periodical *Kumudam* has crossed half-million
mark.

Out of 1,264 daily newspapers, only 32 have a circulation
of one lakh or more. Out of 17,800 periodicals, only 49 have
a circulation of one lakh or more.

According to the circulation data furnished by the newspapers (dailies and periodicals), there were 177 big, 358
medium and 6,798 small newspapers. The remaining newspapers could not be classified as their circulation figures were
not available.

Among daily newspapers, 66 were big, 125 medium and
586 small. The circulation figures of the remaining newspapers
were not available.

Notes : A small newspaper has a circulation up to 15,000
copies per issue;

A medium newspaper has a circulation between
15,000 copies and 50,000 copies per issue; and

A big newspaper has a circulation above 50,000
copies per issue.

Languages

Newspapers were published in the country in 84 languages in 1981. These include 16 principal languages and 68
other languages. The largest number of newspapers was
brought out in Hindi (5,329), followed by English (3,583),
Bangla (1,463), Urdu (1,299) and Marathi (1,098).

Daily newspapers were published in 15 principal and 7
other languages. Kashmiri was one principal language that
did not have a daily newspaper. Out of 1,264 dailies, 105 were
published in English, 407 in Hindi, 128 in Urdu, 120 in Marathi, 101 in Malayalam and the rest in other languages.

State Press

Arunachal Pradesh and Lakshadweep remained out of the
list of publishers in 1981 also. Uttar Pradesh continued to be
the publisher of largest number of newspapers (2,702), followed by Maharashtra (2,560), Delhi (2,325), West Bengal

(2,115), Tamil Nadu (1,216), Andhra Pradesh (1,068) and Kerala (1,005).

With a total circulation of 8.66 million copies, the Maharashtra Press continues to claim the first position. The Press in Delhi comes second with 7.3 million copies followed by Tamil Nadu, U.P., and West Bengal, respectively, in that order.

Ownership pattern

Out of 19,144 newspapers, 12,521 were owned by individuals, 3,240 by societies and associations, 956 by firms and partnerships, 782 by joint stock companies and 597 by Central and State governments. The ownership pattern of the remaining newspapers is not available.

However, newspapers brought out by joint stock companies had the largest circulation with 19.6 million copies.

Foreign Mission Publications

100 publications were brought out by 26 foreign missions stationed in India. All these periodicals were published from the four metropolitan cities. The Embassy of U.S.S.R. with 49 publications remained the largest publisher.

Constitution of India

(RELEVANT EXTRACTS)

*　　　　　*　　　　　*

19. Protection of certain rights regarding freedom of speech, etc.

(1) All citizens shall have the right—

(a) to freedom of speech and expression;

(b) to assemble peaceably and without arms;

(c) to form associations or unions;

(d) to move freely through the territory of India;

(e) to reside and settle in any part of the territory of India;

*　　　　　*　　　　　*

(g) to practise any profession, or to carry on any occupation, trade or business.

(2) Nothing in sub-clause (a) of clause (1) shall affect the operation of any existing law, or prevent the State from making any law, in so far as such law imposes reasonable restrictions on the exercise of the right conferred by the said sub-clause in the interests of the sovereignty and integrity of India, the security of the State, friendly relations with foreign States, public order, decency or morality, or in relation to contempt of court, defamation or incitement to an offence.

*　　　　　*　　　　　*

(6) Nothing in sub-clause (g) of the said clause shall affect the operation of any existing law in so far as it imposes, or prevent the State from making any law imposing, in the

interests of the general public, reasonable restrictions on the exercise of the right conferred by the said sub-clause, and, in particular, nothing in the said sub-clause shall affect the operation of any existing law in so far as it relates to, or prevent the State from making any law relating to,—

(i) the professional or technical qualifications necessary for practising any profession or carrying on any occupation, trade or business, or

(ii) the carrying on by the State, or by a corporation owned or controlled by the State, of any trade, business, industry or service, whether to the exclusion, complete or partial, of citizens or otherwise.

*   *   *

361A. Protection of publication of proceedings of Parliament and State Legislatures.

(1) No person shall be liable to any proceedings, civil or criminal, in any court in respect of the publication in a newspaper of a substantially true report of any proceedings of either House of Parliament or the Legislative Assembly, or, as the case may be, either House of the Legislature, of a State, unless the publication is proved to have been made with malice : Provided that nothing in this clause shall apply to the publication of any report of the proceedings of a secret sitting of either House of Parliament or the Legislative Assembly, or, as the case may be, either House of the Legislature, of a State.

(2) Clause (1) shall apply in relation to reports or matters broadcast by means of wireless telegraphy as part of any programme or service provided by means of a broadcasting station as it applies in relation to reports or matters published in a newspaper.

Explanation—In this article, newspaper includes a news agency report containing material for publication in a newspaper.

*   *   *

APPENDIX III

The Press and Registration of Books Act, 1967

(RELEVANT EXTRACTS)

1. Interpretation Clause :

*   *   *

"Editor" means the person who controls the selection of the matter that is published in a newspaper;

*   *   *

"Newspaper" means any printed periodical work containing public news or comments on public news;

*   *   *

5. Rules as to publication of newspapers.

No newspaper shall be published in India, except in conformity with the rules hereinafter laid down :

(1) Without prejudice to the provisions of Section 3, every copy of every such newspaper shall contain the name of the person who is the editor thereof printed clearly on such copy as the name of the editor of that newspaper;

(2) The printer and the publisher of every such newspaper shall appear in person or by agent authorised in this behalf in accordance with rules made under Section 20, before a District, Presidency or Sub-divisional Magistrate within whose local jurisdiction such newspaper shall be printed or published....and shall make and subscribe, in duplicate, the following declaration :

"I, *A·B.,* declare that I am the printer (or publisher, or printer and publisher) of the newspaper entitled——and to be printed or published, or to be printed and published, as the case may be at......"

And the last blank in this form of declaration, shall be filled up with a true and precise account of the premises where the printing or publication is conducted.

(2A) Every declaration under Rule (2) shall specify the title of the newspaper, the language in which it is to be published and the periodicity of its publication and shall contain such other particulars as may be prescribed.

(2B) Where the printer or publisher of a newspaper making a declaration under Rule (2) is not the owner thereof, the declaration shall specify the name of the owner and shall also be accompanied by an authority in writing from the owner authorising such person to make and subscribe such declaration.

(2C) A declaration in respect of a newspaper made under rule (2) and authenticated under Section 6 shall be necessary before the newspaper can be published.

(2D) Where the title of any newspaper or its language or the periodicity of its publication is changed, the declaration shall cease to have effect and a new declaration shall be necessary before the publication of the newspaper can be continued.

(2E) As often as the ownership of a newspaper is changed, a new declaration shall be necessary.

*　　　　*　　　　*

(7) Where any other newspaper has ceased publication for a period exceeding twelve months, every declaration made in respect thereof shall cease to have effect, and a new declaration shall be necessary before the newspaper can be republished.

*　　　　*　　　　*

8B. Cancellation of declaration

If, on an application made to him by the Press Registrar or any other person or otherwise, the Magistrate empowered to authenticate a declaration under this Act, is of opinion that any declaration made in respect of a newspaper should be cancelled, he may, after giving the person concerned an opportunity of showing cause against the action proposed to be taken, hold an inquiry into the matter and if, after considering the cause, if any, shown by such person and after giving him an opportunity of being heard, he is satisfied that—

   (i) the newspaper, in respect of which the declaration has been made, is being published, in contravention of the provisions of this Act or rules made thereunder; or

   (ii) the newspaper mentioned in the declaration bears a title which is the same as, or similar to, that of any other newspaper published either in the same language or in the same State; or

   (iii) the printer or publisher has ceased to be the printer or publisher of the newspaper mentioned in such declaration; or

   (iv) the declaration was made on false representation or on the concealment of any material fact or in respect of a periodical work which is not a newspaper;

the Magistrate may, by order, cancel the declaration and shall forward as soon as possible a copy of the order to the person making or subscribing the declaration and also to the Press Registrar.

*   *   *

19E. Returns and reports to be furnished by newspapers

The publisher of every newspaper shall furnish to the Press Registrar such returns, statistics and other information with respect to any of the particulars referred to in sub-section (2) of Section 19B as the Press Registrar may from time to time require.

*   *   *

APPENDIX IV

Official Secrets Act, 1923

(RELEVANT EXTRACTS)

*   *   *

3. Penalties for spying

(1) If any person for any purpose prejudicial to the safety or interests of the State—

    (a) approaches, inspects, passes over, or is in the vicinity of, or enters, any prohibited place; or

    (b) makes any sketch, plan, model, or note which is calculated to be or might be or is intended to be, directly or indirectly, useful to an enemy; or

    (c) obtains, collects, records or publishes or communicates to any other person, any secret official code or pass word, or any sketch, plan, model, article or note or other document or information which is calculated to be or might be or is intended to be, directly or indirectly, useful to an enemy or which relates to a matter the disclosure of which is likely to affect the sovereignty and integrity of India, the security of the State or friendly relations with foreign States;

he shall be punishable with imprisonment for a term which may extend, where the offence is committed in relation to any work of defence, arsenal, naval, military or air force establishment or station, mine, minefield, factory, dockyard, camp, ship or otherwise in relation to the secret official code, to fourteen years and in other cases to three years.

(2) On a prosecution for an offence punishable under this section, it shall not be necessary to show that the accused person was guilty of any particular act tending to show a pur-

pose prejudicial to the safety or interests of the State, and notwithstanding that no such act is proved against him, he may be convicted if, from the circumstances of the case or his conduct or his known character as proved, it appears that his purpose was a purpose prejudicial to the safety or interests of the State; and if any sketch, plan, model, article, note, document, or information relating to or used in any prohibited place, or relating to anything in such a place. or any secret official code or pass word is made, obtained, collected, recorded, published or communicated by any person other than a person acting under lawful authority, and from the circumstances of the case or his conduct or his known character as proved it appears that his purpose was a purpose prejudicial to the safety or interests of the State, such sketch, plan, model, article, note, document or information, code or pass word shall be presumed to have been made, obtained, collected, published or communicated for a purpose prejudicial to the safety or interests of the State.

*   *   *

5. Wrongful communication, etc. of information.

(1) If any person having in his possession or control any secret official code or pass word or any sketch, plan, model, article, note, document or information which relates to or is used in a prohibited place or relates to anything in such a place, or which is likely to assist, directly or indirectly, an enemy or which relates to a matter the disclosure of which is likely to affect the sovereignty and integrity of India, the security of the State or friendly relations with foreign States or which has been made or obtained in contravention of this Act, or which has been entrusted in confidence to him by any person holding office under Government, or which he has obtained or to which he has had access owing to his position as a person who holds or has held office under Government or as a person who holds or has held a contract made on behalf of Government, or as a person who is or has been employed under a person who holds or has held such an office or contract—

>   (a) wilfully communicates the code or pass word, sketch, plan, model, article, note, document or information to any person other than a person to whom he is authorised to communicate it, or a Court of Justice or a person to whom it is, in the interests of the State, his duty to communicate it; or

>   (b) uses the information in his possession for the benefit

of any foreign power or in any other manner prejudicial to the safety of the State; or

(c) retains the sketch, plan, model, article, note or document in his possession or control when he has no right
to retain it, or when it is contrary to his duty to
retain it, or wilfully fails to comply with all directions issued by lawful authority with regard to the
return or disposal thereof; or

(d) fails to take reasonable care of, or so conducts himself as to endanger the safety of, the sketch, plan,
model, article, note, document, secret official code or
pass word or information;

he shall be guilty of an offence under this section.

(2) If any person voluntarily receives any secret official
code or pass word or any sketch, plan, model, article, note,
document or information, knowing or having reasonable
ground to believe, at the time when he receives it, that the
code, pass word, sketch, plan, model, article, note, document
or information is communicated in contravention of this Act,
he shall be guilty of an offence under this section.

(3) If any person having in his possession or control any
sketch, plan, model, article, note, document or information,
which relates to munitions of war, communicates it, directly
or indirectly, to any foreign power or in any other manner
prejudicial to the safety or interests of the State, he shall be
guilty of an offence under this section.

(4) A person guilty of an offence under this section shall
be punishable with imprisonment for a term which may extend to three years, or with fine, or with both.

*   *   *

14. Exclusion of public from proceedings

In addition and without prejudice to any powers which
a Court may possess to order the exclusion of the public from
any proceedings if, in the course of proceedings before a
Court against any person for an offence under this Act or the
proceedings on appeal, or in the course of the trial of a person under this Act, application is made by the prosecution,
on the ground that the publication of any evidence to be given
or of any statement to be made in the course of the proceedings would be prejudicial to the safety of the State, that all
or any portion of the public shall be excluded during any part
of the hearing, the Court may make an order to that effect,
but the passing of sentence shall in any case take place in
public.

*   *   *

Select Bibliography

Report of the First Press Commission.
Report of the Second Press Commission.
Report of the Enquiry Committee on Small Newspapers, 1965.
Report of the First Royal Commission.
Many Voices, One World—Report of the International Commission for the study of Communication Problems (UNESCO, 1980).
Mudholkar, J., *Press Law* (Tagore Law Lectures).
D. Basu, *Law of the Press in India*.
Joseph Minattur, *Freedom of the Press in India*.
Freedom of the Press in India, Edited by A. G. Noorani.
What Ails the Indian Press ? Diagnosis and Remedies
The Third World and Press Freedom, edited by Philip C. Horton.
B. Pattabhai Sitaramayya, *The History of the Indian National Congress*, Vol. II.
A. V. Dicey, *Law of the Constitution*.
May, *Parliamentary Practice*.
Sir Ivor Jennings, *The Law and the Constitution*.
Halsbury, *Laws of England*.
M. Chalapati Rau, *The Press in India*.
Morris Jones, *Parliament in India*.
Roy, *Law relating to Press & Sedition*.
M. Hidayatullah, *The Press and the Judiciary*.
H. M. Seervai, *Constitutional Law of India*.

Concise Index